Understanding God in Our Lives
Year 1 Formation Program

Understanding God in Our Lives

Year 1 Formation Program

by Michael Fonseca, D.Min.

(Edited by Jeffrey Wincel, D.Min)

God's Embrace Publishing
728 E. 8th St. #3
Holland, MI 49423
© 2010 by Dr. Michael Fonseca, D.Min.

No Claim to original U.S. Government works

Printed in the United States of America

International Standard Book Number- 978-0-557-85540-7 (paperback)

Edited by Dr. Jeffrey P. Wincel (D.Min.)

Printed and bound by Lulu Publishing

This book contains information obtained from authentic and highly regarded sources. Reprinted material is quoted with permission, and sources are listed. A wide variety of references are listed. Reasonable efforts have been made to publish reliable data and information, but the author and the publisher cannot assume responsibility for the validity of all material or the consequences of their use.

Except as permitted by U.S. Copyright Law, no part of this book may be reprinted, reproduced, transmitted or utilized in any form by electronic, mechanical, or other means, now know or hereafter invented, including photocopying, microfilming, and recording, or in any information storage or retrieval system, without written permission from the publishers and author.

Trademark Notice: Product or corporate names may be trademarks or registered trademarks, and are used only for identification and explanation without intent to infringe.

Library of Congress Control Number: 2010915256

Note on Websites: The publisher has used its best endeavors to insure that the URLs for external website referred to in this book are correct and active at the time is or will remain appropriate.

Cover and text: based on design by Katherine Robinson Coleman

Foreword

Michael Fonseca's latest text, "Understanding God in Our Lives", the first of three manuals intended for those desiring to grow in the spiritual life of discipleship, is an unusually insightful contribution that leaves the reader hungering for Volumes II and III.

The author is clearly not only a man of prayer himself but also a phenomenal teacher, exploring those themes from the Old Testament that are foundational for a proper understanding of Jesus' role in salvation history.

He writes clearly and uses expertly the Catechism of the Catholic Church and the writings of many of the Church's most well-known saints and scholars. His suggestions for prayer, moreover, are bound to help the beginner as well as the seasoned student of the interior life. I would heartily recommend the text.

Bernard A. Hebda, Bishop of Gaylord

PART ONE

ACKNOWLEDGMENTS   1

PREFACE: THE PURPOSE OF THIS MANUAL   3

PRAYER SESSIONS:

1. Who is God for you?   9
2. Who is God as He says He is   17
3. God's Vision for us   25
4. The Reality of Sin   33
5. God's Mercy   39
6. God's Covenants with us   47
7. The Call of Abraham   55
8. The Call of Moses   63
9. The Passover Meal   71
10. The Sinai Covenant   79
11. The Call of Isaiah   91
12. The Suffering Servant   99
13. The Call of Jeremiah   107
14. The Exile Experience   117
15. Sacrificial Traditions and the Eucharist   123
16. God's Vision for us – Salvation as Theosis   135
17. God as Emmanuel   141
18. Intimacy with God   149

PART TWO

SECTION ONE: HELPS TO PRAYER:

1. The Meaning of Prayer — 159
2. Helpful Practices in Prayer — 165
3. Praying as Jesus Taught — 171
4. The Examination of Consciousness — 177
5. Spiritual Reading — 181
6. Suggestions for Journaling and Spiritual Direction — 185
7. The Purgative Stage of Discipleship — 187
8. The Practice of Renunciation — 193
9. Bibliography — 197

METHODS OF PRAYER:

1. Vocal Prayer — 199
2. The Method of Meditation — 203
3. The Method of Ignatian Contemplation or Imaging — 209
4. Lectio Divina or the Benedictine Method of Prayer — 215
5. Praying with the Psalms — 219

PRACTICES FOR COMMITTED DISCIPLESHIP:

1. Practicing the Presence of God — 223
2. The Prayer of Remembrance — 229
3. Recognizing God's Voice and Presence – 1 — 235
4. Recognizing God's Voice and Presence – 2 — 241

FOUR WEEKEND RETREATS — 251

INDEX — 262

ACKNOWLEDGMENTS

Creating this First Year Manual has been a labor of great love and gratitude. In the first place I offer my gratitude to our Triune God who has instilled within me a profound appreciation for the Father's Gift of His Son, Jesus Christ to us, and the continuing work of the Holy Spirit leading us deeper into the Mystery of God's Life and Love. Without this work of sanctification on the Divine Advocate's part, this ministry of God's Embrace Renewal Centers would simply not have happened. The desire to spread the GOOD NEWS is one result of this inner work of the Holy Spirit.

In the second place, I wish to express my thanksgiving and appreciation to Cherrie, my wife, who has been constant in her love and support, encouraging and strengthening me through prayer and counsel. She has been a key partner and advisor in the formation and visioning of God's Embrace Renewal Centers. With her on the team, this ministry is a joyful gift that is deeply appreciated and cherished. Indeed the Holy Spirit has used her as a valuable spokesperson!

Most especially, Cherrie and I want to thank Jeff Wincel, without whose generosity and unstinting support, God's Embrace Renewal Centers would not have gotten off the ground and become what it is. Jeff is the one who had this ministry registered as an ecclesial non-profit organization in the State of Michigan and with the Internal Revenue Services. Jeff manages the business aspect of the ministry. He oversees the administration of all the programs that we facilitate. Jeff is also on the Formation team and puts in many hours of study and prayer in preparing his presentations.

I am grateful to Heather, Jeff's wife, whose forthright opinions and wisdom have helped shape the vision and functioning of God's Embrace. She is a Board member and her commitment to us is greatly appreciated.

I am deeply grateful for all those sincere and earnestly seeking Christians whose paths have crossed mine in ministry. It has been my privilege to receive their wisdom and understanding of discipleship which has enhanced mine in great measure!

Lastly, I ask for God's continued blessings on this ministry. May this ministry be for His greater Glory and Praise!

INTRODUCTORY REMARKS

The Vision for this Three Volume Manual began some years ago when my wife, Cherrie, and I were led by the Holy Spirit to found God's Embrace Renewal Centers to provide Christians with the opportunity to deepen their discipleship through a loving and generous following of Jesus. With the love and support of our family and friends, especially Jeff and Heather Wincel who shared our calling to serve God, God's Embrace Renewal Centers was incorporated as a Non-Profit Ecclesial Corporation on August 8, 2006. Late 2006 and early 2007 was a period of organization and preparation. During this time we met to create programs for the formation of Christian disciples. We decided to provide a rigorous formation in prayer and spirituality that is Trinitarian in emphasis and contemplative in approach. The formation would be geared to cooperating with the Holy Spirit in the work of our transformation into Christ.

The main feature is our 3-year formation Program geared to facilitate the creation of ardent disciples who would glorify God through the witness of their lives and service of the Church. This 3-year program relies on a _threefold source_: We want to make sure that the participants become very familiar with the Bible, both Old and New Testaments, so that their spirituality is steeped in God's revelation of Himself through Jesus Christ and the Trinity's glorious Plan of salvation for us. Secondly, that we rely on the rich heritage of Catholic Spirituality offered to us through the desert Fathers and Mothers, the mystical writings of the Church Fathers on the Trinity, the contemplative traditions of the great Monastic Orders, and the ineffable teachings of the likes of Saints Francis of Assisi, Ignatius of Loyola, Teresa of Avila and John of the Cross. Thirdly, that we emphasize familiarity with the Catechism of the Catholic Church which stands, in the words of Pope John Paul II, as "a sure norm for teaching the faith" and an "authentic text." The desired outcome is the living of our lives within the Trinitarian embrace, inextricably linked to the divine life of the Trinity and to one another in Christ.

The overarching vision in the first year of the Program is <u>*Understanding God in our Lives*</u>. In <u>PART ONE</u> we look at 18 themes over nine months. During this year we are attempting to become truly familiar with the Old Testament without which our understanding of Jesus and the New Testament will be jeopardized. Hence most of the topics draw extensively, though not exclusively, from the Old Testament. The major focus throughout this year is to get a proper understanding of who God really is from His revelation of Himself. An accompanying focus is to understand who we truly are in God's eyes, so that we live our lives in the appropriate context of a covenant relationship with God. Through prayer and reflection, we trust that the Holy Spirit will make right any skewed understanding of God and ourselves.

As you examine the Table of Contents of this first year, you will see that in topic after topic we are learning more deeply who God is, who we are as God has created us in His image and likeness, and how God wants to be in relationship with us. We will see how God prepared His people over several centuries for the coming of His Son, Jesus Christ, to be the Savior of the world and our Risen Lord. Our hope is that a true understanding of the Old Testament will lead us to appreciate more profoundly God's Plan of Salvation in Jesus Christ!

In this first year, we decided to start from the very beginning, presuming that any participant who does the Program is a beginner even if they are not. We make no apologies for this presumption as we believe that any participant who might be an advanced seeker will appreciate the wisdom of always assuming that they have only just begun! So in <u>PART TWO</u> we have offered **_Helps to Prayer:_** The Meaning of Prayer, Helpful Practices in Prayer, Praying as Jesus Taught, The Examination of Consciousness, Spiritual Reading, Suggestions for Journaling and

Spiritual Direction, The Purgative Stage of Discipleship, The Practice of Renunciation, a Bibliography of 10 books, to help lay a firm foundation for the spiritual life. The *Helps to Prayer* contain the wisdom of our saints as they attempted to pattern their lives on Jesus, their Teacher and Lord! These *Helps to Prayer* need to be read and re-read so that they are truly assimilated and become an integral part of your lifestyle as a disciple.

Since we are starting at the very beginning, we assume that the prayer of the beginner will be discursive and the stage of the Spiritual Life to be Purgative. It must not be assumed that discursive prayer which uses thoughts, words, images, memories, sentiments, as we do in human discourse, is an inferior form of prayer. Discursive prayer is the appropriate way of praying for us human beings. Discursive prayer is an excellent way of satisfying our religious curiosity and hunger about God. The mind is a major player in discursive prayer. However, it must always be at the service of the heart where true prayer happens! It is the Holy Spirit who will determine when we are being invited to contemplative prayer. When that begins to happen, you will undergo a very definite transition, with clear signs that our saints talk about. Contemplative Prayer will be a primary focus in the third year. During this year in PART TWO we will look at discursive **Methods of Prayer:** Vocal Prayer, The Method of Meditation, The Method of Ignatian Contemplation or Imaging, Lectio Divina or the Benedictine Method of Prayer, Praying with the Psalms. Once again, you will need to familiarize yourself with the *Methods of Prayer*, especially by using them on a regular basis so that you begin to experience the wisdom of the saints.

    We hold the assumption that if you made a serious commitment to God's invitation to holiness, already in the first year you would move into a committed discipleship. Hence, in PART TWO the Manual offers you some topics on **Practices for Committed Discipleship:** Practicing the Presence of God, The Prayer of Remembrance, and Recognizing God's Voice and Presence, I and II.

During each year of the 3-year Program, we have included **_4 Weekend Retreats or 4 Day-long Retreats_**, depending on the format for each location. We have found these retreats to be crucial in the formation of seasoned disciples. Over the retreat weekend, we have spent about 15 hours in prayer, spiritual direction, Eucharist, Sacrament of Reconciliation, and spiritual direction. Over the day long retreat, we have done about six hours of prayer. Very little input is offered during these retreats, as plenty of input is offered during our regular sessions. It is after these retreat experiences that several participants have developed a consistent pattern of daily prayer that has made a huge impact on their discipleship.

In the Second Year of the Program, the overarching vision is _Christian Discipleship_. As we did in the first year, this year too we will look at 18 themes over nine months. The topics will draw extensively from the teachings of Jesus and the New Testament. The major focus throughout this year will be to get a proper appreciation of who Jesus is as He reveals Himself in relationship to His Father and the Holy Spirit. We will spend much time and reflection on appreciating God's Plan of Salvation as fulfilled in Jesus who offers us the awesome privilege of participating in God's divine nature (2 Peter 1:4), and the gift of living out our discipleship in and with Jesus who is now Emmanuel, God-with-us! The _Helps to Prayer_ and _Necessary Practices toward Committed Discipleship_ will be geared toward the Illuminative Stage of Prayer. You will be given more information about the dynamics of the second year in the second year Manual.

In the third year of the Program, the overarching vision is _Mentored by the Holy Spirit._ As we did in the first two years, this year too we will look at 18 themes over nine months. The major focus throughout this year will be to get a proper appreciation of what it means to live our life with God as our Center, to learn to wait on the Holy Spirit who will reveal our decisions, and to live our life consistently in the Trinitarian Embrace. The _Helps to Prayer_ and _Necessary Practices toward_

Committed Discipleship will be geared toward the Illuminative and Unitive Stages of Prayer. You will be given more information about the dynamics of the third year in the third year Manual.

HOW THEN TO USE THE MANUAL?

We are looking at a three-pronged approach to formation: prayer, spiritual reading, and spiritual practices throughout the day. **PART ONE** or the Section on the Sessions deals primarily with your prayer experience. We are suggesting that you set aside *20-30 minutes every day*, at least five times a week, to spend time alone with God. The sessions offer you an in-depth reflection on the themes, each theme being prayed over for about two weeks. Your subject matter for prayer is taken from the ***PASSAGES FOR PRAYER*** section. Ordinarily, one passage per prayer session would be more than enough. It is quite possible that a particular passage will give you much matter over which to ponder and converse with God. In that case you might want to use the same passage for more than one prayer period. The reflection on the theme is offered as inspiration and motivation for your prayer. It is also spiritual reading.

PART TWO, SECTION ONE, deals with **HELPS TO PRAYER**. This section is to be done for your spiritual reading. The recommendation is that you do *15 minutes daily* for at least five days a week. The suggestions for spiritual reading on a daily basis would require more than 15 minutes. Assuming that you will not have enough time during the week, you might want to make up the difference over the weekend. You will want to read and re-read this section as it will provide answers to many questions that will arise about the dynamics of your prayer and relationship with God. **PART TWO, SECTION TWO,** deals with **METHODS OF PRAYER.** This section is to be done as spiritual reading as well, but it serves the specific purpose of helping you become more familiar with the ways our Christian forebears have related to God in prayer. **PART TWO, SECTION THREE,** deals with

PRACTICES FOR COMMITTED DISCIPLESHIP. These practices are the result of a sustained life of prayer done consistently and faithfully. They permeate the whole day, continuing the prayer that began when the disciple sat down at the feet of the Master for their daily visit. These disciplines make prayer a lifestyle which slowly but surely makes God the Center of one's life! **PART TWO, SECTION FOUR,** deals with **RETREATS** which can either be weekend or overnight. These retreats serve the purpose of strengthening and deepening our daily habit of prayer as well as enhancing prayer as lifestyle. They are done every other month or so during the year.

SESSION ONE: WHO IS GOD FOR YOU?

SCRIPTURE:

But Zion said, "The Lord has forsaken me, my Lord has forgotten me." Can a mother forget her infant, be without tenderness for the child of her womb? Even should she forget, I will never forget you. See, upon the palms of my hands I have written your name (NAB, Isaiah 49:14-16).

WHERE ARE YOU WITH GOD?

As Isaiah 49:14-16 suggests, our relationship with God and the assessment we make of it can depend so much on life's daily circumstances. Israel had fallen on harsh times. As a kingdom they were divided into two and were being plundered and ravaged by their neighboring kingdoms to the point where they would be exiled to Babylon for seventy years. In their misery they were convinced that the Lord had forsaken them, leaving them to destruction and humiliation at the hands of their captors. In this context of overwhelming anxiety and daunting despair, God speaks to Israel through Isaiah, the prophet. God chooses two images to convey divine compassion and covenant love towards them. He first compares himself to mothers who have such an indomitable commitment to their children. Mothers being human, in rare instances, fall short of this noble and intrepid passion for the well being of their children. Knowing that such devotion to their children is the bedrock on which the well-being and security of our human lives are based, the Lord portrays himself as being more faithful and devoted than even the best of mothers! No matter what the circumstances of our lives might be or even the deterioration of our relationship with Him, He will never forsake Israel and us.

The second image is that of an adolescent lover who writes the name of his beloved on the palms of his hands. Is it ironic or paradoxical that God sees himself as a youthful lover and therefore with dreams and enthusiasm about the future even though his beloved is in the throes of destruction and death? How then does this passage affect us and what kind of assessment do we make about our relationship with God?

FROM THE SECULAR TO THE DEVOUT:

Most of us engage in some form of prayer and relationship with God. There are some, however, who want to have nothing to do with God. This is a stance that they have taken for personal reasons, like a difficult crisis in life that soured their willingness to trust and be vulnerable, or as a way of dealing with the complex questions around the problem of evil in human life. At times people want to have nothing to do with God by default. They have been raised in an environment that negates the existence of the supernatural and limits all of human experience to the realm of the visible and discernible.

There are others who pray sporadically, engaging in prayer as ritual because of certain circumstances in their lives around religious feasts, or important passages in life like birth, marriage, and death, or when they are in crisis. For such persons who are experiencing hardship, God seems to be sought out mostly as a problem-solver or trouble-shooter. God is an important resource, to be used in times of emergency, but otherwise shelved in the recesses of their minds and hearts. Such persons are deists. They believe in the existence of God as a benign and transcendent power who lives and operates at a far distance from them. They don't have a real sense of God being involved in their lives and genuinely interested in their welfare. The question of having an intimate relationship with God is just beside the point. Earnest petitions arising out of the complexities of life never seem to get adequately answered because their understanding of God is so impersonal. Consequently they live with much confusion and disillusionment. Why pray, they ask, when God does not seem to be interested in them? If God really cared, God would take care of us. In this view of prayer, the seeker is at the center of his/her universe, left to fend for self, and God is at their beck and call, but not really, because God is inscrutable. Clearly, this is a topsy-turvy understanding of the Creator-creature relationship.

Others have learnt to give God a more significant place in their lives. They have endeavored to learn about God from God Himself, through His revelation. They pray more often and include hard times as well as good times in their conversations and relationship with God. God is sought as their refuge and strength. God is praised and offered thanks when blessings and graces come their way. God is not beholden to them. At the same time, God, through Jesus, has become Emmanuel, God-among-us, and will always be inextricably linked to our human lives! They have an abiding trust in God's tender love for them. Even when their prayers have not been answered the way they wanted, God still heard them. To them God has become a meaningful Presence and so they bring the daily circumstances of their lives to God. In time the significance of God's Presence dominates their lives and probably becomes their most important Presence. They trust this Presence and know they are in good hands, regardless of the circumstances. In gradual increments their relationship might evolve to the point where God has become the Center of their universe and they want to be at God's beck and call.

Persons who relate to God as the center of their lives are individuals who have a true appreciation of the biblical perspective on the relationship between God and humans. We are told in the Book of Genesis, "God created man in his image, in the divine image he created him, male and female he created them" (NAB: Genesis 1: 27). At the end of the sixth day, God's spontaneous response to His creation of humans is that "God looked at everything he had made, and he found it <u>very</u>

good (Genesis 1:31)." God's exclamation that everything he created was very good suggests his immense pleasure and satisfaction at the creation of humans, and the very intimate and strong bond He wished to establish with us by creating us in His image and likeness. The creation story highlights two important facts about our creation as humans. Our creation comes at the climax of God's immense work of love, and humans are seen as the apex of God's wonderful creation, given the privilege and responsibility of being caretakers of God's creatures. Of all earthly creatures, only humans have been created in God's image and likeness. No wonder the Psalmist is agog with wonder and amazement when he exclaims in Psalm 8: "You have made him little less than the angels, and crowned him with glory and honor. You have given him rule over the works of your hands, putting all things under his feet (NAB)." Psalm 139 speaks with deep reverence and appreciation for the work of God's hands on our behalf: "Truly you have formed my inmost being; you knit me in my mother's womb. I give you thanks that I am fearfully, wonderfully made; wonderful are your works (NAB: 13-14)."

The Fathers of the Church never stopped glorifying this irreducible greatness of humanity, this bottomless depth in the human being. Gregory of Nyssa, *On the Creation of Man,* II (PG 44,155) says, "An image is not truly an image if it does not possess all the characteristics of its pattern... It is characteristic of divinity to be incomprehensible: this must also be true of the image. If the image could be essentially understood while the original remained incomprehensible, the image would not be an image at all. But our spiritual dimension, which is precisely that wherein we are the image of our Creator, is beyond our ability to explain... by this mystery within us we bear the imprint of the incomprehensible godhead."

One of the mysterious facts of human life is our rejection or lukewarm acceptance of our Creator's vision and designs for us. The reality of sin and its allure away from God is ever present in our lives.

And Scripture highlights this ambivalence toward God which leads us to choose ourselves over God. Psalm 1 compares and contrasts the good man with the wicked one. The good man who delights in the law of the Lord and meditates on his law day and night is like "a tree planted near running water that yields its fruit in due season, and whose leaves never fade. What he does prospers." The wicked person, on the other hand, is "like chaff which the wind drives away." The Psalm also highlights a seeming fact of our human condition where evil forces appear to dominate the forces of good. "The kings of the earth rise up, and the princes conspire together against the Lord and against his anointed."

Another powerful example of this human dichotomy is illustrated in the story of Abraham's intercession for Sodom and Gomorrah in Genesis 18:16-32. The Lord takes Abraham into his confidence and reveals to him his intention of destroying Sodom and Gomorrah. And God's reason for taking Abraham into confidence is an interesting one. "Shall I hide from Abraham what I am about to do, now that he is to become a great and populous nation, and all the nations of the earth are to find blessing in him? Indeed, I have singled him out that he may direct his sons and his posterity to keep the way of the Lord by doing what is right and just, so that the Lord may carry into effect for Abraham the promises he made about him (NAB: Genesis 18: 17-18)." In this dialogue that takes place between God and Abraham, the latter appeals to God's justice to prevent the destruction of Sodom and Gomorrah because of their sinful ways and rejection of God. At first God agrees that He cannot destroy Sodom and Gomorrah if there were fifty just men in those towns. From fifty, Abraham whittles the number down to 10 and God is still willing to spare the two towns. Finally even Abraham relents when he realizes that there are no just men who will be destroyed in the disaster.

There are countless other examples of men and women both in the Bible and in human history who have chosen to be with or against

God. Cain and his brother Abel come to mind. Abel lived according to God's ways, whereas Cain was jealous of his brother and killed him because he was found pleasing in God's sight. King Solomon was upright and God-fearing in the first years of his reign. Later on, he forsook his God and worshipped the false gods or Baals of his numerous wives.

TOTAL DEPENDENCE ON GOD:

The important fact of our lives is that we will only experience ourselves as God's image and likeness when we are *totally dependent* on God for everything. We are speaking of a lifestyle where God becomes the beginning and end of our life, where every question is asked in God's presence and every answer received from the Holy Spirit. If then we lived life according to our true nature, we would understand that in our relationship with God, we are the satellite and God is the Center of our world. We would therefore seek constantly to be at God's beck and call.

HELPFUL ATTITUDES FOR PRAYER:

- It is important to understand that we can't be half-hearted with God. We might as well give this relationship with the Divine our utmost!
- Our relationship with God is different from all our other relationships. When we come before God, we are in the presence of Truth and Holiness. Hence any falsehood in us will have to be addressed.
- Prayer blossoms when we take the stance of being transparent before God, being willing to lay bare our souls, and being open to allowing the Holy Spirit to guide our lives and actions. The next time you pray, remember to dispose yourself in such a way that you are willing to be transparent before God and willing to allow the Holy Spirit to be your teacher and guide.

- You will realize that there will be much resistance within you to allow God to hold sway over your destiny. It is for this reason that Jesus tells us to ask for whatever we need to live in God's will.
- It is important to remember that we have feet of clay and will always be in need of forgiveness. It is the measure of a true disciple to acknowledge sin and ask for forgiveness.

GUIDELINES FOR PRAYER:

- Be faithful to your time of prayer, and make it between 20 and 30 minutes daily.
- Begin every prayer session with an earnest prayer to the Holy Spirit like the one I have composed for you: *Come, Holy Spirit, and overshadow me with your gentle wisdom and power as I endeavor to sit at the feet of Jesus during this period of prayer. Purify my mind and heart as I seek to make the teachings of Jesus my priority in life, thinking, speaking and doing as He desires. You are the keeper of my soul, leading me into God's heart. May I be docile and submissive to your wisdom and guidance, and may my life be a pleasing offering in your sight. Amen.*
- Take one of the passages suggested for your prayer. During the duration of this session you might want to ponder the question, **"Who is God for me?"**
- Lastly, during your prayer make sure that along with reflection you also address God directly and listen for answers that you need.
- You can end your prayer with the following: *Father, Son, and Holy Spirit, I thank you for your gracious companionship. I praise you for being my Creator, Savior and Lord. May I take your blessings to my day, and may your presence envelop and permeate all my thoughts and actions. Through Christ our Lord. Amen.*

PASSAGES FOR PRAYER:

Genesis, Chapters 1 & 2: Our Creation as God's image and likeness.

Genesis, Chapter 4: The Story of Cain and Abel
Psalm 1: True Happiness
Psalm 8: The Psalmist reflects on our creation as God's image and likeness.
Psalm 65: Thanksgiving for God's Blessings
Psalm 104: Praise of God the Creator
Psalm 139: The all-knowing and ever-present God
Matthew 18: 10-14: The Straying Sheep
Mark 7: 24-37: A Canaanite Woman & Healing of a Deaf Mute
Luke 1:46-55: Mary's Canticle: Mary's glorification of God.
Luke 1: 67-79: Zechariah's praise of God.
Luke 18: 9-14: The Pharisee and the Tax Collector
John 1: 1-14: The Prologue
John 3: 11-21: Salvation through Jesus

JOURNALING: *HELPS TO PRAYER, # 6*

SPIRITUAL READING: *HELPS TO PRAYER, # 4 AND 5*

Manual: Read Sessions One and Two for the first month, and delve into the topics in *Helps to Prayer* and *Methods of Prayer* from session 1 through 10.

New Testament: Try to read the New Testament over Sessions 1 through 10

Old Testament: Try to Read the first five books of the Bible or *Pentateuch* over Sessions 1 through 10.

Imitation of Christ: Follow the suggestions in *Helps to Prayer # 5*.

Catechism of the Catholic Church: Follow the suggestions in *Helps to Prayer #5*

SESSION TWO: WHO IS GOD AS HE SAYS HE IS?

SCRIPTURE:

But now, thus says the Lord, who created you, O Jacob, and formed you, O Israel: "Fear not, for I have redeemed you; I have called you by name: you are mine. When you pass through the water, I will be with you; in the rivers you shall not drown. When you walk through fire, you shall not be burned; the flames shall not consume you. For I am the Lord, your God, the Holy One of Israel, your savior. (NAB: Isaiah 43: 1-3)"

UNDERSTANDING GOD THROUGH HIS WORKS:

St. Ignatius of Loyola hits the nail on the head when in his 'Contemplation to attain the love of God' in the Spiritual Exercises, he describes love as needing to manifest itself in deeds rather than in words. Secondly, the true nature of love consists in a mutual sharing. Thus one always gives to the other. According to this understanding of love, talking the talk makes sense only when one walks the talk. In Scripture God reveals who He is in one way or another by fulfilling His promises.

In the Scripture passage from Isaiah 43, the Lord is speaking to a beleaguered and defeated people. They are definitely going into exile. Yet God offers them a powerful message of hope and reassurance because, as He describes Himself "I am the Lord, your God, the Holy One of Israel, your savior." This statement is like a reverberating "Amen" to God's marvelous deeds among His people. This description reminds Israel of her history with God. In times past, especially during the Exodus and settlement of the Promised Land, God had been 'holy,' totally other than the other gods and their adherents from whom He had always protected and delivered them. God was also totally other than what the Israelites could ever have imagined or expected. As a result they adored, praised, and thanked the Living God for His mighty and marvelous deeds through which He expressed His love for them! He was truly the God of their history!

God reminds them that it is He who redeemed them from slavery in Egypt. Traditionally redemption from slavery occurred when the family member of a slave took his/her place, acting as the price which bought the slave's freedom. You can read Leviticus 25 to know more about this tradition of redemption from slavery. This understanding of redemption was later fulfilled beyond measure by Jesus who bought with the price of his own life and blood, not only the salvation of Israel but that of the whole world. "Though he (Jesus) was in the form of God, he did not deem equality with God something to be grasped at. Rather, he emptied himself and took the form of a slave, being born in the likeness of men. He was known to be of human estate, and it was thus that he humbled himself, obediently accepting even death, death on a cross! Because of this, God highly exalted him and bestowed upon him the name above every other name, so that at Jesus' name every knee must bend in the heavens, on the earth, and under the earth, and every tongue proclaim to the glory of God the Father: JESUS CHRIST IS LORD! (NAB: Philippians 2: 6-11)"

CALLED BY NAME:

God reminds them that it is He who called them by name and they are His. Naming a person in Scripture has particular relevance as it signifies a very special bond between the one naming and the named. In several places God changed the name of the individual as a way of signifying this special relationship of intimacy between God and the individual. Abram's name was changed to Abraham as was Sarai's to Sarah. In the New Testament, among others, Simon's name was changed to Peter.

As Christians we experience this special bond and intimacy on three levels in baptism. In giving us a name our parents were telling themselves and everyone concerned that we belonged to them in a very special way and they were forever committed to us as family. Similarly, the Church expressed her special connection with us by receiving and claiming us as children of the ecclesial community or the Body of Christ. And most importantly, through baptism God claimed us as His own children. Jesus took upon himself our sins and therefore our slavery, so that He could present us to his Father as God's sons and daughters and as his own brothers and sisters.

This wondrous act of redemption is captured eloquently in the vision that John the beloved disciple has in Revelation 5:11-12: "As my vision continued, I heard the voices of many angels who surrounded the throne and the living creatures and the elders. They were countless in number, thousands and tens of thousands, and they all cried out: "Worthy is the Lamb that was slain to receive power and riches, wisdom and strength, honor and glory and praise! (NAB)"

GOD AS PROTECTOR:

God is reminding the Israelites that in the midst of their suffering and humiliation in their land of exile, He will be with them when they pass through the water and river. Clearly there are echoes here of the crossing of the Red Sea which was a mighty crossing over from danger at the hands of Pharaoh and his army to the security and power of God's protection and sovereignty. This passage also echoes Daniel 3: 22-24, where God preserves Shadrach, Meshach, and Abednego from the fiery furnace: "So huge a fire was kindled in the furnace that the flames devoured the men who threw Shadrach, Meshach, and Abednego into it. But these three fell, bound, into the midst of the white-hot furnace. They walked about in the flames, singing to God and blessing the Lord. (NAB)"

MOSES' ENCOUNTER WITH "I AM":

Both the Old and New Testaments are replete with special reference to God's love for humans and faithfulness to His promises. Let us look at just a few references. In Exodus 3, Moses has a life-altering encounter with the Lord God. He is reluctant however to heed God's instructions to go to Egypt as His messenger to bring the Hebrews to freedom and the Promised Land. Moses is obviously intimidated by God's request and concerned about being prosecuted for murdering an Egyptian. So he tries to find any and every excuse to get out of God's mission to him.

At one point Moses says to God, "when I go to the Israelites and say to them, 'The God of your fathers has sent me to you,' if they ask me, 'What is his name?' what am I to tell them?" God replied, "I am who am." Then he added, "This is what you shall tell the Israelites: I AM sent me to you." Apparently this utterance is the source of the word *Yahweh*, the proper personal name of the God of Israel. It is commonly explained in reference to God as the absolute and necessary Being. It may be understood of God as the Source of all created beings.

Out of reverence for this name, the term *Adonai*, "my Lord," was later used as a substitute. In the gospel of John, Jesus repeatedly refers to himself as I AM! In John 8: 24-27, this is what Jesus says about himself while preaching at the temple treasury: "You will surely die in your sins unless you come to believe that I AM...When you lift up the Son of Man, you will come to realize that I AM and that I do nothing by myself." If as the name suggests God is the ultimate Power and Being, the Hebrews and we, the disciples of Jesus, need never fear for our ultimate security and destiny.

GOD'S WAYS ARE NOT OUR WAYS:

There is a beautiful invitation to grace in Isaiah, Chapter 55. We will always be afraid of God's justice if we do not appreciate deeply His mercy and compassion. Chapter 55 of Isaiah helps to give us such an appreciation. There are several images in this chapter that capture the wonderfully mysterious nature of God's love and compassion for us. For instance, "all you who are thirsty come to the water! You who have no money, come, receive grain and eat; come, without paying and without cost, drink wine and milk (NAB: Isaiah 55: 1)!" God will provide abundantly at no cost to us!

Similarly, "let the scoundrel forsake his way, and the wicked man his thoughts; let him turn to the Lord for mercy; to our God who is generous in forgiving. For my thoughts are not your thoughts, nor are your ways my ways, says the Lord. As high as the heavens are above the earth, so high are my ways above your ways and my thoughts above your thoughts (NAB: Isaiah 55:7-9)."

The depths of love contained in these words defy any verbal description. They are words that can only be pondered and appreciated in one's heart where hopefully one day the Mystery of God's love will blossom into the transformation of our lives!

CREATED IN GOD'S IMAGE AND LIKENESS:

Finally, "God created man in his image; in the divine image he created him; male and female He created them. God blessed them, saying: Be fertile and multiply; fill the earth and subdue it. Have dominion over the fish of the sea, the birds of the air, and all the living things that move on the earth" (NAB: Genesis 1: 27-28). The first chapters of the Book of Genesis capture vividly the depths of God's inexhaustible love for us. God's decision is to offer the human inhabitants of a new universe the privilege of participating in the divine life and heritage. In his second letter, 1:4, Peter says, "He has bestowed on us the great and precious things he promised, so that through these you who have fled a world corrupted by lust might become sharers of the divine nature." And Paul in his letter to the Ephesians 1:3-6, captures this amazing and baffling reality that we can participate in God's very own life: "Praised be the God and Father of our Lord Jesus Christ, who has bestowed on us in Christ every spiritual blessing in the heavens! God chose us in him before the world began, to be holy and blameless in his sight, to be full of love; he likewise predestined us through Christ Jesus to be his adopted sons – such was his will and pleasure – that all might praise the glorious favor he has bestowed on us in his beloved." This decision on God's part can only be an act of pure love, as God doesn't need humans to complete Him. As God's image and likeness we participate in the continuing act of creation by exercising authority over creatures the way God would.

HELPFUL ATTITUDES FOR PRAYER:

- You will never become comfortable with God's justice if you do not come to a deep appreciation of God's overwhelming love and compassion for you.
- Your creation as God's image and likeness is an unadulterated blessing and privilege you will never fully understand. However, your life will be profoundly transformed if you live in constant gratitude for this divine gift.
- There will be times when your heart will be racked with doubt and confusion. Your thoughts will be laced with anxiety and you might even wonder about God's faithfulness to you. In those moments it helps to remember Isaiah 55: 9: "As high as the heavens are above the earth, so high are my ways above your ways and my thoughts above your thoughts."

- The Christian learns to be patient and long-suffering in crisis and tribulation because of the conviction that God is faithful to His promises.

<u>GUIDELINES FOR PRAYER:</u>

- Be faithful to your time of prayer, and make it between 20 and 30 minutes daily.
- Begin every prayer session with an earnest prayer to the Holy Spirit like the one I have composed for you: *Come, Holy Spirit, and overshadow me with your gentle wisdom and power as I endeavor to sit at the feet of Jesus during this period of prayer. Purify my mind and heart as I seek to make the teachings of Jesus my priority in life, thinking, speaking and doing as He desires. You are the keeper of my soul, leading me into God's heart. May I be docile and submissive to your wisdom and guidance, and may my life be a pleasing offering in your sight. Amen.*
- Take one of the passages suggested for your prayer. During the duration of this session you might want to ponder the question, **"Do I take seriously who God says He is?"**
- Lastly, during your prayer make sure that along with reflection you also address God directly and listen for answers that you need.
- You can end your prayer with the following: *Father, Son, and Holy Spirit, I thank you for your gracious companionship. I praise you for being my Creator, Savior and Lord. May I take your blessings to my day, and may your presence envelop and permeate all my thoughts and actions. Through Christ our Lord. Amen.*

<u>PASSAGES FOR PRAYER:</u>

Genesis, Chapters 1 & 2: Our Creation as God's image and likeness.
Exodus 3: The Call of Moses
Exodus 15: The Canticle of Moses

Psalm 8: The Psalmist reflects on our creation as God's image and likeness.
Psalm 105: God's Fidelity to His Promise
Psalm 139: The All-Knowing and Ever-Present God
Psalm 145: The Greatness and Goodness of God
Isaiah 43: Promises of Redemption and Restoration
Isaiah 49: 1-7: The Servant of the Lord
John 10: 1-18: The Good Shepherd
John 13: 1-17: Jesus washes the feet of his disciples
John 15: 1-17: The Vine and the Branches & a Disciple's Love
Acts 2: 14-41: Peter's Discourse
Ephesians 1: 1-10: God's Plan of Salvation
Philippians 2: 5-11: Imitating Christ's Humility

JOURNALING: *HELPS TO PRAYER, # 6*

SPIRITUAL READING: *HELPS TO PRAYER, # 4 AND 5*
<u>Manual:</u> Read Sessions One and Two for the first month, and delve into the topics in *Helps to Prayer* and *Methods of Prayer* over Sessions 1 through 10.
<u>New Testament:</u> Try to read the New Testament over Sessions 1 through 10.
<u>Old Testament:</u> Try to Read the first five books of the Bible or *Pentateuch* over Sessions 1 through 10.
<u>Imitation of Christ</u>: Follow the suggestions in *Helps to Prayer # 5*.
<u>Catechism of the Catholic Church</u>: Follow the suggestions in *Helps to Prayer #5*

SESSION THREE: GOD'S VISION FOR US

SCRIPTURE:

God chose us in him before the world began, to be holy and blameless in his sight, to be full of love; he likewise predestined us through Christ Jesus to be his adopted sons (NAB: Ephesians 1: 4-6).

NURTURED IN GOD'S EMBRACE:

A personal and intimate relationship with God is a pure gift. God was never beholden to us when deciding to create us. We were non-existent. God's decision to create us was an act of selfless and overwhelming love. And in creating us in the divine image and likeness, God made the irrevocable decision to be involved intimately in our lives and be the God of our history. Scripture is replete with passages portraying God's predilection for us. We have already looked at a few examples. In the Creation story the author captures God's vision for us in a pithy statement that reveals much more than it says: "God created man in his image; in the divine image he created him; male and female he created them (NAB: Genesis 1:27)."

DISCONCERTING REALITY OF HUMAN LIFE:

Even with such a noble identity many of us struggle with low self-esteem, shame and guilt. Life is summed up as the perennial half empty glass. Some never get past a pessimistic assessment of their lives because they are so trapped in their mistakes and failures. Others have wandered through the wilderness of addictions and degradation. The question of our identity is a complex one, as it is multi-layered. As we go through life, we realize that our families and genes have shaped our identity in significant ways.

At the same time, we have been able to alter our characters in meaningful ways through gaining experience and wisdom, thus replacing some of our maladjusted habits with life-enhancing attitudes. Trends and influences around us play an important role in shaping and grounding our identity. We absorb the positive influences of mentors and friends when we open ourselves to their wisdom and effective lifestyle. By the same token our chances of assuming bad habits are high when we surround ourselves with negative and harmful influences.

It is only on a true understanding of our nature that God's continued providence and grace can build. It is encouraging when we meet a person who believes with every fiber of their being that he or she has been created in God's image and likeness and lives in joy and hope. The Psalmist is one such person who is subdued into wonder and gratitude as he tries to appreciate the mystery of our being in Psalm 8: "What are humans that you are mindful of them, mere mortals that you care for them? Yet you have made them little less than a god, crowned them with glory and honor (NAB: 5-6)."

In Psalm 139 the Psalmist continues to express great awe and gratitude at the way we have been created by God: "How weighty are your designs, O God; how vast the sum of them! Were I to recount them, they would outnumber the sands: did I reach the end of them, I should still be with you (NAB: 17-18)." Whatever our assessments of who we are, or even what others think of us, in our essence we belong to God's own family and lineage. Our destiny is a noble one because it has originated in the heart of God.

GOD IS ABBA:

In Matthew 6, in teaching his disciples how to pray Jesus asks them and us to address God as "Father." "Abba" is a word similar to words in other languages that infants use to address their parents when they are beginning to utter intelligible sounds. Given the nature of the infant such names or terms are easy to pronounce. They are names that are also life lines for the toddler. At one year of age an infant has no choice except to depend totally on its parents. Given its helplessness to fend for itself it has no other option. When this fundamental trust in its parents is reverenced, an infant grows up healthy and secure. When parents abuse this sacred trust society deals with the consequences of abuse and neglect. In the prayer Jesus taught us, he is asking us as adults to put on the mind and heart of an infant and address God with total confidence and trust, believing that no other option would be in our best interests than this one. In a very real sense Jesus is asking us to trust his Father completely even though our ability to trust others might have been marred because of our own suffering and sin.

As Michael Fonseca says in his book, "Living in God's Embrace," "The seeker who calls on God as Abba with trust and conviction soon realizes that being God's child is at the core of his or her reality. And such a truth sets us free. In other words, God's way of understanding us is very different from the way we understand ourselves. True spiritual and psychological health and freedom begin only when we learn to look at and understand ourselves through God's eyes and thoughts (Chapter 2: *Nurtured in God's Embrace*, page 64)." Isaiah55:8, reiterates this security in trusting God when he says, "For my thoughts are not your thoughts, nor are your ways my ways, says the Lord."

There is another even more radical dimension to Jesus' exhortation that we address God as Father. This radical dimension acts as the foundation of the Lord's Prayer. Until Jesus, nowhere in the Bible is God addressed as 'Father.' Jesus is the only Person who addresses God as 'My Father.' While 'I AM' is the Triune God's name that has been revealed to us, Jesus always addressed God as 'My Father.' In giving us the Lord's Prayer, Jesus is inviting us into the bosom of God's divine Life. In enabling us to address God as 'Father,' Jesus is sharing with us the intimacy of His relationship with His Father. Through Jesus the Father claims us as His own. In offering us the gift of His relationship with His Father to make our own, Jesus is sharing with us as well the gift of their Holy Spirit who is the bond of love and tenderness between Father and Son!

GOD'S PLAN OF SALVATION:

A reading of Ephesians 1:3-10 provides an inkling of God's dynamic love for us. To the human mind, God's commitment to us is utterly incomprehensible. More than we can ever imagine or conceive, God knows and abhors the reality of sin. God also knows how enslaved humankind has been to the treachery and deceit of Satan and sin. In spite of or because of our sinfulness, God holds on to the bold and enthusiastic decision made from all eternity that we would be the divine image and likeness. And in his letter to the Ephesians, Paul spells out what this means when he says, "Praised be the God and Father of our Lord Jesus Christ who has bestowed on us in Christ every spiritual blessing in the heavens! God chose us in him before the world began, to be holy and blameless in his sight, to be full of love (NAB)"

It is incomprehensible to the human mind that God would desire holiness, blamelessness, and full love from each of us. Only God is holy by essence. To be holy is to be totally other than. That is why God is Mystery. God wants to transform us so that we will know that we are other than whom we think we are, or as God knows us. Similarly only God is blameless. God desires that we too become blameless. In other words God will forgive us all our sins and help us live transformed lives of service and love, the opposite fruits of sin. We will become like the unblemished victim of sacrifice, offered in devotion and love to God on behalf of His people, the Body of Christ!

Lastly, only God is full of love. God desires that we too be full of love, that we forgive and let go of all hatred, anger, resentment, and anything that soils our spirits so that we can be a pleasing offering in God's sight. And this transformation has been made possible through the sacrifice of Jesus on the cross. He has washed us clean and brought us into the bosom of the Father where God desires that we live our lives. It is therefore very fitting for Jesus to say in Matthew 5:48: "In a word, you must be made perfect as your heavenly Father is perfect (NAB)."

HELPFUL ATTITUDES FOR PRAYER:

- It is important to understand that God decided to make you extraordinary by human standards. You have been made God's own son/daughter through Jesus Christ.
- Being God's child is your privilege and destiny. This identity should produce profound gratitude and humility.
- If ever your divine heritage became a source of pride and elitism, you would have committed the sin of idolatry, making a possession and idol out of God's gift to you.
- In offering us the gift of His relationship with His Father to make our own, Jesus is sharing with us as well the gift of their Holy Spirit who is the bond of love and tenderness between Father and Son!
- Jesus says that he and the Father are one. The best way to understand and appreciate Abba's tenderness towards us is by examining the life of Jesus.
- Our transformation into sons and daughters of the Living God has been made possible through the sacrifice of Jesus on the cross. He has washed us clean and brought us into the bosom of the Father where God desires that we live our lives.

GUIDELINES FOR PRAYER:

- Be faithful to your time of prayer, and make it between 20 and 30 minutes daily.
- Begin every prayer session with an earnest prayer to the Holy Spirit like the one I have composed for you: *Come, Holy Spirit, and*

overshadow me with your gentle wisdom and power as I endeavor to sit at the feet of Jesus during this period of prayer. Purify my mind and heart as I seek to make the teachings of Jesus my priority in life, thinking, speaking and doing as He desires. You are the keeper of my soul, leading me into God's heart. May I be docile and submissive to your wisdom and guidance, and may my life be a pleasing offering in your sight. Amen.

- Take one of the passages suggested for your prayer. During the duration of this session you might want to ponder the question, **"Have I taken the time to appreciate and thank God for His vision and plan of salvation?"**
- Lastly, during your prayer make sure that along with reflection you also address God directly and listen for answers that you need.
- You can end your prayer with the following: *Father, Son, and Holy Spirit, I thank you for your gracious companionship. I praise you for being my Creator, Savior and Lord. May I take your blessings to my day, and may your presence envelop and permeate all my thoughts and actions. Through Christ our Lord. Amen.*

PASSAGES FOR PRAYER:

Psalm 23: The Lord, Shepherd and Host
Isaiah 65: 17-25: The World Renewed
Isaiah 66: 18-24: Gathering of the Nations
Jeremiah 31:31-34: The New Covenant
Ezekiel 36:24-32: Regeneration of the People
Matthew 11: 25-30: Jesus and His Father
John 3: 11-21: Salvation through Christ
John 6: 25-71: Discourse on the Bread of Life
John 12: 44-50: Summary Proclamation
John 13: 1-17: The Washing of the Feet
Ephesians 1: 1-10: The Father's Plan of Salvation
Ephesians 2: 1-10: The Generosity of God's Plan

Colossians 1: 15-23: Fullness and Reconciliation

JOURNALING: *HELPS TO PRAYER, # 6*

SPIRITUAL READING: *HELPS TO PRAYER, # 4 AND 5*

<u>Manual:</u> Read Sessions Three and Four for the second month, and delve into the topics in *Helps to Prayer* and *Methods of Prayer* over Sessions 1 through 10.

<u>New Testament:</u> Try to read the New Testament over Sessions 1 through 10.

<u>Old Testament:</u> Try to Read the first five books of the Bible or *Pentateuch* over Sessions 1 through 10.

<u>Imitation of Christ</u>: Follow the suggestions in *Helps to Prayer # 5*.

<u>Catechism of the Catholic Church</u>: Follow the suggestions in *Helps to Prayer #5*

SESSION FOUR: THE REALITY OF SIN

SCRIPTURE:

The woman answered the serpent: "We may eat of the fruit of the trees in the garden; it is only about the fruit of the tree in the middle of the garden that God said, 'You shall not eat it or even touch it, lest you die.'" But the serpent said to the woman: "You certainly will not die! No, God knows well that the moment you eat of it your eyes will be opened and you will be like gods who know what is good and what is bad. The woman saw that the tree was good for food, pleasing to the eyes, and desirable for gaining wisdom. So she took some of its fruit and ate it; and she also gave some to her husband, who was with her, and he ate it. Then the eyes of both of them were opened, and they realized that they were naked; so they sewed fig leaves together and made loincloths for themselves (NAB: Genesis 3: 2-7).

THE DECEPTION OF SIN:

Genesis 3 offers us the most original understanding of sin and its devious nature. Every other description of sin in the Bible reflects this foundational portrayal of sin. In the above passage the woman states a fact and a prohibition. The fact is that she and the man may eat of the fruit of the trees in the garden; the prohibition, however, is that they are not to eat or touch the fruit of the tree in the middle of the garden. If the prohibition is broken, death will ensue.

It is then that Satan as represented by the serpent enters the scene. He is a master at deceit and trickery. He twists the facts given to him by the woman and makes God out to be a liar. Satan argues that God is in fact afraid that the creature He created will become equal to Him and like other gods. Through this web of deception, sin creates a gravitational allure away from God toward self. Satan's argument against God seems convincing and it is difficult for the man and woman to detect any flaws, because they have already begun thinking along those lines. Agreeing with Sin incarnate becomes well-nigh irresistible.

To return to the passage, at first we are told that the tree in the middle of the garden was good for food, pleasing to the eye, and desirable for gaining wisdom. This statement presents a fact and a mirage. The fact is that all creatures are good in themselves because they have been created by God. As St. Ignatius says in the *First Principle and Foundation* in the Spiritual Exercises, "Man is created to praise, reverence, and serve God our Lord, and by this means to save his soul. The other things on the face of the earth are created for man to help him in attaining the end for which he is created. Hence, man is to make use of them in as far as they help him in the attainment of his end, and he must rid himself of them in as far as they prove a hindrance to him." While all creatures are good in themselves, there is a tendency in humans to thwart the proper use of creatures, misusing them for self-aggrandizement rather than for God's glory. The man and woman in stating the goodness of the tree in the middle of the garden are agreeing with God that "it is good (refer to the Creation story)." But judging from the context they are implying that this good and beautiful creature can be used for their own self-serving purposes to become like and compete with God! The woman then convinced herself that eating the fruit would further her own ambitions even when they violated God's purposes. She ate of the fruit and gave it to her husband who also ate of it. And then they faced a painful reality – the consequences of sin.

THE CONSEQUENCES OF SIN:

All along they were naked and felt no shame (Genesis 2:25). However, after they had eaten of the fruit, they realized that they were <u>naked</u>! This time around they are experiencing their nakedness differently. Shame and confusion have entered the picture. Their identity has been affected. When God wants to visit them at the breezy time of day, "the man and his wife hid themselves from the Lord God among the trees of the garden (NAB: Genesis 3:8)." In response to God's question about their whereabouts, the man answers, "I heard you in the garden; but I was afraid, because I was naked, so I hid myself." Before sin, their nakedness was a blessing and joy as they were in harmony with God and themselves. Now their nakedness is a source of shame and fear as they feel alienated from God and themselves.

Their alienation manifests itself through signs that are foreign to truth and transparency. The Lord God draws the inevitable conclusion from their desire to hide from Him by saying, "You have eaten, then, from the tree of which I had forbidden you to eat (NAB: Genesis 3:11)!" The man replies by excusing himself and blaming his wife for eating of the fruit. And when the Lord God asked the woman the same question, she passed the buck by blaming the serpent. Blaming others for one's own misdeeds or not taking responsibility by making excuses is clearly one of the characteristics of sin. As the story reads, God does not ask the serpent the same question. Satan is the Father of Lies and relishes deceit and opposition to God. Satan will not make excuses about executing plots of evil.

The story continues to reveal the consequences of sin. Turning toward the serpent, God says, "Because you have done this, you shall be banned from all the animals and from all the wild creatures; on your belly shall you crawl, and dirt shall you eat all the days of your life (NAB: Genesis 3:14)." Satan's identification with evil causes a separation and alienation from all creatures. It is necessary to remember this equation: Satan=alienation. Anytime we listen to evil always masquerading under the guise of good, we will suffer isolation and alienation from God, ourselves, and others.

The Lord God goes on to say in Genesis 3:15: "I will put enmity between you and the woman, and between your offspring and hers; He will strike at your head, while you strike at his heel (NAB)." The theme of Satan being our enemy continues in this passage. But there is a more important theme. We will never be able to win our battle against Satan and sin without outside help. Satan's eventual defeat seems implied in the contrast between *head* and *heel*. The passage can be understood as the first promise of a Redeemer for fallen humankind because "the Son of God appeared that he might destroy the works of the devil (NAB: 1 John 3:8)." The woman's offspring then is primarily Jesus Christ.

Another consequence of sin is that human life will have its fair share of travail and hardship. The woman is told that she will bear children in pain and "he (her husband) shall be your master (Genesis 3:16)." Until they sinned, the relationship between the man and woman had been harmonious. There had been no rivalry or need to lord it over each other. The two of them operated as one body. With sin this significant relationship has become disordered; from now on there will always be the need to work at improving relationships. And to the man God said that he would earn his living by the sweat of his brow. There would be no productivity without labor and hardship. The last consequence of sin results in life seeming like an exile from God. While the Lord God will still be very involved with us and solicitous about our welfare, we will always be pining for God, as "the deer pants for running waters (NAB: Psalm 41)."

HELPFUL ATTITUDES FOR PRAYER:

- It is necessary to understand that we are on a slippery slope when we make even the slightest move toward dabbling with sin. If you flirt with sin beyond five seconds, you run the risk of compromising yourself, according to the wisdom of Alcoholics Anonymous.
- Sin has a willful and defiant quality about it. It is the willful disregard of the welfare of others for the satisfaction of self.
- It is always helpful to have a very concrete sense of sin, understanding how it expresses itself in specific behaviors. Part of your spiritual formation is to think concretely about sin.

- Proverbs 6:17-19 tells us of the seven things God hates: "Haughty eyes, a lying tongue, and hands that shed innocent blood; a heart that plots wicked schemes, feet that run swiftly to evil, the false witness who utters lies, and he who sows discord among brothers.
- Paul tells us what proceeds from the flesh: "lewd conduct, impurity, licentiousness, idolatry, sorcery, hostilities, bickering, jealousy, outbursts of rage, selfish rivalries, dissensions, factions, envy, drunkenness, orgies, and the like....those who do such things will not inherit the kingdom of God (NAB Galatians 5:19-21)!"

GUIDELINES FOR PRAYER:

- Be faithful to your time of prayer, and make it between 20 and 30 minutes daily.
- Begin every prayer session with an earnest prayer to the Holy Spirit like the one I have composed for you: *Come, Holy Spirit, and overshadow me with your gentle wisdom and power as I endeavor to sit at the feet of Jesus during this period of prayer. Purify my mind and heart as I seek to make the teachings of Jesus my priority in life, thinking, speaking and doing as He desires. You are the keeper of my soul, leading me into God's heart. May I be docile and submissive to your wisdom and guidance, and may my life be a pleasing offering in your sight. Amen.*
- Take one of the passages suggested for your prayer. During the duration of this session you might want to ponder the question, **"Do I have an appreciation of the disorder of my actions and the ungodly spirit of the world that I encounter on a daily basis?"**
- Lastly, during your prayer make sure that along with reflection you also address God directly and listen for answers that you need.
- You can end your prayer with the following: *Father, Son, and Holy Spirit, I thank you for your gracious companionship. I praise you for being my Creator, Savior and Lord. May I take your blessings to*

my day, and may your presence envelop and permeate all my thoughts and actions. Through Christ our Lord. Amen.

PASSAGES FOR PRAYER:
Genesis 3: 1-24: The Fall of Man; Genesis 4: 1-16: Cain and Abel
Genesis 19: The Destruction of Sodom and Gomorrah
Genesis 32: 1-35: The Golden Calf
Genesis 37: Joseph sold into Egypt
1 Samuel 2: 12-36: Wickedness of Eli's sons
2 Samuel 11: 1-27: David's Sin
1 Kings 11: 1-13: The Sins of Solomon
Psalm 32: Remission of Sin
Psalm 36: Human Wickedness and Divine Providence
Psalm 38: Prayer of an Afflicted Sinner
Psalm 51: Prayer of Repentance
Matthew 4: The Temptations of Jesus
Matthew 7: Avoiding Judgment and the Golden Rule
Matthew 21: 12-17: Cleansing out the Temple
Romans 6: 12-23: Freedom from sin; life in God

JOURNALING: *HELPS TO PRAYER, # 6*

SPIRITUAL READING: *HELPS TO PRAYER, # 4 AND 5*
Manual: Read Sessions Five and Six for the third month, and delve into the topics in *Helps to Prayer* and *Methods of Prayer* over Sessions 1 through 10.
New Testament: Try to read the New Testament over Sessions 1 through 10.
Old Testament: Try to Read the first five books of the Bible or *Pentateuch* over Sessions 1 through 10.
Imitation of Christ: Follow the suggestions in *Helps to Prayer # 5*.
Catechism of the Catholic Church: Follow the suggestions in *Helps to Prayer #5*,
Or Pages 505 to 611: The Ten Commandments

SESSION FIVE: GOD'S MERCY

SCRIPTURE:
Fear not, you shall not be put to shame; you need not blush, for you shall not be disgraced. The shame of your youth you shall forget, the reproach of your widowhood no longer remember. For he who has become your husband is your Maker. - NAB: Isaiah 54: 4-5

REPENTANCE OPENS THE DOOR TO GOD'S MERCY:

This theme is intimately connected with the last session. There would be no need of mercy without the existence of sin. Because of sin our relationship with God is severed or ruptured. Bridging the chasm between God and us is beyond our means. If we were capable of doing so there would be no need of God's help. Our experience of trying not to sin and failing in our endeavor, tells us clearly that we cannot span this gap on our own. Mercy is God's compassion or willingness to suffer with our pain and ignominy and restore us to an authentic relationship with the Divine once again. Mercy is God's bridge by which we can enter God's heart. Isaiah 54, from which the Scripture quote has been taken, captures the essence of God's compassion.

God is speaking to Israel sunk to its lowest depths in its religious history. They are in exile. Their identity has been shattered through their own doing. They have been humiliated and shamed. In the process they have widowed themselves because they abandoned their 'Husband-God': "The LORD calls you back, like a wife forsaken and grieved in spirit, a wife married in youth and then cast off, says your God. For a brief moment I abandoned you, but with great tenderness I will take you back. In an outburst of wrath, for a moment I hid my face from you; but with enduring love I take pity on you, says the LORD, your redeemer (NAB: Isaiah 54:6-8). God's compassion oozes out towards 'his wife,' as God restores Israel to integrity and wholeness: "This is for me like the days of Noah, when I swore that the waters of Noah should never again deluge the earth; so I have sworn not to be angry with you, or to rebuke you (NAB: Isaiah 54: 9)."

While God will always be eager to offer us mercy and forgiveness, on our part we will not be able to receive it without a contrite and repentant heart. Acknowledging our sinfulness and asking for God's forgiveness with the assurance that it will be given, is essential to an authentic relationship with God. Psalm 51 captures this sentiment of repentance very palpably. Nathan the prophet has confronted King David of his twofold sin: of taking Bathsheba unlawfully to be his wife, and having her husband Uriah, killed on the battlefield. David knows that he has sinned grievously against God and his people, especially Uriah. In spite of his grievous sins, he is confident that God will forgive him because he has a repentant heart and is willing to make amends: "Have mercy on me, O God in your goodness; in the greatness of your compassion wipe out my offense (v.1)... I acknowledge my offense, and my sin is before me always (v.5)... A clean heart create for me, O God, and a steadfast spirit renew within me (v.12)... Give me back the joy of your salvation and a willing spirit sustain in me (v.14)... My sacrifice, O God is a contrite spirit; a heart contrite and humbled, O God, you will not spurn (v.19)."

MERCY AT THE HEART OF GOD'S COVENANT WITH US:

Of all God's attributes, mercy is probably the one most appealing to us. Our merciful God is willing to help us in need simply because we are in need. The divine mercy extends itself to us in a faithful, loving kindness that the Hebrew Scriptures frequently speak of as *hesed*. In the Psalms especially, God is praised as faithful, loving, kind, and constant in helping the people: "Hasten to answer me, O LORD, for my spirit fails me. Hide not your face from me lest I become like those who go down into the pit. ...Show me the way in which I should walk, for to you I lift up my soul. Rescue me from my enemies, O LORD, for in you I hope (NAB: Psalm 143:7-9)."

The ground for both understanding and expecting God's faithful mercy is the covenant which will be the topic of our next session. God's mercy is not a fitful and arbitrary action where God splashes into our lives in whimsical fashion. Rather, divine mercy is an ongoing and constant activity because it is grounded in God's covenant relationship with us. Constancy is fundamental to mercy: "Though the mountains leave their place and the hills be shaken, my love shall never leave you nor my covenant of peace be shaken, says the LORD who has mercy on you (NAB: Isaiah 54:10)."

EXPECTING GOD'S MERCY IS THE DISCIPLE'S PRIVILEGE:

The covenant establishes a unique relationship between God and us. While we can never earn mercy, we know that we can expect it because of God's commitment to us. Like all that pertains to God's goodness, mercy is both a much sought after gift and a life-giving action. In Matthew 15: 22 we are told that "a Canaanite woman living in that locality presented herself, crying out to him, "Lord, Son of David, have pity on me! My daughter is terribly troubled by a demon." After testing her and being amazed at her great faith in him, Jesus healed her daughter and offered the family new life and hope. In other instances God is given praise and adoration when people recognize the presence of that mercy. Mary proclaims it in her Canticle when she says that "His mercy is from age to age on those who fear him (NAB: Luke 1:50)." So does Zechariah when he proclaims in his Canticle that "all this is the work of the kindness of our God; he, the Dayspring, shall visit us in his mercy to shine on those who sit in darkness and in the shadow of death to guide our feet into the way of peace (NAB: Luke 1:78-79)."

JESUS, THE REVELATION OF GOD'S MERCY:

Most importantly, Jesus is the very embodiment of salvation, the pure gift of God's mercy which enables us to participate in God's life. He made it very clear that he had come for sinners. His miracles were signs of God's mercy. He brought healing and hope to all those who were afflicted and in despair. There is the remarkable story of the man born blind in John 9. It is a moving testimony to Jesus' power and compassion as well as the man's developing discipleship. The man is willing to obey Jesus' command to wash himself. He then acknowledges that it was Jesus who healed him. He witnesses to the Pharisees that Jesus was indeed a prophet; he is expelled from the Synagogue for acknowledging Jesus as the Messiah. Finally, he bows down in adoration of Jesus. Indeed he has found God's Temple in Jesus!

Jesus' parables are incomparable icons of God's mercy. They make clear to us that God's way of thinking and doing is not our way. We all have our favorite parables. In the history of Christianity there is perhaps no more powerful story about God's mercy and compassion than the Parable of the Prodigal Son. In the story the younger son commits the unpardonable sin of demanding his share of the inheritance while his father is still able-bodied and well. Ordinarily the father divided the inheritance between his male offspring at his discretion and generally when he was nearing death. The younger son displayed great callousness toward his father by asking for his share of the inheritance. As far as he was concerned his father was already dead and he did not really care for this very significant relationship.

True to character he moves out of the house and squanders his wealth on dissolute living. After he had spent everything, a great famine broke out in that country. The young man is in dire need. He secures a job on a farm taking care of the pigs. Jesus is now painting a picture of degradation and hell. This young man has been reduced to the level of pigs which he is tending, an abomination for a Jew! What is even worse is that "he longed to fill his belly with the husks that were fodder for the pigs, but no one made a move to give him anything (NAB: Luke 15:16)." While he is in this hell-hole, he realizes that his father is his only source of salvation. He begins to rethink his relationship with his father and is moving toward repentance. "Coming to his senses at last he said: '…I will break away and return to my father, and say to him, Father, I have sinned against God and against you; I no longer deserve to be called your son. Treat me like one of your hired hands' (NAB: Luke 15: 17-19)"

What is truly amazing is that his father initiates the reconciliation before his son can express any contrition: "While he was still a long way off his father caught sight of him and was deeply moved. He ran out to meet him, threw his arms around his neck, and kissed him (NAB: Luke 15: 20)." It is within his father's embrace that his son acknowledged his offense: "Father, I have sinned against God and against you. I no longer deserve to be called your son (NAB: Luke 15:21)." The Father is so carried away with his joy that he doesn't seem to hear his son's confession. "The father said to his servants: 'Quick! Bring out the finest robe and put it on him; put a ring on his finger and shoes on his feet. Take the fatted calf and kill it. Let us eat and celebrate because this son of mine was dead and has come back to life. He was lost and is found' (NAB: Luke 15: 22-24)."

The son's return seemed to have caused greater joy in the Father than in him. As Jesus said, "There will likewise be more joy in heaven over one repentant sinner than over ninety-nine righteous people who have no need to repent (NAB: Luke 15:7)." This parable can act as a powerful means of entering into the heart of Jesus' teaching: Salvation comes only to the sinner who knows and accepts his or her sinfulness and is aware that only God can bring healing and salvation. Those who believe they are saved on their own merit are not able to hear and assimilate the good news.

WE ARE CALLED TO BE EXPRESSIONS OF GOD'S MERCY:

Relationship with God always implies relationship among people. Mercy is the loving kindness and faithful service we owe each other as members of God's people. Those who know God are called to be merciful with each other. "Be compassionate as your Father is compassionate. Do not judge and you will not be judged. Do not condemn, and you will not be condemned. Pardon and you shall be pardoned (NAB: Luke 6: 36-37)." This is particularly true for the leaders of the people. They are measured by the quality and constancy of their mercy – especially toward those most in need. "Woe to you Pharisees! You pay tithes on mint and rue and all the garden plants, while neglecting justice and the love of God. These are the things you should practice, without omitting the others (NAB: Luke 11: 42)." They are rebuked for their lack of mercy, for the burdens they lay upon the people. The merciful on the other hand belong within the kingdom of God. In Matthew 5:7 Jesus declared the merciful blessed and promised God's mercy toward them as they showed mercy toward others.

HELPFUL ATTITUDES FOR PRAYER:

- Mercy is God's compassion or willingness to suffer with our pain and ignominy and restore us to an authentic relationship with the Divine once again.
- While God will always be eager to offer us mercy and forgiveness, on our part we will not be able to receive it without a contrite and repentant heart.
- Acknowledging one's sinfulness and asking for God's forgiveness with the assurance that it will be given, is essential to an authentic relationship with God.
- Jesus is the very embodiment of salvation, the pure gift of God's mercy which enables us to participate in God's life.

- Relationship with God always implies relationship among people. Mercy is the loving kindness and faithful service we owe each other as members of God's people.
- "Though the mountains leave their place and the hills be shaken, my love shall never leave you nor my covenant of peace be shaken, says the Lord who has mercy on you (NAB: Isaiah 54: 10)."

GUIDELINES FOR PRAYER:

- Be faithful to your time of prayer, and make it between 20 and 30 minutes daily.
- Begin every prayer session with an earnest prayer to the Holy Spirit like the one I have composed for you: *Come, Holy Spirit, and overshadow me with your gentle wisdom and power as I endeavor to sit at the feet of Jesus during this period of prayer. Purify my mind and heart as I seek to make the teachings of Jesus my priority in life, thinking, speaking and doing as He desires. You are the keeper of my soul, leading me into God's heart. May I be docile and submissive to your wisdom and guidance, and may my life be a pleasing offering in your sight. Amen.*
- Take one of the passages suggested for your prayer. During the duration of this session you might want to ponder the question, **"When I ask God for forgiveness either in personal prayer or in the Sacrament of Reconciliation, do I believe I am forgiven by God?"**
- Lastly, during your prayer make sure that along with reflection you also address God directly and listen for answers that you need.
- You can end your prayer with the following: *Father, Son, and Holy Spirit, I thank you for your gracious companionship. I praise you for being my Creator, Savior and Lord. May I take your blessings to my day, and may your presence envelop and permeate all my thoughts and actions. Through Christ our Lord. Amen.*

PASSAGES FOR PRAYER:

Psalm 6: Prayer in time of Distress

Psalm 38: Prayer of an Afflicted Sinner

Psalm 51: The Miserere: Prayer of Repentance

Psalm 102: Prayer in time of Distress

Psalm 130: Prayer for Pardon and Mercy

Isaiah 54: The New Zion

Jeremiah 3: Restoration of Israel and Conditions for Forgiveness

Luke 10: 25-37: The Good Samaritan

Luke 15: Parables of Divine Mercy

John 9: The man born blind

John 10: 1-21: The Good Shepherd

JOURNALING: HELPS TO PRAYER, # 6

SPIRITUAL READING: HELPS TO PRAYER, # 4 AND 5

Manual: Read Sessions Five and Six for the third month, and delve into the topics in *Helps to Prayer* and *Methods of Prayer* over Sessions 1 through 10.

New Testament: Try to read the New Testament over Sessions 1 through 10.

Old Testament: Try to Read the first five books of the Bible or *Pentateuch* over Sessions 1 through 10.

Imitation of Christ: Follow the suggestions in *Helps to Prayer # 5*.

Catechism of the Catholic Church: Follow the suggestions in *Helps to Prayer #5,*

Or Pages 505 to 611: The Ten Commandments

SESSION SIX: GOD'S COVENANT WITH US

SCRIPTURE:

The days are coming, says the Lord, when I will make a new covenant with the house of Israel and the house of Judah. It will not be like the covenant I made with their fathers the day I took them by the hand to lead them forth from the land of Egypt; for they broke my covenant and I had to show myself their master, says the Lord. But this is the covenant which I will make with the house of Israel after those days, says the Lord. I will place my law within them, and write it upon their hearts; I will be their God, and they shall be my people. – NAB: Jeremiah 31: 31-33

THE SIGNIFICANCE OF COVENANT:

A covenant is a solemn agreement between people or between God and a person or persons. A covenant is different from a contract which focuses on keeping an agreement regarding an external object, like a home or property. In a covenant the two parties, through mutual promises, pledge themselves <u>to each other</u> in order to become one entity. Christian marriage is a covenant between the spouses because in a real sense the two have become one. The 'I' is subordinated in the development and growth of the 'We.' Such a 'death' brings new life.

THE COVENANT WITH ADAM AND EVE:

There is no explicit mention of a covenant in the Creation story. However, the context suggests that God desires a covenant relationship with our first parents. God makes a free and loving offer to share His divine life with Adam and Eve so that they (and we, I might add) would understand themselves as God's image and likeness. God promises Adam and Eve that they will live in bliss and harmony with God in the

Garden of Paradise. All their needs will be satisfied and they will experience no shame or conflict. Further they will share in God's loving dominion over all the other creatures. On their part they are to promise to live in accordance with God's desires for them. Refusing to do so will result in empty futility, resulting in their identity as God's image and likeness being jeopardized. They renege on their promise, succumb to the serpent's temptation, disobey God and find themselves in shameful nakedness. Sin and evil have now entered their lives. Adam and Eve's failure to keep their promise does not lead God to sever the covenant once and for all, a decision God could have made. Rather, God fortifies the bonds of the covenant through mercy and compassion, by promising a Savior.

THE COVENANT WITH NOAH:

Early in the Bible we are beginning to notice a familiar pattern in the dynamics of covenant-relationship. Human beings are unfaithful to God and God responds with compassion and invigorating commitment. It is evil dwelling in the human heart that breaks the covenants with God. There is the heart-rending verse in Genesis 6 which captures God's grief and seeming regret for having created humans. Given the context of God's unremitting commitment to us, these moments reveal more the intense depravity of evil rather than any regret on God's part. "When the Lord saw how great was man's wickedness on earth, and how no desire that his heart conceived was ever anything but evil, he regretted that he had made man on the earth, and his heart was grieved (6: 5-6)." The great flood is the story of the consequences of sin: evil is incompatible with God, and un-repented evil brings ultimate destruction.

God then enters into a covenant with Noah: "See, I am now establishing my covenant with you and your descendants after you and with every living creature that was with you: all the birds, and the various tame and wild animals that were with you and came out of the ark. I will establish my covenant with you, that never again shall all bodily creatures be destroyed by the waters of a flood; there shall not be another flood to devastate the earth. This is the sign that I am giving for all ages to come, of the covenant between me and you and every living creature with you: I set my bow in the clouds to serve as a sign of the covenant between me and the earth (NAB: Genesis 9:9-13)." While all non-human creatures are important to God as their Creator, they seem to have an even greater significance from the fact that they are intimately associated with humans: "I am now establishing my covenant with you and your descendants after you and with every living creature that was with you: all the birds, and the various tame and wild animals that were with you and came out of the ark."

THE COVENANTS WITH ABRAHAM AND MOSES:

We will look at these two covenants in greater detail when we look more closely at God's call to Abraham and Moses. For now it is important to appreciate the fact that the covenants tell us a whole lot about God's constant faithfulness to us and our own ingratitude and tendency to thwart and even abort God's deepest desires for communion with us. With Abraham God begins small, but this small family grows into a big clan, and through his grandson Jacob, multiplies into the twelve tribes of Israel in the land of Egypt. Through Moses God then enters into covenant with the descendants of Abraham and Jacob, and over the course of forty years in the desert forms them into a nation. This people have originated from Abraham and they now become as numerous "as the stars in the heavens." As I said, we will look into these covenants in more detail in the next four sessions.

COVENANTS AMONG THE PROPHETS:

The mission of the prophets was to call the people back to their covenant relationship with God. This appeal was made because the people had chosen to worship other gods, to allow and encourage sinful practices, and to strike up alliances with foreign nations who worshiped false gods, thereby placing their reliance on these foreign gods than on the God of Israel. Following a familiar pattern of succumbing to sin and rebellion against God, the Israelites were forced into exile by the Assyrians and Babylonians. In these dire circumstances God reinforces His profound love and compassion for Israel. The new element in the prophetic preaching regarding the covenant relationship is that it will no longer be limited to Israel alone. In fact God desires a covenant relationship with all of humanity and this divine desire will be fulfilled in Jesus Christ.

Micah for instance challenges the corruption among priests and prophets, and condemns the fraudulent merchants and unjust judges, holding them to the standards of the covenant relationship with God. Yet he speaks of the restoration of Israel in the midst of these condemnations: "But you, Bethlehem-Ephrathah too small to be among the clans of Judah, from you shall come forth for me one who is to be ruler in Israel; whose origin is from of old, from ancient times... for now his greatness shall reach to the ends of the earth; he shall be peace (NAB: Micah 5:1, 3)." Jeremiah offers the same message of hope in the midst of doom and destruction. The opening Scripture passage, Jeremiah 31:31-33, voices God's plan for a new covenant. The prophet Ezekiel became a prophet in the Babylonian exile. His first task was to prepare his countrymen for the final destruction of Jerusalem which they believed to be inviolable. After that his message changes to the promise of salvation in a new covenant: "For I will take you away from among the nations, gather you from all the foreign lands, and bring you back to your own land. I will sprinkle clean water upon you to cleanse you from all your impurities, and from all your idols I will clean you. I will give you a new heart and place a new spirit within you, taking from your bodies your stony hearts and giving you natural hearts. I will put my spirit within you and make you live by my statutes, careful to observe my decrees. You shall live in the land I gave your fathers; you shall be my people, and I will be your God (NAB: Ezekiel 36: 24-29)."

The prophet Isaiah probably has the most hopeful message. The Servant-of-the-Lord oracles say it all. In the first oracle the Messiah will bring forth justice to the nations through compassion and mercy: "A bruised reed he shall not break, and a smoldering wick he shall not quench, until he establishes justice on the earth (NAB: Isaiah 42:3-4)." In the second oracle the messiah will bring about the conversion of the whole world: "It is too little, he says, for you to be my servant, to raise up the tribes of Jacob, and restore the survivors of Israel; I will make you a light to the nations, that my salvation may reach to the ends of the earth (NAB: Isaiah 49:6)." In the third oracle the redeemer submits willingly to insults and injury on our behalf: "I gave my back to those who beat me, my cheeks to those who plucked my beard; my face I did not shield from buffets and spitting (NAB: Isaiah 50:6)." In the final oracle, Isaiah 52:13-53:12, the suffering servant atones for the sins of his people and saves them from divine retribution. These prophecies find their fulfillment in Jesus Christ.

HELPFUL ATTITUDES FOR PRAYER:

- In a covenant the two parties, through mutual promises, are pledging themselves *to each other* in order to become one entity.
- Adam and Eve's failure to keep their promise does not lead God to sever the covenant once and for all, a decision God could have made. Rather, God enforces the bonds of the covenant through mercy and compassion, by promising a Savior.
- The great flood is the story of the consequences of sin: evil is incompatible with God, and un-repented evil brings ultimate destruction.
- It is important to appreciate the fact that the covenants tell us a whole lot about God's constant faithfulness to us and our own ingratitude and tendency to thwart and even abort God's deepest desires for communion with us.
- The new element in the covenantal relationship with God is that it will no longer be limited to Israel alone. In fact God desires a

covenantal relationship with all of humanity and this divine desire will be fulfilled in Jesus Christ.

GUIDELINES FOR PRAYER:

- Be faithful to your time of prayer, and make it between 20 and 30 minutes daily.
- Begin every prayer session with an earnest prayer to the Holy Spirit like the one I have composed for you: *Come, Holy Spirit, and overshadow me with your gentle wisdom and power as I endeavor to sit at the feet of Jesus during this period of prayer. Purify my mind and heart as I seek to make the teachings of Jesus my priority in life, thinking, speaking and doing as He desires. You are the keeper of my soul, leading me into God's heart. May I be docile and submissive to your wisdom and guidance, and may my life be a pleasing offering in your sight. Amen.*
- Take one of the passages suggested for your prayer. During the duration of this session you might want to ponder the question, **"Have I reflected on the immense significance of my covenantal relationship with God, that God desires the two of us to become one?"**
- Lastly, during your prayer make sure that along with reflection you also address God directly and listen for answers that you need.
- You can end your prayer with the following: *Father, Son, and Holy Spirit, I thank you for your gracious companionship. I praise you for being my Creator, Savior and Lord. May I take your blessings to my day, and may your presence envelop and permeate all my thoughts and actions. Through Christ our Lord. Amen.*

PASSAGES FOR PRAYER:
Genesis 9: 1-17
Isaiah 42: 1-9: The Servant of the Lord
Isaiah 49: 1-7: The Servant of the Lord
Isaiah 52:13- 53: 12: Suffering and Triumph of the Servant of the Lord

Jeremiah 31: 21-34: Summons to return Home and The New Covenant
Ezekiel 36: 24-32: Regeneration of the People
Luke 22: 14-20: The Holy Eucharist
1 Corinthians 11: 17-34: The Lord's Supper

JOURNALING: HELPS TO PRAYER, # 6

SPIRITUAL READING: HELPS TO PRAYER, # 4 AND 5
Manual: Read Sessions Seven and Eight for the fourth month, and delve into the topics in *Helps to Prayer* and *Methods of Prayer* from sessions 1 through 10.
New Testament: Try to read the New Testament over Sessions 1 through 10.
Old Testament: Try to Read the first five books of the Bible or *Pentateuch* over Sessions 1 through 10.
Imitation of Christ: Follow the suggestions in *Helps to Prayer # 5*.
Catechism of the Catholic Church: Follow the suggestions in *Helps to Prayer #5,*
Or Pages 505 to 611: The Ten Commandments

SESSION SEVEN: THE CALL OF ABRAHAM

SCRIPTURE:

The Lord said to Abram: "Go forth from the land of your kinsfolk and from your father's house to a land that I will show you. I will make of you a great nation, and I will bless you; I will make your name great, so that you will be a blessing. I will bless those who bless you and curse those who curse you. All the communities of the earth shall find blessing in you." – NAB: Genesis 12: 1-3

GOD'S COVENANT WITH ABRAM:

The Lord is clearly the God of human history. God wants to be inextricably linked to the life and destiny of Abram by entering into a covenant relationship with him and his descendants. God begins small, but this small family will grow into a big clan, and through his grandson Jacob, will multiply into the twelve tribes of Israel in the land of Egypt. Eventually Abram's people will become a nation, and Jesus, Savior of the world, will spring from the root of David of the tribe of Judah.

As is typical in a covenant, God makes promises to Abram. Abram's descendants will become a great nation. God will bless him abundantly and make his name great. All the communities of the earth shall find blessing in him. And God is so protective of Abram that his enemies who curse him will be cursed by God. Abram on his part promises to obey God. At the age of seventy-five, with his wife and nephew Lot, he leaves Haran the land of his ancestors, and travels towards Canaan.

ABRAM'S FAITH IS TESTED:

Abram's willingness to trust God's promises is severely tested. Ten years have elapsed and Abram is now eighty-five years old. A part of God's promises has been fulfilled as Abram has become a wealthy man and his flocks have greatly multiplied. However he is childless. In Genesis 15, God reiterates His promise to Abram: "Fear not, Abram! I am your shield; I will make your reward very great (NAB: 15:1)." Abram is not impressed, and says in response, "O Lord God, what good will your gifts be, if I keep on being childless and have as my heir the steward of my house, Eliezer? (NAB: 15:2)" Then God shows Abram the heavens and insists that his children will be uncountable like the stars. And to show Abram the divine resolve, God asks him to prepare for a solemn covenant enactment. Instead of one animal being slaughtered, three animals, a turtle dove and a pigeon are slaughtered. The three year old heifer, three year old she-goat, and three year old ram are split in half and a pathway is made between the split carcasses. According to the tradition of covenant-making, the two parties entering into covenant would walk through the split parts and then sprinkle the blood of the animal(s) on each other as a way of symbolizing their sharing of the same blood or life. In other words, the two have become one entity and through promises to each other will live their lives in meaningful union. Covenant-making was considered so sacred and solemn, that any serious breach of the promises could result in the death of the offending party.

Abram has completed his task of splitting the animals and placing each half opposite the other. As he awaits God's coming, he spends his time shooing away the birds of prey. Given the practice of not addressing God directly as a mark of profound respect and reverence, the Hebrews came up with pseudonyms. Abram falls into a trance and a deep, terrifying darkness envelops him, harbingers announcing the presence of the All Holy One. Then the Lord God appears in the form of a smoking brazier and a flaming torch. God reiterates the promise to

Abram. And then a very unusual thing happens. Only God passes through the split parts, as if to say to Abram, that the Almighty God could be discredited and disowned, the equivalent of 'death', if He reneged on His promises. Then the Lord reiterated the covenant again with Abram, saying: "To your descendants I give this land, from the Wadi of Egypt to the Great River [the Euphrates], the land of the Kenites, the Kenizzites, the Kadmonites, the Hittites, the Perizzites, the Rephaim, the Amorites, the Canaanites, the Girgashites, the Jebusites (NAB: 15:18-21)."

Even after Abram participates in this solemn covenant ceremony, he does not seem to be convinced. For ten years now Sarai had not borne him any children. They find it difficult to take God's promises seriously. Desperate and humiliated, Sarai advises Abram to have a child through her maid, Hagar the Egyptian. Abram heeds her request. During Hagar's pregnancy, Sarai's relationship with Abram sours as there is constant bickering and trading of insults between the two women. Finally Hagar gives birth to Ishmael. Abram was then eighty-six years.

GOD'S CONTINUED COMMITMENT TO A DOUBTING ABRAM:

In Genesis 17, Abram is ninety-nine years old. God continues to reiterate the covenant with Abram by giving it some very specific features that characterize a lasting bond between God and Abram and his descendants. God changes Abram's name to Abraham and Sarai's name to Sarah, thereby indicating very explicitly that they belong to God. Furthermore, circumcision of all males will be the sign of the covenant: "On your part, you and your descendants after you must keep my covenant throughout the ages. This is my covenant with you and your descendants after you that you must keep: every male among you must be circumcised (NAB: 17:9-10)."

Abraham is still unimpressed. He speaks to himself and says, "Can a child be born to a man who is a hundred years old? Or can Sarah give birth at ninety? (NAB: 17:17)" And then he addresses God and says, "Let but Ishmael live on by your favor! (NAB: 17:18)" Abraham asks God to modify the parameters of God's promise of children. In reply God says, "Nevertheless, your wife Sarah is to bear you a son, and you shall call him Isaac. I will maintain my covenant with him as an everlasting pact, to be his God and the God of his descendants after him. As for Ishmael, I am heeding you: I hereby bless him... But my covenant I will maintain with Isaac, whom Sarah shall bear to you by this time next year (NAB: 17:19-21)." Finally, Abraham seems to get it. From here onwards, he takes God seriously. His first step is to obey God and have himself and the male members of his family circumcised.

THE BIRTH OF ISAAC:

In Genesis 18, Abraham and Sarah receive visitors from God to announce the birth of Isaac within a year. There is still anxiety and doubt in Sarah about her ability to bear a son. She voices her disbelief when she overhears one of the visitors say that she would bear a son. "Sarah was listening at the entrance of the tent, just behind him. Now Abraham and Sarah were old, advanced in years, and Sarah had stopped having her womanly periods. So Sarah laughed to herself and said, "Now that I am so withered and my husband is so old, am I still to have sexual pleasure? (NAB: 18:10-12)" God puts up with Sarah's skepticism and the following year to the great rejoicing of this elderly couple, their son, Isaac is born to them.

THE TESTING OF ABRAHAM:

So far in the story, God's fidelity to His promises is doubted and called into question by Abraham and Sarah. And undaunted, God has come through under seemingly impossible circumstances. The Lord God has been patient, steadfast, and inextricably linked to Abraham's life and destiny. Now is the time for Abraham and Sarah to demonstrate their commitment to God that they will obey in all things and be submissive to Him regardless. In response to God putting Abraham to the test by asking him to offer Isaac as a holocaust to Him, Abraham is ready and willing to obey God in every minute detail, even though it might not have made sense to his way of thinking.

Would God want him to sacrifice his son after waiting for so long to have him and now enjoying such wonderful years of joy and happiness with him? If Abraham has any doubts, he sets them aside and promptly obeys God. "God called to him, "Abraham!" "Ready!" he replied. Then God said: "Take your son Isaac, your only one, whom you love, and go to the land of Moriah. There you shall offer him up as a holocaust on a height that I will point out to you (NAB: Genesis 22:1-2)." St. Paul in his letter to the Hebrews, comments on Abraham's steadfast faith: "By faith Abraham, when put to the test, offered up Isaac; he who had received the promises was ready to sacrifice his only son, of whom it was said, "Through Isaac shall your descendants be called." He reasoned that God was able to raise from the dead, and so he received Isaac back as a symbol (NAB: Hebrews 11: 17-19)."

Abraham's life was one hundred and seventy-five years. He breathed his last, dying at a ripe old age, grown old after a full life. His sons Isaac and Ishmael buried him in the cave of Machpelah, next to his wife Sarah. After the death of Abraham, God blessed his son Isaac who made his home near Beer-lahar-roi.

HELPFUL ATTITUDES FOR PRAYER:

- The Lord is clearly the God of human history. God wants to be inextricably linked to the life and destiny of Abram by entering into a covenantal relationship with him and his descendants.

- Now Abraham and Sarah were old, advanced in years, and Sarah had stopped having her womanly periods. So Sarah laughed to herself and said, "Now that I am so withered and my husband is so old, am I still to have sexual pleasure? (NAB: Genesis 18:10-12)" God puts up with Sarah's skepticism and the following year to the great rejoicing of this elderly couple, their son, Isaac is born to them.
- In response to God putting Abraham to the test by asking him to offer Isaac as a holocaust to Him, Abraham is ready and willing to obey God in every minute detail, even though it might not have made sense to his way of thinking.
- "By faith Abraham, when put to the test, offered up Isaac; he who had received the promises was ready to sacrifice his only son, of whom it was said, "Through Isaac shall your descendants be called." He reasoned that God was able to raise from the dead, and so he received Isaac back as a symbol (NAB Hebrews 11: 17-19)."

GUIDELINES FOR PRAYER:

- Be faithful to your time of prayer, and make it between 20 and 30 minutes daily.
- Begin every prayer session with an earnest prayer to the Holy Spirit like the one I have composed for you: *Come, Holy Spirit, and overshadow me with your gentle wisdom and power as I endeavor to sit at the feet of Jesus during this period of prayer. Purify my mind and heart as I seek to make the teachings of Jesus my priority in life, thinking, speaking and doing as He desires. You are the keeper of my soul, leading me into God's heart. May I be docile and submissive to your wisdom and guidance, and may my life be a pleasing offering in your sight. Amen.*
- Take one of the passages suggested for your prayer. During the duration of this session you might want to ponder the question,

"How would I describe *my covenantal relationship* with the Lord God?"

- Lastly, during your prayer make sure that along with reflection you also address God directly and listen for answers that you need.
- You can end your prayer with the following: *Father, Son, and Holy Spirit, I thank you for your gracious companionship. I praise you for being my Creator, Savior and Lord. May I take your blessings to my day, and may your presence envelop and permeate all my thoughts and actions. Through Christ our Lord. Amen.*

PASSAGES FOR PRAYER:
Genesis 12: 1-9: Abram's Call and Migration
Genesis 15: 1-21: The Covenant with Abram
Genesis 16: 1-16: The Birth of Ishmael
Genesis 17: 1-27: Covenant of Circumcision
Genesis 18: 1-15: Abraham's visitors
Genesis 21: 1-8: The Birth of Isaac
Genesis 22: 1-19: The Testing of Abraham
Hebrews 11: 8-12: Abraham's Faith

JOURNALING: HELPS TO PRAYER, # 6

SPIRITUAL READING: *HELPS TO PRAYER, # 4 AND 5*
Manual: Read Sessions Seven and Eight for the fourth month, and delve into the topics in *Helps to Prayer* and *Methods of Prayer* over Sessions 1 through 10.
New Testament: Try to read the New Testament over Sessions 1 through 10.
Old Testament: Try to Read the first five books of the Bible or *Pentateuch* over Sessions 1 through 10.
Imitation of Christ: Follow the suggestions in *Helps to Prayer # 5.*
Catechism of the Catholic Church: Follow the suggestions in *Helps to Prayer #5,*
Or Pages 505 to 611: The Ten Commandments

SESSION EIGHT: THE CALL OF MOSES

SCRIPTURE:

Now a certain man of the house of Levi married a Levite woman who conceived and bore a son. Seeing that he was a goodly child, she hid him for three months. When she could hide him no longer, she took a papyrus basket, daubed it with bitumen and pitch, and putting the child in it, placed it among the reeds on the river bank... Pharaoh's daughter said to her (the child's mother), "Take this child and nurse it for me, and I will repay you." The woman therefore took the child and nursed it. When the child grew, she brought him to Pharaoh's daughter, who adopted him as her son and called him Moses, for she said, "I drew him out of the water." – NAB: Exodus 2: 1-3, 9-10

BIRTH AND ADOPTION OF MOSES:

The Book of Exodus begins with an immediate connection to Abraham. His descendants, specifically his grandson Jacob along with his twelve sons and their families, migrated to Egypt and settled there. In time they prospered and increased greatly in the land. Hebrew power and influence caused great concern to the reigning Pharaoh who knew nothing of Joseph and his outstanding service to the country. Through cunning and intrigue Pharaoh enslaved the Hebrews. God's people remained in slavery for about four hundred years when Moses was born.

Moses' story is similar to that of many others who were called by God. By choosing a most unlikely leader in Moses, God is making a clear statement that He is the Deliverer of His people and not Moses. Moses' circumstances clearly point to God's power and love as the reason for his incredible accomplishments in Egypt. Moses' parents were Levites. After his birth they hid their child for three months. Along with the Hebrew midwife they broke the law of the land which was to slay any newly born

Hebrew male child. When it became impossible for them to hide from the law they made the painful decision of hiding their child among the reeds in the river Nile, leaving their daughter to watch over her little brother. Pharaoh's daughter discovered the baby when she came to the river to bathe. Moses' sister intervened and suggested a Hebrew woman, her own mother, who could nurse the child. When the boy grew up he was brought to Pharaoh's daughter who named him Moses.

MOSES' FLIGHT TO MIDIAN:

Life at Pharaoh's palace is an ambivalent and difficult experience for Moses. He is well aware of his roots and suffers greatly to see his people being abused and reviled as slaves. One day in exasperation he comes to the defense of a slave and ends up slaying the Egyptian guard. Moses knows his secret is out when he tries to act as peace-maker between two Hebrews who are fighting among themselves. One of them creates a panic in him when he asks whether Moses intended to kill him as he did the Egyptian. Soon after Pharaoh himself heard of the incident and sought to put Moses to death. Consequently Moses fled for his life and hid in the land of Midian. He married Zipporah and had a son whom he named Gershom; for he said, "I am a stranger in a foreign land (NAB: Exodus 2:22)."

THE BURNING BUSH:

The call of Moses is intimately linked to God's covenant with Abraham and his descendants. In Exodus 2 we are told that "a long time passed, during which the king of Egypt died. Still the Israelites groaned and cried out because of their slavery. As their cry for release went up to God, he heard their groaning and was mindful of his covenant with Abraham, Isaac and Jacob. He saw the Israelites and knew (NAB: 2: 23-25)...." God makes the decision to send Moses into Egypt as His spokesperson to bring His people out of slavery from the land of Egypt. Moses was tending his flock near Horeb, the mountain of God. "There an angel of the Lord appeared to him in fire flaming out of a bush. As he looked on, he was surprised to see that the bush, though on fire, was not consumed (NAB: 2: 2-3)."

THE CALL OF MOSES:

Moses then decides to investigate. As he approaches the burning bush, God appears to him. God identifies Himself as "the God of your father, the God of Abraham, the God of Isaac, the God of Jacob (NAB: Exodus 3:6)." Moses is overwhelmed. He hides his face as he is afraid to look at God. From his point of view he is given the impossible task of going and telling Pharaoh as God's messenger, to let the enslaved Hebrew people go into the desert to worship their God. Moses is filled with dread and anxiety. He makes several attempts to refuse the summons. He cites many obstacles: his questionable credentials, the people's understandable doubts about God's appearance to him, his own lack of eloquence, among others. God is not easily persuaded. God is persistent with Moses, and very confident that their partnership will work. And God provides Aaron as an able assistant to Moses. Finally, hesitant and relenting, Moses ventures forth into Egypt to confront Pharaoh's might and obduracy.

Clearly, Moses is no match for this impossible mission. In his eyes he is an insignificant presence before the force and cunning of Pharaoh. In slow increments Moses realizes that God is the real architect of the people's liberation. He plays his subordinate but significant role as a malleable instrument as God engages in another incredible transformation. The Exodus story has a sweep similar to the Creation story. It brings order and harmony out of chaos and confusion, and liberation from bondage and ignominy to security and community.

Upon their liberation from Egypt, Moses and the Israelites sing of their jubilation and rescue at the hands of God: "I will sing to the Lord, for he is gloriously triumphant; horse and chariot he has cast into the sea. My strength and my courage is the Lord, and he has been my savior. He is my God, I praise him; the God of my father, I extol him (NAB: Exodus 15:1-2)."

After crossing the Red Sea, it is tempting to think that the Israelites would put the worst of their trials and tribulations behind them. Yet now they are facing a different type of bondage, the slavery of their own sinfulness and wickedness. Now it is their stubbornness and rebellion that Moses has to confront. His commitment to his people and God's faith in them are severely tested. There is that poignant moment in the dialogue between God and Moses when he reminds God that destroying His people would only result in the Egyptians making fun of The LORD, God: " 'With evil intent he brought them out, that he might kill them in the mountains and exterminate them from the face of the earth'? Let your blazing wrath die down; relent in punishing your people. Remember your servants Abraham, Isaac and Israel, and how you swore to them by your own self, saying, 'I will make your descendants as numerous as the stars in the sky; and all this land that I promised, I will give your descendants as their perpetual heritage.' So the Lord relented in the punishment he had threatened to inflict on his people (NAB: Exodus 32: 12-14)."

In the midst of their fickle murmurings and idolatry, God's everlasting love, constancy, and faithfulness to the Israelites shine forth. As God's faithful messenger Moses is subjected to much suffering. Gradually, through trials and tribulations, his leadership and holiness are acknowledged. He is recognized as the Law Giver and intermediary with God. In his later years he is recognized as God's beloved. His countenance is radiant with God's holiness. He successfully leads his people to the boundary of the Promised Land. He himself will enjoy a panoramic view of the Promised Land from a mountain top but it will be Joshua who will lead the Israelites into it (NAB: Numbers 20: 6-13).

Deuteronomy 34:10-12 acts as a fitting encomium to the life and ministry of Moses: "Since then no prophet has arisen in Israel like Moses, whom the Lord knew face to face. He had no equal in all the signs and wonders the Lord sent him to perform in the land of Egypt against Pharaoh and all his servants and against all his land, and for the might and terrifying power that Moses exhibited in the sight of all Israel."

HELPFUL ATTITUDES FOR PRAYER:

- Moses' story is similar to that of many others who were called by God. By choosing a most unlikely leader in Moses, God is making a clear statement that He is the Deliverer of His people and not Moses.
- Moses fled from Egypt and hid in the land of Midian. He married Zipporah and had a son whom he named Gershom; for he said, "I am a stranger in a foreign land."
- Moses is filled with dread and anxiety. He makes several attempts to refuse the summons. He cites many obstacles: his questionable credentials, the people's understandable doubts about God's appearance to him, his own lack of eloquence, among others. God is not easily persuaded. God is persistent and very confident that their partnership will work. Finally, hesitant and relenting, Moses ventures forth into Egypt to confront Pharaoh's might and obduracy.
- The Exodus story has a sweep similar to the Creation story. It brings order and harmony out of chaos and confusion, and liberation from bondage and ignominy to security and community.
- In the midst of their fickle murmurings and idolatry, God's everlasting love, constancy, and faithfulness to the Israelites shine forth.
- As God's faithful messenger Moses is subjected to much suffering. Gradually, through trials and tribulations, his leadership and holiness are acknowledged. He is recognized as the Law Giver and intermediary with God.

GUIDELINES FOR PRAYER:

- Be faithful to your time of prayer, and make it between 20 and 30 minutes daily.
- Begin every prayer session with an earnest prayer to the Holy Spirit like the one I have composed for you: *Come, Holy Spirit, and overshadow me with your gentle wisdom and power as I endeavor to sit at the feet of Jesus during this period of prayer. Purify my mind and heart as I seek to make the teachings of Jesus my priority in life, thinking, speaking and doing as He desires. You are the keeper of my soul, leading me into God's heart. May I be docile and submissive to your wisdom and guidance, and may my life be a pleasing offering in your sight. Amen.*
- Take one of the passages suggested for your prayer. During the duration of this session you might want to ponder the question, **"What has God's call been to me and how have I responded?"**
- Lastly, during your prayer make sure that along with reflection you also address God directly and listen for answers that you need.
- You can end your prayer with the following: *Father, Son, and Holy Spirit, I thank you for your gracious companionship. I praise you for being my Creator, Savior and Lord. May I take your blessings to my day, and may your presence envelop and permeate all my thoughts and actions. Through Christ our Lord. Amen.*

PASSAGES FOR PRAYER:

Exodus 1: 1-22: The Oppression and Command to the Midwives
Exodus 2: 1-22: Birth and Adoption of Moses and his Flight to Midian
Exodus 2: 23-3: 1-22: The Burning Bush and Call of Moses
Exodus 4: 1-31: Confirmation of Moses' Mission and his Return to Egypt
Exodus 5: 1- 6:1-13: Pharaoh's Obduracy and Renewal of God's Promise
Exodus 7: 1- 8: 1-11: The First and Second Plagues
Exodus 8: 12-28: The Third and Fourth Plagues

Exodus 9: 1-35: The Fifth, Sixth, and Seventh Plagues

JOURNALING: REFER TO <u>HELPS TO PRAYER, # 6</u>

SPIRITUAL READING: REFER TO HELPS TO PRAYER, # 4 AND 5
<u>Manual:</u> Read Sessions Nine and Ten for the fifth month, and delve into the topics in *Helps to Prayer* and *Methods of Prayer* over Sessions 1 through 10.
<u>New Testament:</u> Try to read the New Testament over Sessions 1 through 10.
<u>Old Testament:</u> Try to Read the first five books of the Bible or *Pentateuch* over Sessions 1 through 10.
<u>Imitation of Christ</u>: Follow the suggestions in *Helps to Prayer # 5*.
<u>Catechism of the Catholic Church</u>: Follow the suggestions in *Helps to Prayer #5,*
Or Pages 505 to 611: The Ten Commandments

SESSION NINE: THE PASSOVER MEAL

SCRIPTURE:

"This day shall be a memorial feast for you, which all your generations shall celebrate with pilgrimage to the Lord, as a perpetual institution. For seven days you must eat unleavened bread...Keep, then, this custom of the unleavened bread. Since it was on this very day that I brought your ranks out of the land of Egypt, you must celebrate this day throughout your generations as a perpetual institution –NAB: *Exodus 12: 14 &17.*

THE ACTIONS OF GOD-IN-COVENANT:

The God of Abraham, Isaac, and Jacob, is the same God who is now interacting with Moses and the descendants of Abraham. God entered into covenant with Abraham and is therefore being faithful to His promises made to Abraham and his descendants, now enslaved in Egypt. Berit or bond is the preferred meaning of the Old Testament word for covenant. God has entered into a permanent bond with the Hebrew people that can be likened to marriage. Israel will always be looked upon as God's wife, a familiar image that is referred to by the prophets. This bond between God and His people is the core of biblical faith and history.

As we have seen in Session Eight, God has chosen Moses as the divine spokesperson to Pharaoh. Through nine plagues inflicted upon the Egyptians, Moses has grown in stature and respect both among his own people and among the Egyptians. All are beginning to see that Moses is a force to reckon with, as his God is mighty and more powerful than Pharaoh and his gods. However, at the end of Exodus 10, Pharaoh is still obstinate and will not let the Israelites leave for the desert to worship their God. In conclusion Pharaoh said to Moses: "Leave my presence, and see to it that you do not appear before me again! The day you appear before me you shall die! Moses replied, "Well said! I will never appear before you again (NAB: 10:28-29)." And Exodus 11 ends on a similar note. "The Lord said to Moses, "Pharaoh refuses to listen to you that my wonders may be multiplied in the land of Egypt (NAB: 11:9)."

PREPARATIONS FOR FREEDOM AND SALVATION:

The tenth plague is the most crucial one as it serves the purpose of breaking Pharaoh's obstinacy and resolve, and gives the Israelites a true experience of God's powerful commitment to them. In very concrete terms they understand what it means for their God to be in covenant with them. Exodus 11 begins with a definitive word from God to Moses: "One more plague will I bring upon Pharaoh and upon Egypt. After that he will let you depart. In fact, he will not merely let you go; he will drive you away (NAB: 11:1)." In preparation for their exodus from Egypt, the people are told specifically what will happen. Every first-born in the land of Egypt will die, from the first-born of Pharaoh on the throne to the first-born of the slave-girl at the hand mill, as well as all the first-born of the animals. Among the Israelites and their animals, not even a dog shall growl, so that all will know that the Lord distinguishes between the Egyptians and the Israelites.

THE PASSOVER RITUAL PRESCRIBED:

God gives this exodus event a very specific ritual. "Tell the whole community of Israel: On the tenth of this month every one of your families must procure for itself a lamb, one apiece for each household...The lamb must be a year-old male and without blemish.... You shall keep it until the fourteenth day of this month, and then, with the whole assembly of Israel present, it shall be slaughtered during the evening twilight. They shall take some of its blood and apply it to the two doorposts and the lintel of every house in which they partake of the lamb. That same night they shall eat its roasted flesh with unleavened bread and bitter herbs. It shall not be eaten raw or boiled, but roasted whole, with its head and shanks and inner organs.... This is how you are to eat it, with your loins girt, sandals on your feet and your staff in hand you shall eat like those who are in flight. It is the Passover of the Lord. For on this same night I will go through Egypt, striking down every first-born of the land, both man and beast, and executing judgment on all the gods of Egypt – I, the Lord! But the blood will mark the houses where you are. Seeing the blood, I will pass over you; thus, when I strike the land of Egypt, no destructive blow will come upon you. This day shall be a memorial feast for you, which all your generations shall celebrate with pilgrimage to the Lord as a perpetual institution (NAB: Exodus 12: 3-14)."

THE SIGNIFICANCE OF THE MEAL:

It would be rich food for the soul to ponder the immense depths and significance of this Passover Meal. Imagine you were an Israelite at the time. You have heard countless stories of oppression and brutality meted out to your people for four hundred years. You have even heard of Moses' stab at freedom for your people, when he killed the Egyptian guard and then fled for his life, thereby causing harsher punishment and treatment of them. You have wondered about the God of your fathers who seemingly has been absent in the lives of your people. But now it has been several months when stirrings of hope and salvation are echoing throughout the Hebrew ghettoes, as this same Moses has returned in God's name, and has been challenging the indomitable Pharaoh through nine plagues that have been disasters to the Egyptians and blessings to the Israelites.

And now the Israelite community is abuzz with excitement and anticipated liberation as tonight is the night of salvation, a time of reckoning with "I AM" who will deliver them from their captivity, and set them free to worship their true God and become God's people! After these centuries of enslavement, can this summons to partake of a covenant meal, re-affirming and sealing God's bond with the Israelites, be for real? And will the Lord God deliver on His promise against the might of Pharaoh and the gods he worships? Tonight will be the night of Israel's greatest salvation event. God will pass over the Egyptian houses wreaking havoc against their enemies and His, and providing security and salvation to His own people. By the same token the Israelites will pass over from Egypt, the land of slavery, to the Promised Land flowing with milk and honey. The bond between God and His people will be strengthened. Israel will belong to God, and God will be their everlasting Protector! This is the great news then that is being celebrated and savored during the Passover Meal, in a mighty hurry and with extreme urgency!

No wonder God wants them to make it a perpetual institution to celebrate every year as a memorial feast. It was God's way of saying that this salvation event would remain the bedrock of the covenant between the Israelites and God. It would need to be savored and experienced in an ongoing manner for the rest of their lives! And so the term 'memorial' has special significance for God's people. Every year when they celebrated this salvation event, they knew they would not merely be remembering their ancestors' redemption from Egypt which took place in the past. Rather, they would be experiencing the same event and depth of relationship with God in their present lives the way their forebears did. While the Exodus was an event that took place in the history of Israel, it was at the same time an ever-present reality etched into the very fiber of its covenant relationship with God.

JESUS INSTITUTES THE EUCHARIST DURING THE PASSOVER MEAL:

Jesus instituted the Eucharist during the Passover meal, thereby expanding the depths of its meaning beyond anything the Israelites could ever imagine. At one and the same time, Jesus presents himself at various depths of meaning. Jesus is the new Moses leading his people from slavery to sin to the freedom of becoming the sons and daughters of the Living God. Jesus is also the Passover Lamb through whose blood we have been spared God's wrath and justice and have been clothed in the mantel of God's love and forgiveness. Jesus instructs his disciples to celebrate Eucharist as a memorial feast. Every time we celebrate Eucharist we are not merely remembering our redemption from sin and death when Jesus died for us on the cross. Rather, in truth engendered by faith, we are participating in the saving event of Christ's death and resurrection which is an eternal and ever-present reality in the person of the Risen Lord.

HELPFUL ATTITUDES FOR PRAYER:

- Berit or *bond* is the preferred meaning of the Old Testament word for covenant. God has entered into a permanent bond with the Israelites that can be likened to marriage. Israel will always be looked upon as God's wife, a familiar image that is referred to by the prophets.
- The tenth plague serves the purpose of breaking Pharaoh's obstinate resolve, and gives the Israelites a true experience of God's powerful commitment to them. Very concretely they understand what it means for their God to be in covenant with them.
- Through the covenant meal, the Israelites will pass over from slavery to freedom in the Promised Land. The bond between God and His people will be strengthened. Israel will belong to God, and God will be their everlasting Protector! This is the great news then that is being celebrated and savored, albeit with extreme urgency!
- The term 'memorial' has special significance for God's people. They knew they would not merely be remembering their people's redemption from Egypt in the past. Rather, they would be experiencing the same event and depth of relationship with God in their present lives, the way their ancestors did.
- Jesus is the new Moses leading his people from slavery to sin to the freedom of becoming children of the Living God.

- Jesus is the Passover Lamb through whose blood we have been spared God's wrath and justice and have been clothed in the mantel of God's love and forgiveness.

GUIDELINES FOR PRAYER:

- Be faithful to your time of prayer, and make it between 20 and 30 minutes daily.
- Begin every prayer session with an earnest prayer to the Holy Spirit like the one I have composed for you: *Come, Holy Spirit, and overshadow me with your gentle wisdom and power as I endeavor to sit at the feet of Jesus during this period of prayer. Purify my mind and heart as I seek to make the teachings of Jesus my priority in life, thinking, speaking and doing as He desires. You are the keeper of my soul, leading me into God's heart. May I be docile and submissive to your wisdom and guidance, and may my life be a pleasing offering in your sight. Amen.*
- Take one of the passages suggested for your prayer. During the duration of this session you might want to ponder the question, **"What significance does the Eucharist have in my following of Jesus?"**
- Lastly, during your prayer make sure you also address God directly and listen for the Holy Spirit's responses.
- You can end your prayer with the following: *Father, Son, and Holy Spirit, I thank you for your gracious companionship. I praise you for being my Creator, Savior and Lord. May I take your blessings to my day, and may your presence envelop and permeate all my thoughts and actions. Through Christ our Lord. Amen.*

PASSAGES FOR PRAYER:

Exodus 11: Tenth Plague: Death of the First-born
Exodus 12: 1-36: The Passover Meal
Exodus 12: 37-51: Departure from Egypt and Passover Regulations
Exodus 13: 1-14:9: Consecration of First-Born and Toward the Red Sea
Exodus 14: 10-31: Crossing of the Red Sea
I Corinthians 11: 17-24: The Lord's Supper
Matthew 26: 17-30: The Holy Eucharist
Luke 22: 1-20: The Paschal Meal

JOURNALING: REFER TO HELPS TO PRAYER, # 6

SPIRITUAL READING: REFER TO HELPS TO PRAYER, # 4 AND 5

Manual: Read Sessions Nine and Ten for the fifth month, and delve into the topics in Helps to Prayer and Methods of Prayer over Sessions 1 through 10.

New Testament: Try to read the New Testament over Sessions 1 through 10.

Old Testament: Try to Read the first five books of the Bible or Pentateuch over Sessions 1 through 10..

Imitation of Christ: Follow the suggestions in Helps to Prayer # 5.

Catechism of the Catholic Church: Follow the suggestions in Helps to Prayer #5,

Or Pages 505 to 611: The Ten Commandments

SESSION TEN: THE SINAI COVENANT

SCRIPTURE:

Then Moses went up to God; the LORD called to him from the mountain, saying, "Thus you shall say to the house of Jacob, and tell the Israelites: You have seen what I did to the Egyptians, and how I bore you on eagles' wings and brought you to myself. Now therefore, if you obey my voice and keep my covenant, you shall be my treasured possession out of all the peoples. Indeed, the whole earth is mine, but you shall be for me a priestly kingdom and a holy nation. These are the words that you shall speak to the Israelites." So Moses came, summoned the elders of the people, and set before them all these words that the Lord had commanded him. The people all answered as one: "Everything that the LORD has spoken we will do." – NRSV: Exodus 19: 3-8.

GOD THE PROMISE KEEPER:

A monumental moment of intimacy between God and His people has arrived. In the past God had set up covenants with individuals like Noah and Abraham and their descendants. Now God is making this bond much more expansive. The Lord is entering into a significant union with the whole Israelite nation. In our Scripture passage several divine characteristics are revealed. God is the Promise Keeper: "Thus shall you say to the house of Jacob, and tell the Israelites: You have seen what I did to the Egyptians, and how I bore you on eagle wings and brought you to myself (NRSV: Exodus19:3-4)." The people have had first-hand experience in their immediate past of how their God is more powerful than all the gods of the earth, especially the gods of the Egyptians. Pharaoh and his mighty army is no match for the Lord of Hosts. The Israelites witnessed God's power through the ten plagues.

And they were probably still marveling in wondrous disbelief how they got out of the land of slavery.

Among these mighty deeds they would remember the crossing of the Red Sea when in great fright they sought the Lord to save them from the powerful chariots of Pharaoh's army. Moses reassured them: "Do not be afraid, stand firm, and see the deliverance that the LORD will accomplish for you today; for the Egyptians whom you see today you shall never see again. The Lord will fight for you, and you have only to keep still (NRSV: Exodus14:13-14)." Then a sense of urgency overwhelms them as Moses splits the sea in half and tells the Israelites to pass through it on dry land. The Egyptians follow in pursuit. Pharaoh's horses and chariots go after them right into the midst of the sea. Meanwhile God's protection of His people continues: "At the morning watch the LORD in the pillar of fire and cloud looked down upon the Egyptian army, and threw the Egyptian army into panic. He clogged their chariot wheels so that they turned with difficulty. The Egyptians said, "Let us flee from the Israelites, for the LORD is fighting for them against Egypt (NRSV: Exodus 14: 24-25)." As the Egyptians were retreating, Moses stretched out his hand and the sea flowed back, destroying the entire army of Pharaoh. The Israelites beheld the great power that the Lord had shown against the Egyptians. They feared the Lord and believed in him and in his servant Moses. God is indeed their Protector and Keeper of His promises. The Lord voices this sentiment as well: "You have seen what I did to the Egyptians, and how I bore you on eagles' wings and brought you to myself (NRSV: Exodus 19: 4)."

ISRAEL, GOD'S APPLE OF THE EYE:

God desires a covenant relationship with Israel because of His unabashed love for His people: "Now therefore, if you obey my voice and keep my covenant, you shall be my treasured possession of all the peoples. Indeed, the whole earth is mine, but you shall be for me a priestly kingdom and a holy nation. These are the words that you shall speak to the Israelites (NRSV: Exodus 19: 5-6)." Moses communicates God's intentions to the people and their willing response is, "Everything that the LORD has spoken we will do (NRSV: Exodus 19: 8)." The Israelites will never be able to fathom the reasons for God's outrageous love for them. They know for certain, however, that God's gesture and involvement in their lives has everything to do with God and nothing to do with any merit of theirs.

ENTERING INTO COVENANT WITH GOD:

The details of the Sinai Covenant are worked out from Exodus 20 through 40. God's intent is to make Israel a holy nation. And so Moses is given the Ten Commandments and a constitution of holy living where every aspect of life and worship as it relates to God is spelled out. In their observance they will experience the transforming presence of the Lord in their lives and recognize themselves as God's image moving into greater likeness with the Original!

The first three of the Ten Commandments are clearly directed toward having a right relationship with God. In these commandments, God is presenting Himself as a Covenant-God who has kept His promises toward "my special possession." He is the God of their history, intimately involved in their lives and wholeheartedly committed to their destiny. In covenant the people as well are to become promise keepers. They are to accept Him as their God and no longer worship false gods.

Sin breaks this covenant bond between God and us, leading to our alienation and separation from God, our life-source! Repentance brings us back to integration and union with our Savior and Lord. There are scores of examples in the Old and New Testaments of alienation from God through sin. In the case of Adam and Eve, they chose their own selfish interests over God's wisdom. They listened to the serpent rather than God. In David's case, he chose his own selfish desires and committed adultery with Bathsheba. In pursuit of his selfish interests he had her husband, Uriah, murdered so that he could marry Bathsheba. So it makes sense for God to give us the first commandment: "I am the Lord your God: You shall have no other gods before me!

The context for the second commandment is the covenant relationship. Giving and receiving a name in a covenant relationship implied union and profound respect for one another. It suggested the existence of a very special relationship between the one naming and the named. When God changed the name of an individual He was claiming that person as His own, as was the case with Abraham and Jacob. Jesus changed Simon's name to Cephas or Peter, meaning the 'rock.' In Genesis 2 God gives Adam dominion over all creatures and this is indicated by Adam being asked to name all creatures.

When we take God's name in prayer we are expressing worship and praise for this gift of union. In invoking the name we bring the person and their presence before us. This second commandment reminds us of the very special relationship that exists between God and us. In God we live and move and have our being. We will perish outside of this covenant relationship. It behooves us to take it very seriously as it is the ground of our being. Hence, "You shall not make wrongful use of the name of the LORD your God." To take God's name outside of covenant is vain and self-serving. To claim an intimate connection and relationship with God while living a sinful life is both hypocritical and blasphemous.

The third commandment is a natural segue from the first two commandments. The Sabbath was a day of rest "sanctified to the Lord (Exodus 16:23; 31:15; Deuteronomy 5:14)". Being the day of the Lord, the Sabbath required that man should abstain from working for his own ends and interests, and devote the day to God by special acts of positive worship. Special religious observances were prescribed. The daily sacrifices were doubled; new loaves of proposition were placed before the Lord (Leviticus 24:5; 1 Chronicles 9:32); a sacred assembly was held in the sanctuary for solemn worship (Leviticus 23: 2-3). With the Sinai covenant God became the Lord of that covenant. The observance of the Sabbath thereby became a sign of the covenant, and its observance an acknowledgment of the pact: "You shall keep my Sabbaths, for this is a sign between me and you throughout your generations, given in order that you may know that I, the LORD, sanctify you (NRSV: Exodus 31:13).

The Sabbath had a social and philanthropic side. It was also intended as a day of rest and relaxation, particularly for the slaves. The Sabbath as the sign of the Sinai covenant recalled the deliverance from the bondage of Egypt. Through the observance of the Sabbath, the Israelites were bidden to remember that they were once slaves in Egypt and should therefore in grateful remembrance of their deliverance rest themselves and allow their bond-servants to rest (Deuteronomy 5:14-15).

Keeping holy the Sabbath day is an invitation to enter into God's heart and dwell there for an extended period of time. Keeping holy the Sabbath is God's way of telling us, that being intimate with God and living in His heart is the most significant priority of our lives. The Resurrection is the experience of blessings and holiness in the Risen Lord. In keeping holy the Sabbath, we enter and participate in the everlasting Rest of the Trinity. We enter into the dimension of eternity.

The remaining seven commandments concern our relationships with our parents, neighbors, and other human beings. These seven commandments emphasize the fact that we cannot love God and not love our neighbor. In Matthew 22 there is an interesting encounter that takes place between Jesus and a lawyer whose intent is to trip Jesus up. He asks Jesus which commandment of the Law is the greatest. Jesus said to him: "you shall love the Lord your God with all your heart, and with all your soul, and with all your mind.' This is the greatest and first commandment. And a second is like it: 'You shall love your neighbor as yourself.' On these two commandments hang all the law and the prophets (NRSV: 22:37-40)."

Human life is the greatest blessing we could have received from God. God created us in His image and likeness, and Jesus in unmitigated obedience to his Father, assumed our human nature and became our Savior, thus granting us the awesome privilege of participating in God's life and divine nature (2 Peter 1:4). God knew what He was doing when he chose us to be the children of our parents. Our parents were God's chief instruments in offering us the gift of life and nurturing it generously for so many years. No amount of bad behavior on our parents' part can diminish this precious gift that we have received from God. Hence honoring our parents is befitting of them and especially of God, the Source of all blessings! Here is some desert wisdom to help us keep this holy commandment of honoring our parents: One of the elders was asked by a brother, 'What is humility?" And he answered, 'It is to do good to those who do evil to us.' The brother put a further question, 'If one cannot go as far as that, what should one do?' The elder replied, 'Flee those who offend us and keep silent.' (Sayings of the Desert Fathers, Anonymous Series)."

The primary reason God hates murder is that out of all creatures, only humans are made in the image and likeness of God (Genesis 1: 26-27). Even before the Sinai covenant, the murder of other human beings was wrong: "Then the LORD said to Cain, "Where is your brother Abel?" He said, "I do not know. Am I my brother's keeper?" And the LORD said, "What have you done? Listen: your brother's blood is crying out to me from the ground! And now you are cursed from the ground, which has opened its mouth to receive your brother's blood from your hand (NRSV: Genesis 4: 9-11)."

In his teachings, Jesus amplified the meaning of the fifth commandment. Committing murder is more than killing someone. It means having an angry and unforgiving attitude towards them: "You have heard that it was said to those of ancient times, 'You shall not murder'; and 'whoever murders shall be liable to judgment.' But I say to you that if you are angry with a brother or sister, you will be liable to judgment; and if you insult a brother or sister, you will be liable to the council; and if you say, 'You fool,' you will be liable to the hell of fire (Matthew 5: 21-22)." In his first letter John equates hatred with murder: "All who hate a brother or sister are murderers, and you know that murderers do not have eternal life abiding in them (NRSV: 1John:3:15)." Anytime we 'kill' someone else with our anger/ resentment/ hatred/ bitterness/cynicism/revenge, we 'kill' ourselves. It is our mandate to create, not to destroy; to re-create when people are being destroyed. The instruments of creation are love, peace, joy, and forgiveness. "In a word, you must be made perfect as your heavenly Father is perfect" (NAB: Matthew 5: 48).

The sixth and tenth commandments are inter-related: You shall not commit adultery nor shall you covet your neighbor's wife. Quite simply, because we are a covenant-people, we are expected to have the same attitudes and dispositions toward others that God has, in this case men and women who are spouses: respect and reverence for the integrity and uniqueness of their personhood. Jesus tells us in Matthew 5:27-28: "You have heard the commandment, 'You shall not commit adultery.' What I say to you is: anyone who looks lustfully at a woman has already committed adultery with her in his thoughts."

The seventh and ninth commandments are inter-related as well: You shall not steal nor shall you covet your neighbor's goods. Jesus gives us excellent advice in obeying these two commandments: "Do not store up for yourselves treasures on earth, where moth and rust consume and where thieves break in and steal; but store up for yourselves treasures in heaven, where neither moth nor rust consumes and where thieves do not break in and steal. For where your treasure is, there your heart will be also (NRSV: Matthew 6:19-21)."

The eighth commandment has to do with perjury: You shall not bear false witness against your neighbor. This is what the Catechism says in Article 8 on The Eighth Commandment #2464: "The eighth commandment forbids misrepresenting the truth in our relationship with others. This moral prescription flows from the vocation of the holy people to bear witness to their God who is the truth and wills the truth. Offenses against the truth express by word or deed a refusal to commit oneself to moral uprightness: they are fundamental infidelities to God and, in this sense, they undermine the foundations of the covenant."

WORSHIP OF THE GOLDEN CALF:

In the Old Testament saga of covenant-building between God and His people, for every silver lining there is a dark and impenetrable cloud. To the consternation of God and Moses, about three thousand of the Israelites persuaded Aaron to make them a god who would be their leader. Aaron had them bring their golden earrings to him that he fashioned into a golden calf. The people then cried out, "These are your gods, O Israel, who brought you out of the land of Egypt (NRSV: Exodus 32: 4)." On seeing this Aaron built an altar before the calf and proclaimed, "Tomorrow shall be a festival to the Lord (NRSV: Exodus 32:5).

One moment of grace in this very sacrilegious episode is Moses' intervention on behalf of God's people. This self-proclaimed stutterer now waxes eloquent and convinces God that the destruction of His people because of their sin of rebellion and ingratitude would only bring a smirk to Egyptian lips. "Why should the Egyptians say, 'It was with evil intent that he brought them out to kill them in the mountains, and to consume them from the face of the earth'? Turn from your fierce wrath; change your mind and do not bring disaster on your people (NRSV: Exodus 32:12).'" Then Moses reminds God of His promise to Abraham, Isaac and Israel and how He swore to them that He would make them as numerous as the stars in the sky and would give them the Promised

Land as their perpetual heritage. And God relented in the punishment He had threatened to inflict on His people.

Another moment of grace occurs when Moses discovers to his horror the extent of the rebellion of his people under Aaron's leadership. He decides to make atonement for his people and enters the following plea before God: "Alas, this people has sinned a great sin; they have made for themselves gods of gold. But now, if you will only forgive their sin – but if not, blot me out of the book that you have written (NRSV: Exodus 32:31-32)." God's answer is appropriate. Only those who had sinned against God will be struck down. And Moses is told to go and lead the people to the Promised Land with the promise of God's guidance through His angel.

HELPFUL ATTITUDES FOR PRAYER:

- In the past God had set up covenants with individuals like Noah and Abraham and their descendants. Now God is making this bond even more expansive. The Lord and is entering into a significant union with the whole Israelite nation.
- God is the Promise Keeper. "Thus shall you say to the house of Jacob, and tell the Israelites: You have seen what I did to the Egyptians, and how I bore you on eagles' wings and brought you to myself (NRSV: Exodus19: 3-4)."
- God's clear intent to enter into covenant with Israel is because of His unabashed love for His people. "Therefore, if you hearken to my voice and keep my covenant, you shall be my special possession, dearer to me than all other people, though all the earth is mine. You shall be to me a kingdom of priests, a holy nation. That is what you must tell the Israelites (Exodus 19: 5-6)."
- The first three of the Ten Commandments are clearly directed toward having a right relationship with God. In these commandments, God is presenting Himself as a Covenant-God who has kept His promises toward "my special possession."

- Keeping holy the Sabbath is God's way of telling us, that being intimate with God and living in His heart is the most significant priority of our lives.
- The surest and shortest way to union with God is to love our families and neighbors and all human beings as God loves and respects them.
- Throughout the Old Testament saga of covenant-building between God and His people, for every silver lining there is a dark and impenetrable cloud.

GUIDELINES FOR PRAYER:

- Be faithful to your time of prayer, and make it between 20 and 30 minutes daily.
- Begin every prayer session with an earnest prayer to the Holy Spirit like the one I have composed for you: *Come, Holy Spirit, and overshadow me with your gentle wisdom and power as I endeavor to sit at the feet of Jesus during this period of prayer. Purify my mind and heart as I seek to make the teachings of Jesus my priority in life, thinking, speaking and doing as He desires. You are the keeper of my soul, leading me into God's heart. May I be docile and submissive to your wisdom and guidance and may my life be a pleasing offering in your sight. Amen.*
- Take one of the passages suggested for prayer. During the duration of this session you might want to ponder the question, **"Do I take seriously my role as promise keeper in my covenant bond with God and His Church?"**
- Lastly, during your prayer make sure you also address God directly and listen for the Holy Spirit's responses.
- You can end your prayer with the following: *Father, Son, and Holy Spirit, I thank you for your gracious companionship. I praise you for being my Creator, Savior and Lord. May I take your blessings to my day, and may your presence envelop and permeate all my thoughts and actions. Through Christ our Lord. Amen.*

PASSAGES FOR PRAYER:

Exodus 14: Crossing of the Red Sea
Exodus 15: Moses Canticle of Praise
Exodus 19: Arrival at Sinai
Exodus 20: The Ten Commandments
Exodus 32: The Golden Calf
Deuteronomy 5: The Covenant at Horeb and Moses as Mediator
Hebrews 11: 24-31: Moses' Steadfastness extolled

JOURNALING: REFER TO HELPS TO PRAYER, # 6

SPIRITUAL READING: REFER TO *HELPS TO PRAYER, # 4 AND 5*
Manual: Read Sessions Eleven and Twelve for the sixth month, and delve into the topics in Helps to Prayer and Methods of Prayer over Sessions 1 through 10.
New Testament: Try to read the New Testament over Sessions 1 through 10.
Old Testament: Try to Read the first five books of the Bible or Pentateuch over Sessions 1 through 10.
Imitation of Christ: Follow the suggestions in Helps to Prayer # 5.
Catechism of the Catholic Church: Follow the suggestions in Helps to Prayer #5
Or Pages 505 to 611: The Ten Commandments.

SESSION ELEVEN: THE CALL OF ISAIAH

SCRIPTURE:

In the year that King Uzziah died, I saw the Lord seated on a throne, high and lofty; and the hem of his robe filled the temple. Seraphs were in attendance above him; each had six wings: with two they covered their faces, and with two they covered their feet, and with two they flew. And one called to another and said: "Holy, holy, holy is the Lord of hosts; the whole earth is full of his glory." The pivots on the thresholds shook at the voices of those who called, and the house filled with smoke. And I said: "Woe is me! I am lost, for I am a man of unclean lips, and I live among a people of unclean lips, yet my eyes have seen the King, the LORD of hosts!" Then one of the seraphs flew to me, holding a live coal that had been taken from the altar with a pair of tongs. The seraph touched my mouth with it and said: "Now that this has touched your lips, your guilt has departed and your sin is blotted out." Then I heard the voice of the Lord saying, "Whom shall I send, and who will go for us?" And I said, "Here am I; send me!" – NRSV: Isaiah 6: 1-8

ISAIAH'S CALL TO BE GOD'S PROPHET:

Isaiah is considered the greatest of the prophets. He appeared at a crucial time in Israel's history. God's people had already been divided between Judah, the Southern Kingdom, and Israel, the Northern Kingdom. This was the result of intrigue, division, and a departure from covenant with God. Israel collapsed in 722 B.C. under the overwhelming might and power of Assyria. Twenty one years later, in 701 B.C., Jerusalem, part of the Southern Kingdom, saw itself surrounded on all sides by the army of Sennacherib.

Prior to the devastation of Israel at the hands of the Assyrians, in 742 B.C., the year Uzziah, king of Judah died, Isaiah received his call to the prophetic office in the Temple of Jerusalem. The vision of the Lord enthroned in glory left an unforgettable mark on Isaiah's ministry and provides the key to the understanding of his message. In beholding the majesty, glory, and holiness of God, Isaiah was deeply aware of his own sinfulness and gained a new awareness of human pettiness, rebellion, and sin. He experienced in the depths of his being the enormous chasm between God's sovereign holiness and man's sin, leading him to exclaim, "Woe is me! I am lost, for I am a man of unclean lips, and I live among a people of unclean lips." Only the purifying coal of the Seraph could cleanse his lips and prepare him for acceptance of the call: "Here am I, send me!"

THE INSTITUTION OF PROPHETISM:

Israel saw itself as a theocracy. God was its ruler and God's rule was established through the Mosaic Law. When the Israelites first entered the Promised Land, the Mosaic Law was interpreted and enacted by the Priests and Judges. The Judges were military leaders sent by God to aid and relieve His people in time of external danger. They exercised their activity between the death of Joshua who led the Israelites into the Promised Land and the institution of monarchy during the time of Samuel, the last of the Judges.

During Samuel's term, Israel desired an earthly king, like the neighboring kingdoms. "But the thing displeased Samuel when they said, "Give us a king to govern us." Samuel prayed to the LORD, and the LORD said to Samuel, "Listen to the voice of the people in all that they say to you; for they have not rejected you, but they have rejected me from being king over them. Just as they have done to me, from the day I brought them up out of Egypt to this day, forsaking me and serving other gods, so also they are doing to you. Now then, listen to their voice;

only – you shall solemnly warn them, and show them the ways of the king who shall reign over them (NRSV: 1 Samuel 8: 6-9)."

These words from 1 Samuel are a painful indictment of Israel's leadership. The institution of monarchy did not improve matters. Corruption and abandonment of God and God's law continued unabated, leading to the ultimate dissolution of the monarchy and exile of God's people. Given that both the monarchy and the priesthood were lax in preserving God's central role in the Israelite nation, God chose a succession of Israelites to transmit in His name the divine communications to the people. The office of prophet was a direct call from God and was subject entirely to the divine will.

Already in Deuteronomy 18: 15-20, the office of prophet gets instituted. "The LORD your God will raise up for you, a prophet like me (Moses), from among your own people; you shall heed such a prophet. This is what you requested of the LORD your God at Horeb on the day of the assembly when you said: "If I hear the voice of the LORD my God any more, or ever again see this great fire, I will die." Then the LORD replied to me: "They are right in what they have said. I will raise up for them a prophet like you from among their own people; I will put my words in the mouth of the prophet, who shall speak to them everything that I command. Anyone who does not heed the words that the prophet shall speak in my name, I, myself, will hold accountable (NRSV: Deuteronomy 18:15-19)." The prophets were intermediaries between God and His people. Their communications from God came through visions, dreams, and ecstasies and were transmitted through sermons, writings and symbolic actions. The prophets preserved and developed revealed religion (1 Samuel 12:1-15), gave counsel in political matters (Isaiah 31:1ff), and in matters of private life (1 Samuel 9:6-9). Their predictions of the future intensified the expectation of the Messiah and his kingdom.

The prophecies express judgments of the people's moral conduct on the basis of the Mosaic covenant between God and Israel. They teach sublime truths and lofty morals. In the affairs of men, their prime concern is the interests of God, especially in what pertains to the chosen people through whom the Messiah is to come: hence their denunciations of idolatry and ritualism in worship that excludes the interior spirit of religion. They are concerned also with the universal nature of the moral law, with personal responsibility, with the person and office of the Messiah, and with the conduct of foreign nations.

THE BOOK AND MINISTRY OF ISAIAH:

The ministry of Isaiah may be divided into three periods, covering 7 years of the reign of Jotham from 742-735 B.C., 20 years of the rule of Ahaz from 735-715 B.C., and 28 years of the reign of Hezekiah from 715-687 B.C. The early oracles found in Chapters 1 through 5, belong to the first period covering the reign of Jotham. They exposed the moral breakdown of Judah and its capital, Jerusalem. When Ahaz became king, the prophet became his adviser. The king's throne was threatened by the Syro-Ephraimite coalition. Ephraim was Israel, the Northern Kingdom. Instead of heeding Isaiah's advice to rely on God and do God's bidding, in his anxiety and haste, Ahaz rejected Isaiah's plea to have faith and courage, and instead sought Assyria's help. The majority of the messianic oracles found in Chapters 6 through 12 came from this period.

Hezekiah succeeded his father and undertook a religious reform which Isaiah supported enthusiastically. But the old intrigues began again, and the king was soon won over to the pro-Egyptian party. Isaiah denounced this "covenant with death: "Alas for those who go down to Egypt for help and who rely on horses, who trust in chariots because they are many and in horsemen because they are very strong, but do not look to the Holy One of Israel or consult the LORD!...The Egyptians are human, and not God; their horses are flesh, and not spirit. When the LORD stretches out his hand, the helper will stumble, and the one helped will fall, and they will all perish together (NRSV: Isaiah 31:1-3)."

Isaiah kept summoning Judah to faith in Yahweh as her only hope. But it was too late; the revolt had already begun. Assyria acted quickly and her army, after ravaging Judah, laid siege to Jerusalem in 701 B.C. "I shut up Hezekiah like a bird in his cage," boasts the famous inscription of Sennacherib. But Yahweh delivered the city, as Isaiah had promised (Isaiah 29, 36, 37). God is the Lord of history, and Assyria but an instrument in his hands. Little is known about the last days of this great religious leader, whose oracles, of singular poetic beauty and power, constantly reminded his wayward people of their destiny and God's fidelity to His promises.

The complete book of Isaiah is a collection of poems composed chiefly by the great prophet, but also by disciples, some of whom came many years after Isaiah. In Chapters 1 through 39, most of the oracles come from Isaiah and faithfully reflect the situation in eighth-century Judah. Some sections like the Apocalypse of Isaiah, chapters 24 through 27, the oracles against Babylon, chapters 13 and 14, and probably the poems of chapters 34 and 35 belong to disciples deeply influenced by the prophet. Chapters 40 through 55, sometimes called Deutero-Isaiah or Second-Isaiah, are generally attributed to an anonymous poet who prophesied toward the end of the Babylonian exile, in the sixth century, B.C. From this section come the great messianic oracles known as the Songs of the Servant whose mysterious destiny of suffering and glorification is fulfilled in Christ's passion and glorification. Chapters 56 through 66 were composed by disciples who inherited the spirit of the great prophet and continued his work.

THE MESSAGE OF ISAIAH:

Isaiah has a twofold message: of judgment and hope, or exile and homecoming. In the first book, Chapters 1-39, the message is one of judgment and exile. There is a deep sense of impending doom, destruction, and great loss. In Second-Isaiah, Chapters 40-66, the message is one of great hope and tenderness. The narrative of Jesus replicates the story of Jerusalem. Jesus accepts our 'loss and degradation' by taking it upon himself through his passion, crucifixion, and death, and transforming Himself and us through His Resurrection!

HELPFUL ATTITUDES FOR PRAYER:

- The majesty, holiness and glory of the Lord took possession of his spirit and, conversely, he gained a new awareness of human pettiness and sinfulness.
- The enormous abyss between God's sovereign holiness and man's sin overwhelmed the prophet. Only the purifying coal of the seraphim could cleanse his lips and prepare him for acceptance of the call: "Here am I, send me!"
- The institution of monarchy did not improve matters. Corruption and abandonment of God and God's law continued unabated, leading to the ultimate dissolution of the monarchy and exile of God's people.
- Given that both the monarchy and the priesthood were lax in preserving God's central role in the Israelite nation, God chose a succession of Israelites to transmit in His name the divine communications to the people. The office of prophet was a direct call from God and was subject entirely to the divine will.
- The prophets were intermediaries between God and His people. Their communications from God came through visions, dreams, and ecstasies and were transmitted through sermons, writings and symbolic actions.
- In the affairs of men, the prophets' prime concern is the interests of God, especially in what pertains to the chosen people through whom the Messiah is to come; hence their denunciations of idolatry and that externalism in worship which excludes the interior spirit of religion.

GUIDELINES FOR PRAYER:

- Be faithful to your time of prayer, and make it between 20 and 30 minutes daily.

- Begin every prayer session with an earnest prayer to the Holy Spirit like the one I have composed for you: *Come, Holy Spirit, and overshadow me with your gentle wisdom and power as I endeavor to sit at the feet of Jesus during this period of prayer. Purify my mind and heart as I seek to make the teachings of Jesus my priority in life, thinking, speaking and doing as He desires. You are the keeper of my soul, leading me into God's heart. May I be docile and submissive to your wisdom and guidance and may my life be a pleasing offering in your sight. Amen.*
- Take one of the passages suggested for prayer. During the duration of the session you might want to ponder the question, **"In what way is Isaiah speaking to me directly through his oracles and messianic prophecies?"**
- Lastly, during your prayer make sure you also address God directly and listen for the Holy Spirit's responses.
- You can end your prayer with the following: *Father, Son, and Holy Spirit, I thank you for your gracious companionship. I praise you for being my Creator, Savior and Lord. May I take your blessings to my day, and may your presence envelop and permeate all my thoughts and actions. Through Christ our Lord. Amen.*

PASSAGES FOR PRAYER:

Isaiah 1 & 2: Indictment of Israel and Judah & Zion, the Messianic Capital
Isaiah 3: Judgment of Judah & Jerusalem & the Messianic Branch
Isaiah 6: 1-13: The Call of Isaiah
Isaiah 7: Birth of Emmanuel
Isaiah 9: The Promise of the Messiah and Fall of the Northern Kingdom
Isaiah 11: Emmanuel's Rule; Union of Ephraim (Northern) & Judah (Southern) kingdoms
Isaiah 12: Song of Thanksgiving

JOURNALING: *REFER TO **HELPS TO PRAYER, # 6***

SPIRITUAL READING: *REFER TO **HELPS TO PRAYER, # 4 AND 5***
Manual: Read Sessions Eleven and Twelve for the sixth month, and delve into the topics in *Helps to Prayer, Methods of Prayer, and Practices for Committed Discipleship.*
New Testament: Try to read the New Testament over Sessions 11 through 18
Old Testament: Try to Read 1 & 2 Samuel, and 1 & 2 Kings.
Imitation of Christ: Follow the suggestions in *Helps to Prayer # 5.*
Catechism of the Catholic Church: Follow the suggestions in *Helps to Prayer #5*

SESSION TWELVE: THE SUFFERING SERVANT

SCRIPTURE:

"A bruised reed he will not break, and a dimly burning wick he will not quench; he will faithfully bring forth justice. He will not grow faint or be crushed until he has established justice in the earth." –NRSV: Isaiah 42:2-3

"It is too little a thing that you should be my servant to raise up the tribes of Jacob and to restore the survivors of Israel; I will give you as a light to the nation, that my salvation may reach to the end of the earth." –NRSV: Isaiah 49: 6

"Surely he has borne our infirmities and carried our diseases; yet we accounted him stricken, struck down by God, and afflicted. But he was wounded for our transgressions, crushed for our iniquities; upon him was the punishment that made us whole, and by his bruises we are healed. All we like sheep have gone astray; we have all turned to our own way, and the LORD has laid on him the iniquity of us all." –NRSV: Isaiah 53:4-6

PROMISE OF SALVATION:

First Isaiah was an indictment of the idolatrous ways of Israel and Judah which culminated in exile. The Vineyard Song is an appropriate summary of this period: "Let me sing for my beloved my love-song concerning his vineyard: My beloved had a vineyard on a very fertile hill. He dug it and cleared it of stones, and planted it with choice vines; he built a watchtower in the midst of it, and hewed out a wine vat in it; he expected it to yield grapes, but it yielded wild grapes...What more was there to do for my vineyard that I have not done in it? When I expected it to yield grapes, why did it yield wild grapes? And now I will tell you what I will do to my vineyard. I will remove its hedge, and it shall be devoured; I will break down its wall, and it shall be trampled down. I will make it a waste; it shall not be pruned or hoed, and it shall be overgrown with briers and thorns; I will also command the clouds that they rain no rain upon it. For the vineyard of the LORD of hosts is the house of Israel, and the people of Judah are his pleasant planting; he expected justice, but saw bloodshed; righteousness but heard a cry (NRSV: Isaiah 5:1-7)."

Second Isaiah (Chapters 40-55) proclaims a message of salvation and restoration. Isaiah 40 rings in a promise of salvation: "Comfort, O comfort my people, says your God. Speak tenderly to Jerusalem, and cry to her that she has served her term, that her penalty is paid, that she has received from the LORD's hand double for all her sins (NRSV: 40:1-2)." Isaiah is summoned to prepare Israel to return from exile to the amazement of the nations: "A voice cries out: In the wilderness prepare the way of the LORD, make straight in the desert a highway for our God. Every valley shall be lifted up, and every mountain and hill be made low; the uneven ground shall become level, and the rough places a plain. Then the glory of the LORD shall be revealed, and all people shall see it together, for the mouth of the Lord has spoken (NRSV: Isaiah 40:3-5)." Isaiah can be seen as someone who, like John the Baptist, prepared the way of the Lord.

MESSIANIC SALVATION:

Several significant strands are woven together to develop the theme of salvation and restoration in this Second Book of Isaiah. The first is the idea of messianic salvation coming through the hands of the meshiah or the anointed one. Only the kings, and later the priests, were anointed with oil in the ceremony of installation (1 Samuel 10:1). Much later, after the Old Testament, the term applied to God's mediators in the future salvation of Israel, for instance in the Dead Sea scrolls and the New Testament. In First Isaiah, the prophet relied upon the Israelite kings who ruled from Jerusalem for the fulfillment of divine promises. Even in their failure the prophet expected a new, still more glorious Son of David to lead the people into the final age: "But a shoot shall sprout from the stump of Jesse, and from his roots a bud shall blossom (Isaiah 11: 1)." In Second Isaiah (Chapters 40-55), the Davidic dynasty has been swept away, the people have been sent into exile, and the divine promises have been returned to the people.

A second strand in the understanding and development of salvation is the title "redeemer" or Goel in Hebrew. This title came into usage in early biblical times and was used as the word for kinsperson of the same family or tribe. Leviticus 25 gives us a detailed explanation of the implications of being a redeemer in the community. Second Isaiah turns this secular word into a sacred title for God. In redeeming Israel, God is living up to his role as Parent: "Do not fear, for I have redeemed you; I have called you by name, you are mine… For I am the LORD your God, the Holy One of Israel, your Savior (NRSV: Isaiah 43: 1-3)" As redeemer, God is also spouse to Israel: "Do not fear, for you will not be ashamed; do not be discouraged, for you will not suffer disgrace; for you will forget the shame of your youth, and the disgrace of your widowhood you will remember no more. For your Maker is your husband, the LORD of hosts is his name; the Holy One of Israel is your Redeemer, the God of the whole earth he is called (NRSV: Isaiah 54: 4-5)." Applied to Jesus, the title reminds us that Jesus acted out of "obligation" for us, his kinsfolk. This obligation was freely undertaken in voluntary obedience to His Father's will.

"Redeemer" brings Christians to another aspect of Second Isaiah's theology, that of Suffering Servant which is the third strand. Several identifications have been proposed, e.g. historical Israel, ideal Israel, an Old Testament historical character before or during the lifetime of the prophet, and even the prophet himself. The revelation of the Servant is that salvation comes through suffering. Such a conception must have referred to the future in the mind of the writer. The New

Testament and Christian tradition have seen a fulfillment of these prophecies in Jesus Christ.

Second Isaiah also prophesied that God would use Cyrus, king of Persia (559-529 B.C.), as a new Moses. He was God's anointed one to bring about the destruction of Babylon and the return from exile of the Israelites. "Thus says the LORD to his anointed, to Cyrus, whose right hand I have grasped to subdue nations before him and strip kings of their robes, to open doors before him – and the gates shall not be closed: I will go before you and level the mountains, I will break in pieces the doors of bronze and cut through the bars of iron, I will give you the treasures of darkness and riches hidden in secret places, so that you may know that it is I, the LORD, the God of Israel, who call you by your name. (NRSV: Isaiah 45:1-3)." However, Second Isaiah's hopes were repudiated by the people as perhaps too liberal in accepting foreigners into the ranks of God's chosen people and in considering the Persian Cyrus as a new Moses. It is at this point in the exile experience of Israel that Second Isaiah composed the Suffering Servant songs and identified with Israel, depressed and humiliated in Babylon. The Servant's weakest moment became the best moment for Israel. As the Servant experienced rejection for reaching out to the nations, Israel glimpsed in the Servant her own call for a mission to the Gentiles: "Hear me, O coastlands, listen, O distant peoples (Isaiah 49:1-6)."

By remaining bonded with sinful Israel, the Servant became the source of salvation for those who rejected him. They contemplate this silent servant in a song of thanksgiving: "Who has believed what we have heard? And to whom has the arm of the LORD been revealed? For he grew up before him like a young plant, and like a root out of dry ground; he had no form or majesty that we should look at him, nothing in his appearance that we should desire him. He was despised and rejected by others; a man of suffering and acquainted with infirmity; and as one from whom others hide their faces he was despised and we held him of no account (NRSV: Isaiah 53:1-4)." This description of the suffering servant was modeled upon Moses ("Even with me the LORD was angry on your account, saying, "You also shall not enter there. Joshua son of Nun, your assistant, shall enter there (Promised Land); encourage him, for he is the one who will secure Israel's possession of it –NRSV: Deuteronomy 1:37-38) and Jeremiah ("Woe is me, my mother that you ever bore me, a man of strife and contention to the whole land! I have not lent, nor have I borrowed, yet all of them curse me –NRSV: Jeremiah 15:10), and influenced the writing of Psalm 22, and so became the typical expression of innocent sufferers who contribute to redemption of a community that persecutes them.

JESUS, THE SUFFERING SERVANT

Only in Jesus Christ are these sweeping prophecies fulfilled. The idea of saving the world through a humble, suffering servant rather than a glorious king is contrary to human thought. Religious Jews assumed that Israel would receive a political Messiah, a king who would deliver his people from their enemies and colonizers. Yet the Messiah's strength would be shown in humility, suffering, and mercy. Isaiah's prophecies reveal the future Redeemer through four Servant-of-the-Lord oracles. In the First Oracle he is described as God's chosen one who is filled with God's spirit. He will bring forth justice to the nations through mercy and compassion. "A bruised reed he will not break, and a dimly burning wick he will not quench; he will faithfully bring forth justice (NRSV: Isaiah 42:3-4)."

In the Second Oracle Isaiah speaks of a redeemer designated by God from conception for a special station in life. He is a suffering servant whose vocation will be not only the restoration of Israel, but also the conversion of the world. "It is too light a thing that you should be my servant to raise up the tribes of Jacob and to restore the survivors of Israel; I will give you as a light to the nations, that my salvation may reach to the end of the earth – (NRSV: Isaiah 49:6)." In the Third Oracle the redeemer is portrayed as one who speaks words of consolation and inspiration to the weary. He does not refuse the divine vocation and as a result submits willingly to insults and beatings. "I gave my back to those who struck me, and my cheeks to those who pulled out the beard; I did not hide my face from insult and spitting – (NRSV: Isaiah 50: 6)." In the last Oracle, Chapters 52: 13-53:12, Isaiah gives us an extraordinary description of the sinless Servant, who by his voluntary suffering atones for the sins of his people and saves them from just punishment at the hands of God.

In the New Testament, Jesus is servant in various ways: at his baptism, which identifies him with Israel in search of redemption (NRSV: Mk 1:11: "And a voice came from heaven, "You are my Son, the Beloved; with you I am well pleased."). He identifies with suffering and disabled people (Mt 8:17: "This was to fulfill what had been spoken through the prophet Isaiah, "He took our infirmities and bore our diseases."). Jesus is one with people in their humility and sinfulness (NRSV: Philippians 2:7: "He emptied himself, taking the form of a slave, being born in human likeness."). Jesus thus appears as redeemer by plunging his own life and goodness into the midst of Israel and the entire world, bearing the full brunt of sin and sorrow, and thus overcoming evil by his own divine goodness. This tradition of an innocent sufferer, of Israel at its prophetic best, sustained Jesus in his own rejection (Mt 8:17) and inspired the Church in its understanding of a Suffering Messiah (Phil 2: 6-11). Jesus identified with this tradition and brought the theology of redemption to a sublime perfection.

HELPFUL ATTITUDES FOR PRAYER:

- The first strand of salvation is the idea of messianic salvation coming through the hands of the *meshiah, the anointed one*. Only the kings, and later the priests, were the anointed ones. Much after the Old Testament was the term applied to God's mediators in the *future* salvation of Israel, as in the Dead Sea scrolls and the New Testament.

- A second strand in the understanding of salvation is the title "redeemer." This title came into usage in early biblical times and was used as the word for kinsperson of the same family or tribe. Second Isaiah turns this secular word into a sacred title for God. In redeeming Israel God is living up to his role as Parent and Husband.
- Applied to Jesus, the title "redeemer" reminds us that Jesus acted out of "obligation" for us, his kinsfolk. This obligation was freely undertaken.
- The revelation of the Suffering Servant, the third strand, is that salvation comes through suffering. In the mind of the writer, such a conception must have been in the future. The New Testament and Christian tradition have seen a fulfillment of these prophecies in Jesus Christ.
- This tradition of an innocent sufferer, of Israel at its prophetic best, sustained Jesus in his own rejection (Mt 8:17) and inspired the church in its understanding of a suffering Messiah (Phil 2: 6-11).

GUIDELINES FOR PRAYER:

- Be faithful to your time of prayer, and make it between 20 and 30 minutes daily.
- Begin every prayer session with an earnest prayer to the Holy Spirit such as: *Come, Holy Spirit, and overshadow me with your gentle wisdom and power as I endeavor to sit at the feet of Jesus during this period of prayer. Purify my mind and heart as I seek to make the teachings of Jesus my priority in life, thinking, speaking and doing as He desires. You are the keeper of my soul, leading me into God's heart. May I be docile and submissive to your wisdom and guidance and may my life be a pleasing offering in your sight. Amen.*
- Take one passage a day suggested for prayer. During the duration of the session you might want to ponder the question, **"What is the connection between loving others and suffering on their behalf?"**
- Lastly, during your prayer make sure you also address God directly and listen for the Holy Spirit's responses.

- You can end your prayer with the following: *Father, Son, and Holy Spirit, I thank you for your gracious companionship. I praise you for being my Creator, Savior and Lord. May I take your blessings to my day, and may your presence envelop and permeate all my thoughts and actions. Through Christ our Lord. Amen.*

PASSAGES FOR PRAYER:

Isaiah 42: 1-7: The First Servant-of-the-Lord Oracle
Isaiah 43: 1-7: God as Redeemer and Restorer of His Kinsfolk
Isaiah 49: 1-7: The Second Servant-of-the-Lord Oracle
Isaiah 49: 14-21: Restoration of Zion
Isaiah 50: 4-9: Third Salvation-through-the-Lord's-Servant Oracle
Isaiah 52:13- 53:12: Fourth Suffering-&-Triumph-of-the-Lord's-Servant Oracle
Isaiah 54: 1-10: Yahweh redeeming Israel, His Spouse
Psalm 22: The Suffering and Triumph of Jesus, Suffering Servant and Messiah
Philippians 2: 5-11: Jesus, the Suffering Servant

JOURNALING: REFER TO *HELPS TO PRAYER, # 6*

SPIRITUAL READING: REFER TO *HELPS TO PRAYER, # 4 AND 5*

Manual: Read Sessions Eleven and Twelve for the sixth month, and delve into the topics in *Helps to Prayer, Methods of Prayer, Practices for Committed Discipleship.*

New Testament: Try to read the New Testament over Sessions 11 through 18

Old Testament: Try to Read 1 & 2 Samuel, and 1 & 2 Kings.

Imitation of Christ: Follow the suggestions in *Helps to Prayer # 5.*

Catechism of the Catholic Church: Follow the suggestions in *Helps to Prayer #5*

SESSION THIRTEEN: THE CALL OF JEREMIAH

SCRIPTURE:

Now the word of the LORD came to me saying, "Before I formed you in the womb I knew you, and before you were born I consecrated you; I appointed you a prophet to the nations." Then I said, "Ah, Lord God! Truly I do not know how to speak, for I am only a boy." But the Lord said to me, "Do not say, 'I am only a boy'; for you shall go to all to whom I send you, and you shall speak whatever I command you. Do not be afraid of them, for I am with you to deliver you, says the Lord."
—NRSV: Jeremiah 1: 4-8

JEREMIAH THE PROPHET:

Ancestry: Jeremiah came from a priestly family in Anathoth, a town about 4 miles northeast of Jerusalem. His ancestry was traced to Abiathar, the great-great grandson of Eli and a priest who had been exiled by King Solomon to Anathoth. Jeremiah's father Hilkiah, may have been the high priest who found the book of Deuteronomy during the repair of the Temple: "The high priest Hilkiah informed the scribe Shaphan, "I have found the book of the law in the temple of the Lord (2 Kings 22:8)." This could have been the reason why Jeremiah was influenced by the book of Deuteronomy.

Politics: The politics of the period shaped the message of Jeremiah. Once the last great Assyrian king, Ashurbanipal slipped into old age, opposition and rebellion against Assyrian power and hegemony began to emerge on all sides. During this period King Josiah reigned. As a result of his religious conversion, he took the risk of repudiating publicly the Assyrian gods. This action would have been treated as treason in Assyria's heyday and Josiah would have been dethroned. At the death of Ashurbanipal in 627 B.C., civil war broke out in the empire and Babylon successfully wrested its independence and became the new colossus. This was the same year that Jeremiah received the call to prophesy.

In 621 B.C. King Josiah introduced his "Deuteronomic reform (2 Kings 22: 1-23: 27)" Here is a flavor of the actions the king took: "Then the king commanded the high priest Hilkiah, his vicar, and the door-keepers to remove from the temple of the Lord all the objects that had been made for Baal, Asherah, and the whole host of heaven. He had these burned outside Jerusalem on the slopes of the Kidron and their ashes carried to Bethel. He also put an end to the pseudo-priests whom the kings of Judah had appointed to burn incense on the high places in the cities of Judah and in the vicinity of Jerusalem, as well as those who burned incense to Baal to the sun, moon, and signs of the Zodiac, and to the whole host of heaven (NRSV 23:4-5)." Both politics and prophecy were seizing the day, each for their own separate purposes.

Ministry: Jeremiah's ministry began in 627 B.C., and he dealt with three kings. As the Assyrian empire collapsed, Jeremiah announced with much hope the return of the northern tribes who had been carried off into exile some hundred years earlier. This ecstatic note is expressed in Chapter 31:3-6: "With age-old love I have loved you; so I have kept my mercy toward you. Again I will restore you, and you shall be rebuilt, O Virgin Israel; carrying your festive tambourines, you shall go forth dancing with the merrymakers. Again you shall plant vineyards on the mountains of Samaria; those who plant them shall enjoy the fruits. Yes, a day will come when the watchmen will call out on Mount Ephraim: "Rise up, let us go to Zion, to the Lord, our God (NRSV)." Jeremiah also condemned idolatry that was prevalent in Jerusalem (Chapters 2-6). During King Josiah's Deuteronomic reform, Jeremiah turned silent. He was in favor of its goals but disagreed with the king's ruthless ways (2 Kings 23: 4-20).

In 600 B.C. Josiah was killed in battle by the Egyptians as he attempted to stop the northward march of the Pharaoh Neco. He was eventually succeeded by his son Jehoiakim whom Jeremiah despised as cunning and wicked: "Woe to him who builds by unrighteousness, and his upper rooms by injustice; who makes his neighbors work for nothing, and does not give them their wages; who says, "I will build myself a spacious house with large upper rooms," and who cuts out windows for it, paneling it with cedar and painting it with vermilion...But your eyes and heart are only on your dishonest gain, for shedding innocent blood, and for practicing oppression and violence (NRSV: Jeremiah 22:13-17)." At this juncture, Nebuchadnezzar was king and Babylon was the world power in place of Assyria. When Jehoiakim revolted, the Babylonians captured and plundered Jerusalem, and took many prominent Israelites into exile. The king died in the debacle and Jehoiachin, his son along with Ezekiel, the prophet, were among the deportees. Jeremiah urged the next king, Zedekiah, to refrain from entering into an alliance with the Egyptians in order to plot another revolt.

Zedekiah, however, was weak and easily swayed. He went against Jeremiah's advice and in July, 587 B.C. the Babylonians stormed Jerusalem again and a month later burned it to the ground: "In the nineteenth year of Nebuchadnezzar, king of Babylon, Nebuzaradan, the captain of the bodyguard who served the king of Babylon, entered Jerusalem. He burned the house of the LORD, the king's house, and all the houses of Jerusalem; every great house he burned down. All the army of the Chaldeans, who were with the captain of the guard, broke down all the walls around Jerusalem (NRSV: Jeremiah 52:12-14)." The Babylonians treated Jeremiah well because he persistently spoke against revolt. They gave him the choice of either living in a palace in Babylon or remaining behind in Judah. The prophet chose the latter (40:1-6). When the remnant in Jerusalem rejected his advice and fled into Egypt, they dragged the prophet with them (Jeremiah 42:1-43:7). Jeremiah died in Egypt.

Character: The Book of Jeremiah gives us a vivid portrait of his character. There is the joyful optimism in Chapter 31 when he prophesies the joyful return of the northern tribes from exile: "For thus says the LORD: Sing aloud with gladness for Jacob, and raise shouts for the chief of the nations; proclaim, give praise, and say, "Save, O LORD, your people, the remnant of Israel." See, I am going to bring them from the land of the north, and gather them from the farthest parts of the earth, among them the blind and the lame, those with child and those in labor, together; a great company, they shall return here. With weeping they shall come, and with consolations I will lead them back, I will let them walk by brooks of water, in a straight path in which they shall not stumble; for I have become a father to Israel, and Ephraim is my firstborn (NRSV: Jeremiah 31:7-9)."

There is courage in confronting kings: "The officials were enraged at Jeremiah, and they beat him and imprisoned him in the house of the secretary Jonathan, for it had been made a prison...Jeremiah also said to King Zedekiah, "What wrong have I done to you or your servants or this people, that you have put me in prison? Where are your prophets who prophesied to you, saying, 'The king of Babylon will not come against you and against this land'?...So King Zedekiah gave orders, and they committed Jeremiah to the court of the guard; and a loaf of bread was given him daily from the bakers' street, until all the bread of the city was gone. So Jeremiah remained in the court of the guard (NRSV: Chapter 37:15-21)."

Then there are his honest and painful struggles with God in Chapters 12, 15, and 20, where he appears as petulant and even revengeful: "O LORD, you have enticed me, and I was enticed; you have overpowered me, and you have prevailed. I have become a laughingstock all day long; everyone mocks me. For whenever I speak, I must cry out, I must shout, "Violence and destruction!" For the word of the LORD has become for me a reproach and derision all day long. If I say, "I will not mention him or speak any more in his name," then within me there is something like a burning fire shut up in my bones; I am weary with holding it in and I cannot (NRSV: Jeremiah 20:7-9)."

Celibacy was not an easy decision and he felt its loneliness severely. He was being asked by God to be a reminder to His people that their ways were leading them to total destruction, making pointless the rearing of families: "The word of the LORD came to me: You shall not take a wife, nor shall you have sons or daughters in this place. For thus says the LORD concerning the sons and daughters who are born in this place, and concerning the mothers who bear them and the fathers who beget them in this land: They shall die of deadly diseases. They shall not be lamented, nor shall they be buried; they shall become like dung on the surface of the ground. They shall perish by the sword and by famine, and their dead bodies shall become food for the birds of the air and for the wild animals of the earth (Jeremiah16:1-4)." Paradoxically, it bonded him with the people in their most difficult moments of loss.

THE MESSAGE OF JEREMIAH:

Jeremiah's message shows up in compassion and prayer as well as in fidelity to a covenant inscribed upon the heart. Let us look at some themes within his message:

The New Covenant: The key passage is found in Chapter 31: 31-34: "The days are surely coming, says the LORD, when I will make a new covenant with the house of Israel and the house of Judah... I will put my law within them, and I will write it on their hearts; and I will be their God, and they shall be my people. No longer shall they teach one another, or say to each other, "Know the LORD," for they shall all know me, from the least of them to the greatest, says the LORD; for I will forgive their iniquity, and remember their sin no more (NRSV)."

The phrase "the days are coming" had a strong impact on the Jewish community that produced the Dead Sea Scrolls, on Jesus and the

New Testament writers, as well as on the early church. Before Jeremiah's time the Israelites thought mostly in terms of a future fulfillment of promises in a single great day of the Lord. Under Jeremiah's influence this future "day" began to appear in stages: an initial time of suffering at first; then an in-between period; and finally, the absolute and definite completion of hopes and promises. The in-between period offered consolation to the followers of Jesus when his ministry and especially his Passion-Resurrection did not immediately usher in the final age. These events of Jesus' earthly life initiated the messianic age and led to the "in-between period," but we still await Christ's Second Glorious Coming!

Jeremiah's "new" covenant written upon the heart is closely tied with the Mosaic covenant of Mount Sinai: Hear, O Israel! The LORD is our God, the LORD alone! You shall love the LORD your God with all your heart, and with all your soul, and with all your might. Keep these words that I am commanding you today in your heart (NRSV: Deuteronomy 6:4-6)." And in the New Testament the old became new within the "coming days" through the Death and Resurrection of Jesus. This new covenant is commemorated every time we celebrate the Eucharist (Luke 22:20; 1 Corinthians 11: 25).

Sin and Atonement: The prophet suggests that sin inevitably brings its own sorrow: "Thus says the Lord: What wrong did your ancestors find in me that they went far from me, and went after worthless things, and became worthless themselves? I brought you into a plentiful land to eat its fruits and its good things. But when you entered you defiled my land, and made my heritage an abomination. The priests did not say, "Where is the LORD?" Those who handle the law did not know me; the rulers transgressed against me; the prophets prophesied by Baal, and went after things that do not profit (NRSV: Jeremiah 2:5-8)." We are changed into that which we desire, for good or for evil.

Jeremiah also draws our attention to another aspect of sin and atonement through the Hebrew word 'yasar' meaning "chastise": "Indeed I heard Ephraim pleading: "You disciplined me, and I took the discipline; I was like a calf untrained. Bring me back, let me come back, for you're the LORD my God. For after I had turned away I repented; and after I was discovered, I struck my thigh; I was ashamed, and I was dismayed because I bore the disgrace of my youth." Is Ephraim my dear son? Is he the child I delight in? As often as I speak against him, I still remember him. Therefore I am deeply moved for him; I will surely have mercy on him, says the LORD (NRSV: Jeremiah 31: 18-20)." This sequence of sin –suffering –repentance – forgiveness – new life stresses the purifying and strengthening results of punishment as well as God's compassion.

In this movement from sin to suffering, Jeremiah was never far removed from the agony of God toward Israel: "I thought how I would set you among my children, and give you a pleasant land, the most beautiful heritage of all the nations. And I thought you would call me, My Father, and would not turn from following me. Instead, as a faithless wife leaves her husband, so you have been faithless to me, O house of Israel, says the LORD (NRSV: Jeremiah 3:19-20).

Faith and Prayer: Jeremiah is continually laying bare the anguish of his heart. He wrestles fiercely with God in his confrontations of God: 12:1-5; 15:10-21; 17:12-18; 18:18-23; 20:7-18. He confronts God with defiant questions, but is always trusting of God's fidelity and concern: "You will be in the right, O LORD, when I lay charges against you; but let me put my case to you. Why does the way of the guilty prosper? Why do all who are treacherous thrive? You plant them, and they take root; they grow and bring forth fruit; you are near in their mouths yet far from their hearts. But you, O LORD, know me; you see me and test me – my heart is with you. Pull them out like sheep for the slaughter, and set them apart for the day of slaughter. How long will the land mourn, and the grass of every field wither? For the wickedness of those who live in it, the animals and the birds are swept away, and because people said, "He is blind to our ways (NRSV: Jeremiah 12:1-4)." God answers Jeremiah's questions by posing his own questions: "If you have raced with foot-runners and they have wearied you, how will you compete with horses? And if in a safe land you fall down, how will you fare in the thickets of the Jordan? (NRSV: Jeremiah 12:5)." Jeremiah understands that things must get worse before they can get better. He will continue to live his life in faith and trust.

HELPFUL ATTITUDES FOR PRAYER:

- Before I formed you in the womb I knew you, before you were born I dedicated you, a prophet to the nations I appointed you. "Ah, Lord God!" I said, "I know not how to speak; I am too young." But the Lord answered me, Say not, "I am too young." To whomever I send you, you shall go; whatever I command you, you shall speak.
- "The days are coming, says the Lord, when I will make a new covenant with the house of Israel and the house of Judah... I will place my law within them, and write it upon their hearts.
- Sin inevitably brings its own sorrow: "What fault did your fathers find in me that they withdrew from me, went after empty idols and became empty themselves? We are changed for good or bad into that which we desire.
- This sequence of sin-suffering, repentance-forgiveness-new life stresses the purifying and strengthening results of punishment as well as God's compassion.
- God answers Jeremiah's question by posing his own question: "If running against human beings wearies you, how will you race against horses? If you are secure only in a land of peace, what will you do in the thickets of the Jordan?" Jeremiah understands that things must get worse before they can get better. He will continue to live his life in faith and trust.

GUIDELINES FOR PRAYER:

- Be faithful to your time of prayer, and make it between 20 and 30 minutes daily.
- Begin every prayer session with an earnest prayer to the Holy Spirit like the one I have composed for you: *Come, Holy Spirit, and overshadow me with your gentle wisdom and power as I endeavor to sit at the feet of Jesus during this period of prayer. Purify my mind and heart as I seek to make the teachings of Jesus my priority in life, thinking, speaking and doing as He desires. You are the keeper of my soul, leading me into God's heart. May I be docile and submissive to your wisdom and guidance, and may my life be a pleasing offering in your sight. Amen.*
- Take one of the passages suggested for prayer. During the duration of the session you might want to ponder the question, **"As Jeremiah was characterized as the "weeping prophet," how would you describe your own pain and sorrow at the existence of evil in your own heart and in the world?"**
- Lastly, during your prayer make sure you also address God directly and listen for the Holy Spirit's responses.
- You can end your prayer with the following: *Father, Son, and Holy Spirit, I thank you for your gracious companionship. I praise you for being my Creator, Savior and Lord. May I take your blessings to my day, and may your presence envelop and permeate all my thoughts and actions. Through Christ our Lord. Amen.*

PASSAGES FOR PRAYER:

Jeremiah 1: 4-10: Call of Jeremiah
Jeremiah 2: 1-13: Infidelity of Israel
Jeremiah 3: 11-18: Restoration of Israel
Jeremiah 8: 18-23: The Prophet's Grief over the People's Suffering.
Jeremiah 12: 1-23: Jeremiah's Lamentation
Jeremiah 20: 7-18: Jeremiah's Interior Crisis

Jeremiah 31: 31-34: The New Covenant

JOURNALING: *REFER TO HELPS TO PRAYER, # 6*

SPIRITUAL READING: *REFER TO HELPS TO PRAYER, # 4 AND 5*
Manual: Read Sessions Thirteen and Fourteen for seventh month, and delve into the topics in *Helps to Prayer, Methods of Prayer and Practices for Committed Discipleship*.
New Testament: Try to read the New Testament over Sessions 11 through 18.
Old Testament: Try to Read 1 & 2 Samuel, and 1 & 2 Kings.
Imitation of Christ: Follow the suggestions in *Helps to Prayer # 5*.
Catechism of the Catholic Church: Follow the suggestions in *Helps to Prayer #5*

SESSION FOURTEEN: THE EXILE EXPERIENCE

SCRIPTURE:

"How lonely sits the city that once was full of people! How like a widow she has become, she that was great among the nations! She that was a princess among the provinces has become a vassal. She weeps bitterly in the night, with tears on her cheeks; among all her lovers she has no one to comfort her; all her friends have dealt treacherously with her, they have become her enemies. Judah has gone into exile with suffering and hard servitude; she lives now among the nations, and finds no resting place; her pursuers have all overtaken her in the midst of her distress." –NRSV: Lamentations 1: 1-3

THE PRACTICE OF EXILE:

Jeremiah predicted the seventy year exile in chapter 25:9-11: "I am going to send for all the tribes of the north, says the LORD, even for King Nebuchadnezzar of Babylon, my servant, and I will bring them against this land and its inhabitants, and against all these nations around; I will utterly destroy them, and make them an object of horror and of hissing, and an everlasting disgrace. And I will banish from them the sound of mirth and the sound of gladness, the voice of the bridegroom and the voice of the bride, the sound of the millstones and the light of the lamp. This whole land shall become a ruin and a waste, and these nations shall serve the king of Babylon seventy years (NRSV)." In 587 BC, Jerusalem was destroyed by the Babylonians and the Israelites were deported to Babylon. The exile lasted some 70 years, commencing in 587 BC. The end of the exile began some fifty years later with the rebuilding of Jerusalem under the Persians which began in 537 BC.

Tiglath-Peleser III of Assyria (745-727 BC) was the first to refine this ancient practice of removing conquered peoples on a large scale. He resettled peoples in different parts of the empire as a way of detaching them from their land and destroying the spirit of resistance by suppressing their national identity. Not everyone was deported. Those selected for exile included the royal and noble families, people of means, the landowners, and skilled artisans, all of whom were most influential in shaping the popular will and inciting resistance. In general the peasants were left on the soil and for them it did not really matter who governed the country.

THE REASON FOR THE EXILE:

Jeremiah tells us very clearly why the exile took place. For twenty three years, beginning in the fourth year of Jehoiakim, son of Josiah, King of Judah, Jeremiah had spoken untiringly to all the people of Judah and all the inhabitants of Jerusalem, but they would not listen: "And though the LORD persistently sent you all his servants the prophets, you have neither listened nor inclined your ears to hear when they said, "Turn now, every one of you, from your evil way and wicked doings, and you will remain upon the land that the LORD has given to you and your ancestors from of old and forever; do not go after other gods to serve and worship them, and do not provoke me to anger with the work of your hands. Then I will do you no harm." Yet you did not listen to me, says the LORD, and so you have provoked me to anger with the work of your hands to your own harm... I will utterly destroy them, and make them an object of horror and of hissing, and an everlasting disgrace. And I will banish from them the sound of mirth and the sound of gladness, the voice of the bridegroom and the voice of the bride, the sound of the millstones and the light of the lamp. This whole land shall become a ruin and a waste, and these nations shall serve the king of Babylon seventy years (NRSV: Jeremiah 25: 4-11)."

THE FORMATIVE EXPERIENCE OF THE EXILE:

Isaiah 40 to 55 was written toward the end of the exile experience. The Israelites had several formative experiences during this painful period in their history. For one they came to understand God's tenderness and covenant love as never before. God projected Himself as Israel's <u>*Redeemer*</u>: "Do not fear, for I have redeemed you; I have called you by name, you are mine (NRSV: Isaiah 43:1)." In spite of Israel's rebellion, God will not abandon Israel, but will claim her for His own and will ransom her. God projected Himself as mother: "Can a woman forget her nursing child, or show no compassion for the child of her womb? Even these may forget, yet I will not forget you (NRSV: Isaiah 49:15)." And God expressed Himself as husband: "For your Maker is your husband, the LORD of hosts is his name; the Holy One of Israel is your Redeemer, the God of the whole earth he is called. For the LORD has called you like a wife forsaken and grieved in spirit, like the wife of a man's youth when she is cast off, says your God. For a brief moment I abandoned you, but with great compassion I will gather you (NRSV: Isaiah 54:5-7)." In the midst of Israel's oppression and misery, God's optimism and hope brims forth to overflowing: "For as the new heavens and the new earth, which I will make, shall remain before me, says the LORD; so shall your descendants and your name remain (NRSV: Isaiah 66:22)."

THE SIGNIFICANCE OF THE EXILE EXPERIENCE:

The importance of the exile lies in the fact that the center of gravity of Israelite life and religious consciousness shifted from Jerusalem to Babylon during the years 587-537 BC. Jeremiah had encouraged them to build houses, plant vineyards, and marry the people among whom they settled. He urged them to accept the exile because it was the will of Yahweh that they should be punished, and to await His good pleasure for the redemption of Israel. The Jews were allowed to live freely in Mesopotamia, and OT allusions suggest that they gathered in their own communities. Some of them prospered so well that the Jewish colony begun by the deportations of Nebuchadnezzar still existed in the medieval period.

The religious importance of the exile appears not only in the survival of national and religious consciousness but also, as most scholars are convinced, in extensive work on the sacred books and traditions of Israel. Most of the historical books of the Old Testament were collected and edited during the exile. The Prophetic books as well were edited during this period, and two major Prophetic works, Ezekiel and Isaiah 40-55, were written during the exile. The codification of Hebrew Law in the form in which it appears in the Pentateuch was at least begun during the exile. Lastly, it is possible that the synagogue, of such vital importance in the subsequent history of Judaism, first made its appearance in the exile as a substitute for the worship of the temple.

HELPFUL ATTITUDES FOR PRAYER:

- "Though you refused to listen or pay heed, the Lord has sent you without fail all his servants the prophets with this message: Turn back, each of you, from your evil way and from your evil deeds; then you shall remain in the land which the Lord gave you and your fathers, from of old and forever.
- "Fear not, for I have redeemed you; I have called you by name: you are mine (Isaiah 43:1)." In spite of Israel's rebellion, God will not abandon Israel, but will claim her for His own and will ransom her.
- "Can a mother forget her infant, be without tenderness for the child of her womb? Even should she forget, I will never forget you (NAB: Isaiah 49:15)."
- "For he who has become your husband is your Maker; his name is the Lord of hosts; ... The Lord calls you back, like a wife forsaken and grieved in spirit, a wife married in youth and then cast off, says your God. For a brief moment I abandoned you, but with great tenderness I will take you back.

Session XIV – The Exile Experience

- In the midst of Israel's oppression and misery, God's optimism and hope brims forth to overflowing: *For as the new heavens and the new earth, which I will make, shall remain before me, says the LORD; so shall your descendants and your name remain* (NRSV: Isaiah 66:22)."
- Jeremiah urged the Israelites to accept the exile because it was the will of Yahweh that they should be punished, and to await His good pleasure for the redemption of Israel.

GUIDELINES FOR PRAYER:

- Be faithful to your time of prayer, and make it between 20 and 30 minutes daily.
- Begin every prayer session with an earnest prayer to the Holy Spirit like the one I have composed for you: *Come, Holy Spirit, and overshadow me with your gentle wisdom and power as I endeavor to sit at the feet of Jesus during this period of prayer. Purify my mind and heart as I seek to make the teachings of Jesus my priority in life, thinking, speaking and doing as He desires. You are the keeper of my soul, leading me into God's heart. May I be docile and submissive to your wisdom and guidance, and may my life be a pleasing offering in your sight. Amen.*
- Take one of the passages suggested for prayer. During the duration of the session you might want to ponder the question, **"Have I looked upon my adversities as steeping stones toward humility and deeper union with God or have they become stumbling blocks in my discipleship?"**
- Lastly, during your prayer make sure you also address God directly and listen for the Holy Spirit's responses.
- You can end your prayer with the following: *Father, Son, and Holy Spirit, I thank you for your gracious companionship. I praise you for being my Creator, Savior and Lord. May I take your blessings to*

my day, and may your presence envelop and permeate all my thoughts and actions. Through Christ our Lord. Amen.

PASSAGES FOR PRAYER:

Jeremiah 29:1-15: Letter to the exiles of Babylon
Jeremiah 30: 4-21: The Restoration
Lamentations: 1: 1-13: Jerusalem abandoned and disgraced
Isaiah 40: 1-8: Promise of Salvation
Isaiah 54: 1-15: The New Zion
Isaiah 57: 14- 21: Comfort for the Afflicted
Ezekiel 36: 24-32: Regeneration of the People

JOURNALING: REFER TO HELPS TO PRAYER, # 6

SPIRITUAL READING: REFER TO HELPS TO PRAYER, # 4 AND 5

<u>Manual:</u> Read Sessions Thirteen and Fourteen for the seventh month, and delve into the topics in *Helps to Prayer, Methods of Prayer and Practices for Committed Discipleship*.

<u>New Testament:</u> Try to read the New Testament over Sessions 11 through 18

<u>Old Testament:</u> Try to Read 1 & 2 Samuel, and 1 & 2 Kings.

<u>Imitation of Christ:</u> Follow the suggestions in *Helps to Prayer # 5*.

<u>Catechism of the Catholic Church:</u> Follow the suggestions in *Helps to Prayer #5*

SESSION FIFTEEN: SACRIFICIAL TRADITIONS AND THE EUCHARIST

SCRIPTURE:

"When the sun had gone down and it was dark, a smoking fire pot and a flaming torch passed between these pieces. On that day the LORD made a covenant with Abram, saying, "To your descendants I give this land, from the river of Egypt to the great river, the river Euphrates…"
-NRSV: Genesis 15: 17

"But he was wounded for our transgressions, crushed for our iniquities; upon him was the punishment that made us whole, and by his bruises we are healed. All we like sheep have gone astray; we have all turned to our own way, and the LORD has laid on him the iniquity of us all. He was oppressed, and he was afflicted, yet he did not open his mouth; like a lamb that is led to the slaughter, and like a sheep that before its shearers is silent, so he did not open his mouth
-NRSV: Isaiah 53: 5-7

SIGNS OF COVENANT:

Before the advent of sin, God's relationship with Adam and Eve was lived in true covenant fashion. The harmony and union between God and our first parents was perfect, modeled on the perfect harmony and oneness of the Three Persons of the Trinity. In the first two chapters of Genesis one gets clear glimpses of this covenant relationship between God and Adam and Eve. Here are three indications found in Genesis 2. In a covenant relationship the sharing between the parties is built upon trust and mutual enhancement. So God asks Adam to name the creatures He has created, thereby giving him the power over creatures that only God has and trusting that Adam will act towards them as God would. Secondly, we are told that Adam and Eve were naked and knew no shame (2:25). When there is true intimacy and harmony between individuals, they can be transparent and naked in the relationship and feel no shame. So Adam and Eve were perfectly at peace with God and themselves. The third sign of covenant was that "a man leaves his father and his mother and clings to his wife, and they become one flesh (NSRV: 2:24)." God always intended for us to live in harmony and unity in our families in the same way that the three Persons of the Trinity live in harmony and oneness.

SACRIFICIAL TRADITIONS IN THE OLD TESTAMENT:

Through sin God's plan was shattered but not destroyed. On His part, God would never tolerate the chasm between Himself and His people. God established several covenants in the Old Testament, beginning with Adam and Eve and culminating in the new and everlasting covenant established between Himself and His people through his Son, Jesus Christ. Circumcision was the sign of covenant in the Old Testament and Baptism is the sign of covenant in the New Testament.

Through what kind of ritual was the covenant established between God and His people? Two important truths were established through the covenant ritual: the parties made clear that they would be sharing the same life, symbolized by blood and a meal. Secondly they made promises to one another as their way of expressing oneness and harmony. In the ritual they took an unblemished lamb or goat or other animal like a heifer and slaughtered it. Then they sprinkled the altar, which symbolized God and themselves with the blood of the victim to denote their sharing in the same life. They then partook of the sacrificial victim in a meal, as the consummation of the covenant treaty. The unblemished animal/victim signified the intentions of the parties concerned, to be pure and in harmony with one another.

Session XV – Sacrificial Traditions and the Eucharist

YOM KIPPUR OR THE FEAST OF ATONEMENT:

Yom Kippur or the Feast of Atonement is one of the sacrificial traditions that helps our understanding of Eucharist. Every year on this feast, the High Priest would enter the Holy of Holies in the temple. He was allowed to do so only on this day. Leviticus 16: 11-16 tells us what the High Priest did: "Aaron shall present the bull as a sin offering for himself, and shall make atonement for himself and for his house; he shall slaughter the bull as a sin offering for himself. He shall take a censer full of coals of fire from the altar before the LORD, and two handfuls of crushed sweet incense, and he shall bring it inside the curtain and put the incense on the fire before the LORD, that the cloud of the incense may cover the mercy seat that is upon the covenant, or he will die. He shall take some of the blood of the bull, and sprinkle it with his finger on the front of the mercy seat, and before the mercy seat he shall sprinkle the blood with his finger seven times. He shall slaughter the goat of the sin offering that is for the people and bring its blood inside the curtain, and do with its blood as he did with the blood of the bull, sprinkling it upon the mercy seat and before the mercy seat. Thus he shall make atonement for the sanctuary, because of the uncleannesses of the people of Israel, and because of their transgressions, all their sins (NRSV)." After making atonement for himself and the Israelites, the high priest would then come out of the temple to continue with the ritual: "Then (Aaron) shall go out to the altar that is before the LORD and make atonement on its behalf, and shall take some of the blood of the bull and of the blood of the goat, and put it on each of the horns of the altar. He shall sprinkle some of the blood on it with his finger seven times, and clean it and hallow it from the uncleannesses of the people of Israel (NRSV: Leviticus 16: 18-19)." Then an attendant would thrust before him a goat. "Then Aaron shall lay both his hands on the head of the live goat, and confess over it all the iniquities of the people of Israel, and all their transgressions, all their sins, putting them on the head of the goat, and sending it away into the wilderness by means of someone designated for the task (NRSV:

Leviticus 16: 21-22)." This is the origin of the word 'scapegoat.' In Hebrews 9 and 10 Paul contrasts the celebration of Yom Kippur with the sacrifice of Jesus, making it clear that Yom Kippur had to be celebrated every year because in essence the sacrifice was imperfect whereas the sacrifice of Jesus was offered once and for all because it was perfect.

THE PASSOVER SACRIFICE AND MEAL:

The Passover sacrifice and meal is the other sacrificial tradition that pertains to our understanding and appreciation of Eucharist. God gives this exodus event a very specific ritual. "Tell the whole community of Israel: On the tenth of this month every one of your families must procure for itself a lamb, one apiece for each household...The lamb must be a year-old male and without blemish.... You shall keep it until the fourteenth day of this month, and then, with the whole assembly of Israel present, it shall be slaughtered during the evening twilight. They shall take some of its blood and apply it to the two doorposts and the lintel of every house in which they partake of the lamb. That same night they shall eat its roasted flesh with unleavened bread and bitter herbs. It shall not be eaten raw or boiled, but roasted whole, with its head and shanks and inner organs.... This is how you are to eat it, with your loins girt, sandals on your feet and your staff in hand you shall eat like those who are in flight. It is the Passover of the Lord. For on this same night I will go through Egypt, striking down every first-born of the land, both man and beast, and executing judgment on all the gods of Egypt – I, the Lord! But the blood will mark the houses where you are. Seeing the blood, I will pass over you; thus, when I strike the land of Egypt, no destructive blow will come upon you. This day shall be a memorial feast for you, which all your generations shall celebrate with pilgrimage to the Lord as a perpetual institution (NAB: Exodus 12: 3-14)."

As a result of this proclamation, the Israelite community is abuzz with excitement and anticipated liberation. Tonight will be the night of Israel's greatest salvation event. God will pass over the Egyptian houses wreaking havoc against their enemies and His, and providing security and salvation to His own people. By the same token the Israelites will pass over from Egypt, the land of slavery, to the Promised Land flowing with milk and honey. The bond between God and His people will be strengthened. Israel will belong to God, and God will be their everlasting Protector! This is the great news then that is being celebrated and savored during this sacrificial Passover Meal, eaten in a mighty hurry and with extreme urgency!

God wants them to make the Passover celebration a perpetual institution to celebrate every year as a memorial feast. It was God's way of saying that this salvation event would remain the bedrock of the covenant between the Israelites and God. It would need to be savored and experienced in an ongoing manner for the rest of their lives! So the term 'memorial' has special significance for God's people. When they celebrated this salvation event, they knew they would not merely be remembering their ancestors' redemption from Egypt which took place in the past. Rather, they would be experiencing the same event and depth of relationship with God in their present lives the way their forebears did. While the Exodus was an event that took place in the history of Israel, it was at the same time an ever-present reality etched into the very fiber of its covenant relationship with God.

JESUS INSTITUTES THE EUCHARIST DURING THE PASSOVER MEAL:

Jesus instituted the Eucharist during the Passover meal, thereby expanding the depths of its meaning beyond anything the Israelites could ever imagine. At one and the same time, Jesus presents himself at various depths of meaning. Jesus is the new Moses leading his people from slavery to sin to the freedom of becoming the sons and daughters of the Living God. Jesus is also the Passover Lamb through whose blood we have been spared God's wrath and justice and have been clothed in the mantel of God's love and forgiveness. Jesus instructs his disciples to celebrate Eucharist as a memorial feast. Every time we celebrate Eucharist we are not merely remembering our redemption from sin and death when Jesus died for us on the cross. Rather, in truth engendered by faith, we are participating in the saving event of Christ's death and resurrection which are an eternal and ever-present reality in the person of the Risen Lord.

THE EUCHARIST AS SOURCE AND SUMMIT:

For the Catholic Church, Eucharist is the source and summit of her understanding of Jesus and Christian discipleship. It is the prayer par excellence. Within Eucharist every other presence of the Lord and every other prayer is contained and expressed. Eucharist is the making present on our altars or the re-presentation of the saving event of Christ's death and resurrection. This re-presentation is not a re-crucifying of Jesus. Rather it is a making present of the very same event of Christ's crucifixion, death, and resurrection that took place in time and human history. This re-presentation is possible because this saving event is ever living and present in the Person of the Risen Lord and the Lord has commanded us to do it in his remembrance. That is why for John, the crucifixion is the hour of glory for Jesus: "The hour has come for the Son of Man to be glorified. Very truly, I tell you, unless a grain of wheat falls into the earth and dies, it remains just a single grain; but if it dies, it bears much fruit (NRSV; John12: 23-24)." The Risen Lord continues to be *"the Lamb standing as if it had been slaughtered (NRSV: Revelation 5:6)."*

We agree with Paul's assertion in Hebrews 9 that Christ's sacrifice was offered <u>once for all</u> because it was perfect unlike the sacrifices offered by the human high priest. If it were not perfect, then we would have to admit that the sacrifice of Jesus on our behalf could not bring about our salvation permanently. "But when Christ came as a high priest of the good things that have come, then through the greater and perfect tent (not made with hands, that is, not of this creation), he entered *once for all* into the Holy Place, not with the blood of goats and calves, but with his own blood, thus obtaining eternal redemption. For if the blood of goats and bulls, with the sprinkling of the ashes of a heifer, sanctifies those who have been defiled so that their flesh is purified, how much more will the blood of Christ, who through the eternal Spirit offered himself without blemish to God, purify our conscience from dead works to worship the living God (NRSV: Hebrews 9: 11-14)!" The author of Hebrews is comparing and contrasting Yom Kippur with the sacrifice of Jesus. Jesus is our 'scapegoat.' During our Eucharistic celebration we make reference to the ritual of Yom Kippur by identifying Jesus as our Scapegoat. Before we receive the Body and Blood of Jesus in communion, we say three times: "Lamb of God, you who take away the sins of the world, have mercy on us (twice) and grant us peace (once)."

In John 6, Jesus makes it clear in numerous ways that *"unless you eat the flesh of the Son of Man and drink his blood, you have no life in you (NRSV: 6:53)."* Only the literal sense does justice to the text, because more than once John uses the expression *"unless you feed on my flesh"* indicating the way an animal feeds, to relay the unmistakable message that it is a real eating and a real drinking of the body and blood of Jesus. We can only partake of his body and blood as real eating because his sacrifice on the Cross is ever present in the person of the Risen Lord. At the end of John's discourse on the Bread of Life, Jesus is absolutely adamant about not compromising his assertion that one can only enter into covenant with God through the actual (and not virtual) eating of his body and drinking of his blood. So he asks Peter and the disciples the following question: *"Do you want to leave me too?"* Peter's answer has always been the Church's answer in our understanding of Eucharist: *"Lord, to whom can we go? You have the words of eternal life. We have come to believe and know that you are the Holy One of God (NRSV: 6:69)."* It doesn't matter whether Jesus' words make sense to our minds or comfort our sensibilities. If He is God's Holy One and we accept Him as our Lord and Savior, then we do as He tells us.

In the words of the Institution narrative, Jesus says: <u>*Do this in remembrance or memory of me...*</u>" <u>*Do*</u> has always been understood by the Church, in keeping with the understanding of the early Church, to mean Jesus giving his disciples and their successors, who for us mean the bishops and priests, the power through ordination, to do as Jesus did. Secondly, <u>*this*</u> has been understood, in keeping with the understanding of the early Church, to mean Jesus telling us to do as He did at the last supper, with the same meaning and intent as He had. <u>*In remembrance*</u> is translated as <u>*Anamnesis*</u> in the Greek, a term which suggests a re-entering or continuing participation in this saving event, because while it occurred in the past it is an ever-living event. So in Exodus 12, when Moses speaking in God's name, exhorted the Israelites and their descendants to celebrate the Passover Meal in remembrance of God's saving event through the Exodus of His people from the land of Egypt, the people knew that they were re-entering this saving event and being transformed by it, because it was always present in their midst through the everlasting love and presence of the Living God. Similarly when Jesus asks us to celebrate his Eucharist in remembrance of Him, he is asking us to make present again (we generally use the term *re-present*) the event of our salvation enacted through his sacrifice on the cross. And through this saving event we have entered into a new and everlasting covenant with the Father of all mercies, the Father of our Lord Jesus Christ, whom we now address as *Abba*. In Romans 8: 15-16, Paul says: "For you did not receive a spirit of slavery to fall back into fear, but you have received a spirit of adoption. When we cry "Abba!, Father!" it is that very Spirit bearing witness with our spirit that we are children of God, and if children, then heirs, heirs of God and joint heirs with Christ – if, in fact, we suffer with him so that we may also be glorified with him (NRSV)." This saving event of Jesus' Death and Resurrection is ever-present in the Person of the Risen Lord!

You would do well to read and ponder Revelation 5 where John is giving us a vivid description of the heavenly Eucharist. Two truths are emphasized in this chapter. One, the most significant question of our lives is posed in the very beginning: "Who is worthy to open the scroll and break its seals? (NRSV: Revelation 5:2)" In other words, God's divine plan of salvation requires the conquest of sin, Satan and death? At first we are told that no one in heaven or on earth or under the earth could be found to open the scroll or examine its contents (Revelation 5: 4), thereby increasing the anxious and desperate suspense both of John the visionary, and us the readers of this Book of Scripture. Such anxiety can and does plague us at times in the trying circumstances of our lives. Then to his great relief, in his vision John sees "a Lamb standing as if it had been slaughtered." This Lamb came and received the scroll. And then we have the continual celebration of the Eucharistic event: The congregation is God's holy people in heaven and on earth washed clean by the blood of the Lamb: "Then I heard every creature in heaven and on earth and under the earth and in the sea, and all that is in them, singing, "To the One seated on the throne and to the Lamb be blessing and honor and glory and might forever and ever (NRSV: Revelation 5:13)!" The offering of praise and adoration to God the Father is perfect because it is being made through the Lamb that was slain. In the process, the Father and all God's holy people look at "the Lamb with blessing and honor and glory and might forever and ever (NRSV: Revelation 5: 13)!" And the prayers of the Faithful are efficacious before the throne of God, symbolized as "golden bowls full of incense (NRSV: Revelation 5: 8)," because they are offered to the Father in and through the sacrifice of the Lamb that was slain. This same Eucharistic celebration taking place continually in heaven before the throne of God is made present on our altars when we participate in this amazing and awe-inspiring event on Sundays and week days. While we can behold only the earthly congregation with our sense faculties, in truth the congregation is enormous because all God's people, in heaven and on earth have come together to celebrate the sacrifice and mystery of the Lamb that was slain. No wonder in the early Church the Eucharist was described as "heaven on earth."

HELPFUL ATTITUDES FOR PRAYER:

- God always intended for us to live in harmony and unity in our families in the same way that the three Persons of the Trinity live in harmony and oneness.
- Jesus is the new Moses leading his people from slavery to sin to the freedom of becoming sons and daughters of the Living God. Jesus is also the Passover Lamb through whose blood we have been spared God's wrath and justice and have been clothed in the mantel of God's love and forgiveness.
- It doesn't matter whether Jesus' words make sense to our minds or comfort our sensibilities. If He is God's Holy One and we accept Him as our Lord and Savior, then we do as He tells us.
- *In remembrance* is translated as *Anamnesis* in the Greek, a term which suggests a re-entering or continuing participation in this saving event, because while it occurred in the past it is an ever-living event.

PASSAGES FOR PRAYER:

Genesis 15: The Covenant with Abram;
Exodus 12: The Passover Ritual prescribed;
Isaiah 43: 1-7: God as Redeemer and Restorer of His Kinsfolk
Isaiah 49: 1-7: The Second Servant-of-the-Lord Oracle
Isaiah 49: 14-21: Restoration of Zion
Isaiah 52: 13- 53:12: Suffering and Triumph of the Lord's Servant – 4th Oracle
Psalm 22: The Suffering and Triumph of Jesus, Suffering Servant and Messiah
Matthew 26: 17-30: The Holy Eucharist
Luke 22: 1-20: The Paschal Meal
John 13: The Washing of the Feet;
1 Corinthians 11: The Lord's Supper;
Hebrews 9: The Worship of the Old Covenant;

Session XV – Sacrificial Traditions and the Eucharist

Hebrews 10: One Sacrifice instead of many;
Philippians 2: 5-11: Jesus, the Suffering Servant
Revelation 4 & 5: Vision of Heavenly Worship

GUIDELINES FOR PRAYER:

- Be faithful to your time of prayer, and make it between 20 and 30 minutes daily.
- Begin every prayer session with an earnest prayer to the Holy Spirit like the one I have composed for you: *Come, Holy Spirit, and overshadow me with your gentle wisdom and power as I endeavor to sit at the feet of Jesus during this period of prayer. Purify my mind and heart as I seek to make the teachings of Jesus my priority in life, thinking, speaking and doing as He desires. You are the keeper of my soul, leading me into God's heart. May I be docile and submissive to your wisdom and guidance and may my life be a pleasing offering in your sight. Amen.*
- Take one of the passages suggested for prayer. During the session you might want to ponder the question, **"Is the Eucharist the source and summit of my life as a disciple?"**
- Lastly, during your prayer make sure you also address God directly and listen for the Holy Spirit's responses.
- You can end your prayer with the following: *Father, Son, and Holy Spirit, I thank you for your gracious companionship. I praise you for being my Creator, Savior and Lord. May I take your blessings to my day, and may your presence envelop and permeate all my thoughts and actions. Through Christ our Lord. Amen.*

JOURNALING: REFER TO HELPS TO PRAYER, # 6

SPIRITUAL READING: REFER TO HELPS TO PRAYER, # 4 AND 5
Manual: Read Sessions Fifteen and Sixteen for eighth month, and delve into the topics in *Helps to Prayer, Methods of Prayer, and Practices for Committed Discipleship*.

New Testament: Try to read the New Testament over Sessions 11 through 18.

Old Testament: Try to read the Psalms.

Imitation of Christ: Follow the suggestions in *Helps to Prayer # 5*.

Catechism of the Catholic Church: Follow the suggestions in *Helps to Prayer #5*

SESSION SIXTEEN: GOD'S VISION FOR US: SALVATION AS THEOSIS

SCRIPTURE:

"Praised be the God and Father of our Lord Jesus Christ who has bestowed on us in Christ every spiritual blessing in the heavens! God chose us in him before the world began, to be holy and blameless in his sight, to be full of love; he likewise predestined us through Christ Jesus to be his adopted sons – such was his will and pleasure – that all might praise the glorious favor he has bestowed on us in his beloved." – NAB: Ephesians 1: 3-6.

SALVATION AS THEOSIS:

Before we attempt to offer a definition of theosis, let us examine several of Jesus' sayings that will both astound and overwhelm us with the scope of God's plan of salvation and His optimism and confidence in bringing about profound union with us. In the prologue, Jesus says in John 1:14: "The Word became flesh and lived among us (NRSV)." In the Creation story we were giddily amazed to know that God created us in His very own image and likeness. In this passage from John we are told that Jesus, our Creator and Lord, took on our human nature and became one of us. To understand the enormous love and tenderness that God has for us in sending His Son to become one of sinful humanity, we have only to notice some of the names in Jesus' genealogy. Jesus was descended from Perez whose mother was Tamar and his father was Judah, Tamar's father-in-law. Perez was therefore a twin child of incest (Genesis 38). Down the line, Salmon was the father of Boaz, whose mother was Rahab, a former prostitute. And Boaz was the father of Obed, whose mother was Ruth, a gentile woman. And Jesus became one of us so that he could be Emmanuel, God-among-us, as God dwelt among his people in the Ark of the Covenant.

John 3:16-17 says, "For God so loved the world that he gave his only Son, so that everyone who believes in him may not perish but may have eternal life. Indeed, God did not send the Son into the world to condemn the world, but in order that the world might be saved through him (NRSV)." In utterly astounding fashion, the Father demonstrates his total love for us by giving us His very own Son. Can there be any greater self-emptying and selfless giving than this act of God surrendering to us His Son Jesus as an infinite gift? And the reason why the Father so benevolently and magnanimously gave us his Son was so that we might not perish but participate in God's very own eternal life. God's passionate desire was to redeem us by His Son becoming our slave (Philippians 2: 5-11), taking upon himself our burden of sin and thus saving us from condemnation and granting us the freedom of the children of God.

In John 6:56-57, Jesus says, "The man who feeds on my flesh and drinks my blood remains in me, and I in him. Just as the Father who has life sent me and I have life because of the Father, so the man who feeds on me will have life because of me (NAB)." Jesus offers us salvation by being our Savior and liberating us from the bondage of sin, Satan and death. Understood positively, Jesus wants covenant union with us. He offers himself to us as our life so that we may remain in him, and he in us. Jesus emphasizes the fact that just as he has life because of the Father, in the same way we who feed on him will have life because of him. This union is so intimate and profound that it is truly beyond description. Through it we are allowed into the Mystery of God's Life, participating in the divine Life and Love in ways only the Holy Spirit can reveal to us.

In John 10: 14-15, Jesus says, "I am the good shepherd. I know my own and my own know me, just as the Father knows me and I know the Father. And I lay down my life for the sheep (NRSV)." Sheep are supposedly dumb, vulnerable and dependent animals which need a watchful and devoted shepherd if they are to survive and thrive in the wild. Jesus contrasts himself with frauds who masquerade as shepherds: thieves, marauders, strangers, hired hands. For his sheep Jesus is willing to give his life. Furthermore his mission as shepherd is to create a covenant relationship between himself, his Father, and his sheep. Through his Holy Spirit, Jesus will bring about our transformation so that we will know him in the same way that the Father knows him and he knows the Father. Jesus is talking about an intimate union with us along the lines of Trinitarian union, a Mystery that is beyond our comprehension and yet stirs our hearts deeply!

In the Great Discourse, John 14 through 17, our transformation into Christ is a Trinitarian mission. In John 15 Jesus tells us that he is the true vine and we are his branches and the Father is the vine-grower. The Father is actively involved in this process of our transformation as He prunes away every barren branch, and trims clean the fruitful ones to increase their yield. Further, through his incarnation, Jesus establishes an inextricable bond with us when he says that he is the vine and we are the branches. If we live in him and he live in us we will produce abundantly. Apart from him we will be withered, rejected branches. When Jesus thinks of himself, He is at one and the same time the Second Person of the Trinity and one of us! In John 14, Jesus tells us that the Father will give us another Advocate – to be with us always! The Holy Spirit will instruct us in everything and remind us of all the things Jesus told us.

The early Church Fathers used different terms to express this very intimate union between the Trinity and us. Theosis or Deification, Union with God, Participation in God, Intermingling with God, were terms they used to try to describe this ineffable intimacy that God desires to have with us. Through this process human beings enter into the divine Life and participate in the communion of divine love that exists in the Trinity. And all of this is offered to us as pure gift through Jesus Christ in whose blood we have been washed clean. For Gregory of

Nazianzus (329-389) theosis was "the blessed telos (end) for which all things were made." Here then is a definition of theosis that I have taken from Dr. Philip De Jonge's Sabbatical Reflections on the Theological Theme of Theosis (Union with Christ) and the Practice of Perichoretic Prayer: "Theosis is the process by which humanity is graciously brought to the telos or goal of creation: loving participation in the communion of the Trinity. Theosis is accomplished by the Holy Spirit when forgiven humanity is incorporated into the person of the incarnate Christ, who, by virtue of the hypostatic union of his divine and human natures, is the bridge of union between humanity and divinity."

HELPFUL ATTITUDES FOR PRAYER:

- To understand the enormous love and tenderness that God had for us in sending his Son to become one of us, we have only to notice some of the names in Jesus' genealogy. Jesus was descended from Perez whose mother was Tamar and his father was Judah, Tamar's father-in-law. Perez was a twin child of incest (Genesis 28). Down the line, Salmon was the father of Boaz, whose mother was Rahab, a former prostitute. And Boaz was the father of Obed, whose mother was Ruth, a gentile woman.
- In utterly astounding fashion, the Father demonstrates his total love for us by giving us His very own Son. Can there be any greater self-emptying and selfless giving that this act of God surrendering to us the infinite gift of his Son, Jesus?
- This union is so intimate and profound that it is truly beyond description. Through it we are allowed into the depths of God's mystery, participating in the divine life and love in ways only the Holy Spirit can reveal to us.
- Jesus tells us that the Father will give us another Advocate – to be with us always! The Holy Spirit will instruct us in everything and remind us of all the things Jesus told us.
- "Theosis is the process by which humanity is graciously brought to the telos or goal of creation: loving participation in the communion of the Trinity. Theosis is accomplished by the Holy Spirit when forgiven

humanity is incorporated into the person of the incarnate Christ, who, by virtue of the hypostatic union of his divine and human natures, is the bridge of union between humanity and divinity."

GUIDELINES FOR PRAYER:

- Be faithful to your time of prayer, and make it between 20 and 30 minutes daily.
- Begin every prayer session with an earnest prayer to the Holy Spirit like the one I have composed for you: *Come, Holy Spirit, and overshadow me with your gentle wisdom and power as I endeavor to sit at the feet of Jesus during this period of prayer. Purify my mind and heart as I seek to make the teachings of Jesus my priority in life, thinking, speaking and doing as He desires. You are the keeper of my soul, leading me into God's heart. May I be docile and submissive, to your wisdom and guidance. And may my life be a pleasing offering in your sight. Amen.*
- Take one of the passages suggested for your prayer. During the duration of this session you might want to ponder the question, **"Have I taken the time to appreciate and thank God for His Vision and Plan of salvation?"**
- Lastly, during your prayer make sure that along with reflection you also address God directly and listen for answers that you need.
- You can end your prayer with the following: *Father, Son, and Holy Spirit, I thank you for your gracious companionship. I praise you for being my Creator, Savior and Lord. May I take your blessings to my day, and may your presence envelop and permeate all my thoughts and actions. Through Christ our Lord. Amen.*

PASSAGES FOR PRAYER:
John 1: 1-14: The Prologue
John 3: 14-18: The Father's gift of his Son
John 6: 53-58: Jesus, the Bread of Life
John 10: 14-18: Jesus, the Good Shepherd

John 11: 25-26: Jesus, the Resurrection and the Life
John 15: 1-8: The Vine and the Branches
Romans 5: 15-21: Grace and Life through Christ
Romans 8: 28-39: God's Love for Man
Ephesians 1: 1-10: The Father's Plan of Salvation
Ephesians 2: 1-10: The Generosity of God's Plan
Colossians 1: 15-23: Fullness and Reconciliation

JOURNALING: *HELPS TO PRAYER, # 6*

SPIRITUAL READING: *HELPS TO PRAYER, # 4 AND 5*
Manual: Read Sessions Fifteen and Sixteen for the eighth, and delve into the topics in *Helps to Prayer, Methods of Prayer, and Practices for Committed Discipleship*.
New Testament: Try to read the New Testament over Sessions 11 through 18.
Old Testament: Try to Read 1 & 2 Samuel and 1 & 2 Kings.
Imitation of Christ: Follow the suggestions in *Helps to Prayer # 5*.
Catechism of the Catholic Church: Follow the suggestions in *Helps to Prayer #5*

SESSION SEVENTEEN: GOD AS EMMANUEL

SCRIPTURE:

"Therefore the Lord himself will give you a sign. Look, the young woman is with child and shall bear a son, and shall name him Immanuel." –NRSV: Isaiah 7:14

Look, the virgin shall conceive and bear a son, and they shall name him Emmanuel," which means, "God is with us." –NSRV: Matthew 1:23

OUR DESTINY IN GOD'S EYES:

From our survey of God's involvement with His people so far, we have seen that Scripture offers us many windows into God's heart. There are many promises and events that signal clearly who God is in relationship to us. The Book of Genesis described the very special relationship that God established with creation and in particular with humans. In a pithy statement the author grasped the awesome mystery that a human person is: "So God created humankind in his image, in the image of God he created them; male and female he created them (NRSV: Genesis 1:27)." Centuries later, God reveals the deeper layers of this wondrous mystery that is our identity through His Son who became flesh of our flesh. Through Jesus Christ we have been made sons and daughters of the Living God, able to call God, our Father and Jesus, our brother. In God's eyes we belong to God's own house and lineage; in God's heart, we are His sons and daughters bought by the blood of his son, Jesus Christ.

GOD'S PASSIONATE COMMITMENT TO US:

We have also seen that the history of God's people is replete with rebellion and infidelity. Some incidents are absolutely shocking, like the absolute commitment to evil on the part of Sodom and Gomorrah, or the idolatry of 3000 Israelites under the leadership of Aaron when they worshiped the Golden Calf. This incident is especially revolting in light of the powerful saving event of the Exodus. In spite of God's unwavering fidelity, the Israelites renege repeatedly on their promises. They embrace sin and idolatry and abandon God. Had God abandoned His covenant love and promises, such a decision would have been fully justified.

The prophets, however, tell us another story. In vivid detail they portray God's decision to be ever faithful and solicitous towards the people. "But now thus says the LORD, he who created you, O Jacob, he who formed you, O Israel: Do not fear, for I have redeemed you; I have called you by name, you are mine (NRSV: Isaiah 43: 1-3)." Redeemer in Hebrew is goel, a kinsperson who frees a family member from slavery and suffering by taking his place (refer to Leviticus 25). In this passage, therefore, God sees Himself as a family member, bringing redemption to his family members by taking upon himself their enslavement. This prophecy is especially fulfilled in Jesus, who through his incarnation became a member of our human family and brought salvation to us by taking upon himself the burden and shame of our sins. There will never be limits to God's passion and love for us. Even in our worst trials and tribulations, many of our own making, God will be with us because our God is the Holy One of Israel, our Savior.

GOD AMONG US:

God's love and compassion are best expressed in Jesus becoming human and identifying with us in all things, except sin. John tells us that, "The Word became flesh and lived among us, and we have seen his glory, the glory as of a father's only son, full of grace and truth (NRSV: John 1:14)." The word for 'dwelling' is 'Shekinah,' the same term that was used for the Ark of the Covenant or dwelling place of God among His people during their travels towards the Promised Land. In the same way Jesus dwells among us. Matthew uses a very moving title 'Emmanuel,' to describe God's compassionate intimacy toward us. God could not have become more immanent to us than by becoming one of us. "Look, the virgin shall conceive and bear a son, and they shall name him Emmanuel, which means, "God is with us (NRSV: Matthew 1: 23)."

There are three images that help us appreciate the significance of Jesus as God among us. There is the understanding of Jesus as goel or kinsperson. Through his death on the cross Jesus paid our ransom, freed us from slavery to sin, and made us children of the Living God. Paul evokes this image in his letter to the Philippians, 2: 7-8: "He emptied himself, taking the form of a slave, being born in human likeness. And being found in human form, he humbled himself and became obedient to the point of death – even death on a cross (NRSV)!" And John describes Jesus as identifying himself as a non-Jewish slave when he washes the feet of his disciples, as only non-Jewish slaves washed the feet of the invited guests (John 13). Through this gesture Jesus was capturing the significance of his journey to Calvary and his impending crucifixion and death. The last image is offered by John the Baptist who refers to Jesus as 'the Lamb of God who takes away the sin of the world (John 1:29)!' John is referring to the Feast of Atonement or Yom Kippur. Jesus is the scapegoat taking upon himself our transgressions to ensure our freedom (refer to Leviticus 16:1-22). During Eucharist we invoke Jesus as the Lamb of God beseeching him to take away our sins before we receive him in Holy Communion.

Jesus will forever be with us, a reality that can be deeply cherished while never being fully grasped. Paul expresses eloquently the ultimate purpose God had in asking Jesus to be our Savior and Lord: "Blessed be the God and Father of our Lord Jesus Christ, who has blessed us in Christ with every spiritual blessing in the heavenly places, just as he chose us in Christ before the foundation of the world to be holy and blameless before him in love. He destined us for adoption as his children through Jesus Christ, according to the good pleasure of his will, to the praise of his glorious grace that he freely bestowed on us in the Beloved (NRSV: Ephesians 1: 4-6)." Paul echoes the same purpose in Colossians 1:19-20: "For in him all the fullness of God was pleased to dwell, and through him God was pleased to reconcile to himself all things, whether on earth or in heaven, by making peace through the blood of his cross (NRSV)."

GOD AMONG US AT CHRISTMAS:

The infancy narratives of Matthew and Luke give us a deep insight into how God understands what it means for Jesus to be Emmanuel. Jesus came for the salvation of sinners. Jesus is very comfortable among the poor and lowly of this world. Mary, his mother will be a virgin, of lowly and humble estate. In her Canticle she proclaims herself as his servant in her lowliness. And she praises God that "He has helped his servant Israel, in remembrance of his mercy (NRSV: Luke 1:46-55)." Jesus was born in a stable, and his first visitors were shepherds, the have-nots and marginalized of society. Wise men came to visit Jesus from the East and they were Gentiles. And the reactions of Anna and Simeon provide much consolation and hope. Anna, the prophetess gave thanks to God and talked about the child to all who looked forward to the deliverance of Jerusalem (Luke 2:38). And Simeon the prophet can now die in peace: "Master, now you are dismissing your servant in peace, according to your word; for my eyes have seen your salvation which you have prepared in the presence of all peoples, a light for revelation to the Gentiles and for glory to your people Israel (NRSV: Luke 2:29-32)"

HELPFUL ATTITUDES FOR PRAYER:

- Redeemer in Hebrew is *goel,* a kinsperson who frees a family member from slavery and suffering by taking his place (refer to Leviticus 25).

- This prophecy is especially fulfilled in Jesus, who through his incarnation became a member of our human family and brought salvation to us by taking upon himself the burden and shame of our sins.
- There will *never* be limits to God's passion and love for us. God will go to any limit to save us. God will be with us when we pass through the water, as God was present when the Israelites passed through the Red Sea.
- "The Word became flesh and made his dwelling among us, and we have seen his glory: the glory of an only Son coming from the Father filled with enduring love (John 1:14)." The word for 'dwelling' is 'shekinah,' the same term that was used for the Ark of the Covenant or dwelling place of God among His people during their travels towards the Promised Land. In the same way Jesus dwells among us.
- Matthew uses a very moving title 'Emmanuel,' to describe God's compassionate intimacy toward us. God could not have become more immanent to us than by becoming one of us.
- John describes Jesus as identifying himself as a non-Jewish slave when he washes the feet of his disciples, as only non-Jewish slaves washed the feet of the invited guests (chapter 13). Through this gesture Jesus was capturing the significance of his journey to Calvary and his impending crucifixion and death.
- John the Baptist refers to Jesus as 'the Lamb of God who takes away the sin of the world (John 1:29)!' John is referring to the feast of Atonement or Yom Kippur. Jesus is the scapegoat who takes upon himself our sinful faults and transgressions to ensure our freedom (refer to Leviticus 16: 1-22).

GUIDELINES FOR PRAYER:
- Be faithful to your time of prayer, and make it between 20 and 30 minutes daily.
- Begin every prayer session with an earnest prayer to the Holy Spirit like the one I have composed for you: *Come, Holy Spirit, and overshadow me with your gentle wisdom and power as I endeavor to sit at the feet*

of Jesus during this period of prayer. Purify my mind and heart as I seek to make the teachings of Jesus my priority in life, thinking, speaking and doing as He desires. You are the keeper of my soul, leading me into God's heart. May I be docile and submissive to your wisdom and guidance, and may my life be a pleasing offering in your sight. Amen.

- Take one of the passages suggested for prayer. During the week you might want to ponder the question, **"What does it mean for you to know Jesus as Emmanuel, God-with-us?"**
- Lastly, during your prayer make sure you also address God directly and listen for the Holy Spirit's responses.
- You can end your prayer with the following: *Father, Son, and Holy Spirit, I thank you for your gracious companionship. I praise you for being my Creator, Savior and Lord. May I take your blessings to my day, and may your presence envelop and permeate all my thoughts and actions. Through Christ our Lord. Amen.*

PASSAGES FOR PRAYER:

Leviticus 25: 47-55: Redemption of a slave
Isaiah 43: 1-8: Promise of Redemption and Restoration
Matthew 1: 18-23: The Birth of Jesus
Luke 1: 26-38: Announcement of the Birth of Jesus
Luke 1: 46-55: Mary's Canticle
Luke 2: 1-20: The Birth of Jesus
John 1: 29-37: John's Testimony to Jesus
John 13: 1-17: The Washing of the Feet

JOURNALING: *HELPS TO PRAYER, # 6*

SPIRITUAL READING: *HELPS TO PRAYER, # 4 AND 5*

Manual: Read Sessions Seventeen and Eighteen for the ninth month, and delve into the topics in *Helps to Prayer, Methods of Prayer, and Practices for Committed Discipleship*.

New Testament: Try to read the New Testament over Sessions 11 through 18

Old Testament: Try to Read 1 & 2 Samuel and 1 & 2 Kings.

Imitation of Christ: Follow the suggestions in *Helps to Prayer # 5*.

Catechism of the Catholic Church: Follow the suggestions in *Helps to Prayer #5*

SESSION EIGHTEEN: INTIMACY WITH GOD

SCRIPTURE:

"For God so loved the world that he gave his only Son, so that everyone who believes in him may not perish but may have eternal life. Indeed, God did not send the Son into the world to condemn the world, but in order that the world might be saved through him." –NRSV: John 3: 16-17

"Blessed be the God and Father of our Lord Jesus Christ, who has blessed us in Christ with every spiritual blessing in the heavenly places, just as he chose us in Christ before the foundation of the world to be holy and blameless before him in love. He destined us for adoption as his children through Jesus Christ, according to the good pleasure of his will, to the praise of his glorious grace that he freely bestowed on us in the Beloved." – NRSV: Ephesians 1: 4-6

THE PARADOX OF INTIMACY WITH GOD:

We are very unequal partners when it comes to our relationship with God. God is merciful and holy; we are recalcitrant and sinful. Were it not for God's passionate desire to transform us into His sons and daughters, it would be audacious and pretentious to imagine that we could enter into intimate union with the Divine. We will never be able to understand why and how, in spite of our rebellious nature, God made the decision from all eternity to accord us the most intimate of invitations: to become the children of Abba, God through Jesus Christ. God chose us in him before the world began, to be holy and blameless in his sight, to be full of love (Ephesians 1:4).

While this invitation boggles the mind, it nourishes the heart and gives us hope and strength even in our darkest passages through life. Whatever objections our finite intelligence may throw up against this plan of salvation, the Author, being God, is immensely credible because His Son, though he was in the form of God, did not cling to his divinity. Rather, he emptied himself and took the form of a slave, being born in the likeness of man. He was known to be of human estate, and it was thus that he humbled himself, obediently accepting even death, death on a cross (NAB Philippians 2: 6-8)! Let us examine further this bedrock of intimacy between God and us, its characteristics and far reaching implications.

GOD'S COMMITMENT AND LOVING KINDNESS:

Salvation history is an amazing story of God's commitment to us. From the very beginning God created us in "the divine image and likeness," desiring that we walk with God in love, harmony, and joy. Yet God's designs for us kept getting frustrated by our recalcitrance. When universal covenants as with Noah did not work, God entered into covenant with Abraham and his family. God continued this steadfast faithfulness to Abraham and his descendants by liberating his family that had now become an enslaved people in Egypt, and formed them into a nation under Moses' leadership so that they understood themselves as God's Chosen People. God sealed this intimate relationship with His people through the Sinai Covenant. Through their history and through covenant after covenant, God invited Israel to intimacy and faithful love. Sadly enough, in numerous chapters of Israel's history, God was the only partner who remained faithful to the covenant. On different occasions, God referred to Israel as His adulterous wife. Matters worsened to the point where Israel brought exile upon itself in 587 B.C. Israel had then entered into the darkest chapter of its history with God.

With the exile it seemed as if God's dreams for Israel, "His first born," were shattered. In these very adverse circumstances, God's commitment to His promises to redeem Israel and bring her back to Him never faltered. Through Isaiah, Jeremiah, and the other prophets, God made reassuring promises that the Messiah would be sent to redeem us from our sins. In Jesus, the Suffering Servant, God established a new and everlasting covenant with us, a covenant that would never need to be renewed and refurbished. In spite of our rebelliousness and untrustworthiness, God's commitment to us has been steadfast and rock solid. Indeed our salvation is a pure and totally gratuitous gift to us from our God and Savior!!

Fortunately for our edification, we have had remarkable models of faithfulness and trust among holy men and women both in the Old and New Testaments. Saints like Abraham, Moses, Esther, Isaiah, Jeremiah are some examples from the Old Testament. Mary, mother of Jesus, Peter and Paul, the other apostles, and the men and women who kept company with Jesus are instances from the New Testament. We can dare to trust in God and indeed become steadfast in our commitment to God, because the Holy Spirit is our Advocate, working within us, bringing to completion the good work begun through our Savior, Jesus Christ. We can derive great comfort and strength from this promise of Jesus: "When the Spirit of truth comes, he will guide you into all the truth; for he will not speak on his own, but will speak whatever he hears, and he will declare to you the things that are to come. He will glorify me, because he will take what is mine and declare it to you (NRSV 16:13-14).

GOD'S MAGNANIMITY:

God does indeed have a magnanimous (can be translated as large-hearted or generous-minded) disposition toward us. A magnanimous spirit hitches its wagon to the stars, never yielding to the temptation of lowered horizons. Magnanimity is best demonstrated in challenging times. Throughout salvation history, through thick and thin, God's commitment to us never wavered. On the contrary, it expressed itself in even stronger and more hopeful terms, the more Israel wavered and sinned. Thanks to God's hope and passionate commitment to us, we can set our sights on heaven itself! God's dreams for us are as inexhaustible as the divine mysteries.

No wonder in his letter to the Ephesians, Paul can assert that God wants to make us holy, blameless, and full of love as God is. In our journey with God, regardless of our personal failures and miserable track record, we need to have limitless horizons because God's designs for us have fathomless depths. We need to believe that we can do anything in Christ who strengthens us. Discipleship wilts and founders when the heart is faint. It blossoms when the spirit is intrepid and indomitable because the Holy Spirit is at the helm of our affairs.

GOD'S LOVING EMBRACE:

In his first letter, John tells us that fear and love are incompatible with each other. The context of our relationship with God will always be one of enduring love and unfailing forgiveness. Imputing motives and descriptions to God that are born of fear and trepidation are an anomaly. The God whom Jesus revealed is a God who is full of love and compassion as Jesus amply demonstrated through his life. Yes, God so loved the world that he gave his only Son, that whoever believes in him may not die but may have eternal life. God did not send the Son into the world to condemn the world, but that the world might be saved through him (NAB John 3: 16-17). When the disciple has gotten in touch with the God of Jesus Christ, he/she is filled with love and an intense desire to reciprocate. Such a desire generally results in the disciple making a serious commitment to live a life of dedicated service to God and God's reign in the world. And as intimacy with God deepens, so does reverence for God's holiness and goodness.

NURTURING INTIMACY WITH GOD THROUGH PRAYER:

Prayer is the place where the love affair between God and the disciple occurs and gathers momentum. Prayer is the place where the disciple develops transparency of spirit, where bondage to sin is loosened, and freedom to act as God desires takes precedence. In the transparency of the disciple's spirit, now being fashioned in the image and likeness of Jesus, God's Life and love can be revealed and the teachings of Jesus can become a life force for holiness and transformation. Ultimately, prayer is the place of worship and adoration of the Triune God who is bringing to completion the work of union with the disciple decided upon from all eternity.

HELPFUL ATTITUDES FOR PRAYER:

- We are very unequal partners when it comes to our relationship with God. Were it not for God's passionate desire to transform us into His sons and daughters, it would be audacious and pretentious to imagine that we could enter into intimate union with the Divine.
- Whatever objections our finite intelligence may throw up against God's plan of salvation for us, the Author, being God, is immensely credible because His Son, though he was in the form of God, did not deem equality with God something to be grasped at. Rather, he emptied himself and took the form of a slave, being born in the likeness of man (Philippians 2: 6-7)!
- In Jesus, the Suffering Servant, God established a new and everlasting covenant with us, a covenant that would never need to be renewed and refurbished. In spite of our rebelliousness and untrustworthiness, God's commitment to us has been steadfast and rock solid.
- The context of our relationship with God will always be one of enduring love and unfailing forgiveness. The God whom Jesus revealed is a God who is full of love and compassion as Jesus amply demonstrated through his life.

- Prayer is the place where the disciple develops transparency of spirit, where bondage to sin is loosened, and freedom to act as God desires takes precedence.
- In the transparency of the disciple's spirit, now being conformed to the image and likeness of God, the mystery of God can be revealed and the teachings of Jesus can become a life force for holiness and transformation.
- Ultimately, prayer is the place of worship and adoration of the Triune God who is bringing to completion the work of union with the disciple decided upon from all eternity.

GUIDELINES FOR PRAYER:

- Be faithful to your time of prayer, and make it between 20 and 30 minutes daily.
- Begin every prayer session with an earnest prayer to the Holy Spirit like the one I have composed for you: *Come, Holy Spirit, and overshadow me with your gentle wisdom and power as I endeavor to sit at the feet of Jesus during this period of prayer. Purify my mind and heart as I seek to make the teachings of Jesus my priority in life, thinking, speaking and doing as He desires. You are the keeper of my soul, leading me into God's heart. May I be docile and submissive to your wisdom and guidance, and may my life be a pleasing offering in your sight. Amen.*
- Take one of the passages suggested for prayer. During the duration of the session you might want to ponder the question, **"Is your prayer the place where God is slowly becoming your breath and your pulse?"**
- Lastly, during your prayer make sure you also address God directly and listen for the Holy Spirit's responses.
- You can end your prayer with the following: *Father, Son, and Holy Spirit, I thank you for your gracious companionship. I praise you for being my Creator, Savior and Lord. May I take your blessings to my*

day, and may your presence envelop and permeate all my thoughts and actions. Through Christ our Lord. Amen.

PASSAGES FOR PRAYER:

Luke 15: 1-10: Parable of Divine Mercy
John 3: 14-21: Salvation in Jesus
John 10: 8-18: Jesus, the Good Shepherd
John 15: 9-17: A Disciple's Love
Romans 8: 28-39: God's Love for Man
Ephesians 1: 1-14: The Father's Plan of Salvation
Philippians 2: 5-11: Imitating Christ's Humility

JOURNALING: *REFER TO HELPS TO PRAYER, # 6*

SPIRITUAL READING: *REFER TO HELPS TO PRAYER, # 4 AND 5*
Manual: Read Sessions Seventeen and Eighteen for the ninth month, and delve into the topics in *Helps to Prayer, Methods of Prayer, and Practices for Committed Discipleship*.
New Testament: Try to read the New Testament over Sessions 1 through 12
Old Testament: Try to read 1 & 2 Samuel and 1 & 2 Kings.
Imitation of Christ: Follow the suggestions in *Helps to Prayer # 5*.
Catechism of the Catholic Church: Follow the suggestions in *Helps to Prayer #5*

PART TWO:

SECTION ONE: HELPS TO PRAYER:
1. The Meaning of Prayer
2. Helpful Practices in Prayer
3. Praying as Jesus Taught
4. The Examination of Consciousness
5. Spiritual Reading
6. Suggestions for Journaling and Spiritual Direction
7. The Purgative Stage of Discipleship
8. The Practice of Renunciation
9. Bibliography

SECTION TWO: METHODS OF PRAYER:
1. Vocal Prayer
2. The Method of Meditation
3. The Method of Ignatian Contemplation or Imaging
4. Lectio Divina or the Benedictine Method of Prayer
5. Praying with the Psalms

SECTION THREE: PRACTICES FOR COMMITTED DISCIPLESHIP:
5. Practicing the Presence of God
6. The Prayer of Remembrance
7. Recognizing God's Voice and Presence – 1
8. Recognizing God's Voice and Presence – 2

SECTION FOUR: FOUR WEEKEND RETREATS

I - THE MEANING OF PRAYER

SCRIPTURE:

My heart is not proud, O LORD, my eyes are not haughty; I do not concern myself with great matters or things too wonderful for me. But I have stilled and quieted my soul; like a weaned child with its mother, Like a weaned child is my soul within me.
 – (NIV: Psalm 131:1-2)

PROVIDING THE RIGHT PERSPECTIVE:

Psalm 131 highlights both the context of prayer and the right relationship that the disciple needs to have with God. This relationship is very special because it is one of Creator to creature, Savior to saved. The passage echoes the wisdom of surrender and filial trust in the loving kindness of God. Prayer is that time with God when "I have stilled and quieted my soul like a weaned child with its mother."

Our relationship with God is the most profound of all our relationships. Given the nature of God, we will change profoundly if we choose to accept God's magnanimous invitation to participate in His enduring love. Jesus tells us that in knowing him we will know the Father and through him we will enter into the life of the Trinity: "I am the way, and the truth, and the life. No one comes to the Father except through me. If you really knew me, you would know my Father as well. From now on, you do know him and have seen him (NIV: John 14: 6-7)." And in talking about the Holy Spirit, Jesus says, "But when he, the Spirit of truth, comes, he will guide you into all truth. He will not speak on his own; he will speak only what he hears, and he will tell you what is yet to come... All that belongs to the Father is mine. That is why I said the Spirit will take from what is mine and make it known to you (NIV: John 16: 13-15)."

Hence it would be more appropriate to describe prayer or our meetings with God as encounters rather than visits. In prayer we are standing before our Creator and Lord, our Savior and Teacher. The only authentic way to stand in God's Presence is by becoming transparent to God and especially to ourselves. Making excuses, offering conditions, and imposing restrictions and compromises, are tantamount to distorting the relationship, to making ourselves the sun instead of the satellite. This distortion is idolatry. We end up worshipping a false god, an idol that we have created in our own likeness and preference. If, however, we enter into the relationship with a deep reverence for the transforming mystery of God, we will experience a profound conversion of heart, mind, and spirit, and come to a deeper appreciation of our true self as well. We will indeed experience Jesus as the Resurrection and the Life. Belief in Jesus and surrender to him will bring us everlasting life.

MAGNANIMITY REQUIRED FOR THE ENCOUNTER WITH GOD:

God does indeed have a magnanimous (can be translated as large-hearted or generous-minded) disposition toward us. Magnanimity is best demonstrated in challenging times. Throughout salvation history God's commitment to us never wavered. On the contrary, it got stronger the more we wavered and sinned. And in Jesus, God-among-us, God's love was especially demonstrated. "Greater love has no one than this, that he lay down his life for his friends...I have called you friends, for everything that I have learned from my Father I have made known to you (NIV: John 15:13-15)." Thanks to God's passionate commitment to us, we can pin our exuberant hopes on God fulfilling His promise to make us His sons and daughters through His son, Jesus Christ. God's dreams for us are as inexhaustible as the divine Mysteries. We need to believe that we can do anything in Christ who strengthens us. We can have this magnanimous spirit because of Christ's power given to us by his Holy Spirit. Discipleship blossoms when the spirit is intrepid and bold because the Holy Spirit is at the helm of our affairs.

There is the mistaken notion that in order to enter into a meaningful relationship with God, we need to be good and upright. The opposite is true. Jesus came precisely for sinners. God asks that we come with hearts and minds that are open and willing to be overwhelmed by God's love and forgiveness. When we have truly experienced God's love and compassion, we will move toward repentance and discipleship. We will desire to love and serve God and our neighbor with all our hearts and minds and souls, imitating Jesus Christ, our teacher and role model.

In this walk with God, having a large heart and generous spirit are essential. Anyone desiring to enter into a significant relationship with God will have to be prepared to take on the characteristics and dispositions of God Himself. It does not make sense to be afraid to look beyond our noses when God's horizons are limitless and all-embracing. Being magnanimous on our part will mean that we truly allow God to be God; we truly trust God to fulfill His promises to us, to make us His own sons and daughters, created in his own image and likeness, and washed in the blood of his son, Jesus Christ.

REVERENCE:

True intimacy with God will always take into consideration the awe-inspiring majesty of God. God is both immanent and transcendent, more intimate to us than our very breath, and totally other than who we are at the same time. It is important that we keep in proper balance the immanence and transcendence of God in our prayer and everyday lives. Moses was rendered speechless at the Burning Bush and Mt. Sinai. A deep sense of unworthiness came upon him as he realized how utterly holy God was, totally other than he. Moses hid his face because he was afraid to look at God (Exodus 3:6). Isaiah, too, felt an acute sense of sinfulness before the holy God who was calling him to be a prophet. He exclaims, "Woe to me!" I cried. "I am ruined! For I am a man of unclean lips, and I live among a people of unclean lips, and my eyes have seen the King, the LORD Almighty (NIV: Isaiah 6:5)." Jesus is both the Good Shepherd who carries his lamb around his shoulders, and the Risen Lord who sits at the right hand of the Father. True reverence for God creates genuine intimacy that enlivens and transforms. Familiarity, without reverence, breeds superficiality and self-centeredness.

Just as we participate in God's magnanimity and receive the grace from the Holy Spirit to be like Jesus, in the same way, reverence is a mutual sharing between God and us. While it is most appropriate that we fall into adoration and praise, wonder and awe at God's revelation of Himself to us, it is equally true that God has a profound reverence for us as well. God created us in his own image and likeness. The Uncreated Original sees a reflection of Himself in us, his image and likeness. Jesus, while being God, became man and took unto himself this image and likeness, to transform it by washing it clean in his blood and making us a pleasing and exhilarating offering in his Father's sight. Prayer then is the place where the heart of God is laid bare to us, enabling us to enter into the divine mystery, and thereby transforming our own feeble hearts and giving us His own!

TRANSITION:

As our relationship with God is unique among all our relationships, it is important that we bring our whole person to the dialogue. It makes sense to create a sacred space when we come to prayer. It is a good idea to set aside some time to transition into our prayer. Transition enables us to close the door to whatever activity we were engaged in and apply our full attention to communing with God. It is a good idea to take as much time as we need to become quiet, or else our prayer period could become more distracting and difficult than it need be.

There are other effective ways of becoming still and creating openness to the Holy Spirit in prayer. The sounds around us are echoes of God's presence. Listening carefully to them, without rejecting any sound either far or near, is a helpful way to arrive at a fair measure of quietness. Similarly, becoming aware of sensations in different parts of the body is another way of creating a helpful transition into prayer. Focusing on our breathing, or on the sensations caused in our nostrils as we inhale and exhale, is also an effective way of becoming still before we enter into God's presence.

SEEKING THE HOLY SPIRIT'S GUIDANCE:

However hard we try to commune with God, it is important to understand that our transformation and union with God is brought about by the Holy Spirit. Without the Holy Spirit's guidance and wisdom, we would be mired in our own selfishness and pride. Our ego would get in the way of our noblest intentions. Hence it is important that we begin every prayer and action under the umbrage of the Holy Spirit. As I said earlier in this reflection, our meetings with God are encounters! So let the Holy Spirit be the one under whose mantle you do your prayer.

As the suggested opening prayer for every session states: "Come, Holy Spirit, and overshadow me with your gentle wisdom and power as I endeavor to sit at the feet of Jesus during this period of prayer. Purify my mind and heart as I seek to make the teachings of Jesus my priority in life, thinking, speaking and doing as He desires. You are the keeper of my soul, leading me into God's heart. May I be docile and submissive to your wisdom and guidance and may my life be a pleasing offering in your sight. Amen."

HELPFUL ATTITUDES FOR PRAYER:

- Our relationship with God is the most profound of all our relationships. Given God's nature we will change profoundly if we choose to accept God's enduring love.
- The only authentic way to stand in God's presence is by becoming transparent to God and especially to ourselves.
- It does not make sense to be afraid to look beyond our noses when God's horizons are limitless and all-embracing. Being magnanimous on our part will mean that we truly trust God to fulfill His promises to us.
- True reverence for God creates genuine intimacy that enlivens and transforms. God has a profound delight and reverence for us as well, having created us in his image and likeness, and Jesus becoming incarnate in order to wash us clean in his blood and make us a pleasing offering in his Father's sight.
- When you are with God, you are in the presence of Holy Mystery. Make an effort to bring your whole being before your Creator and Lord.
- Try coming home to yourself before you make the effort to come into God's presence. Coming home to self is like feeling hushed as a weaned child on its mother's lap.
- If you are wondering why your relationship with God does not have the depth and meaning you would like it to have, one reason could be because you have not developed the attitude of reverence.

II - HELPFUL PRACTICES IN PRAYER

SCRIPTURE:

Come and see the works of the LORD, the desolations he has brought on the earth. He makes wars cease to the ends of the earth; he breaks the bow and shatters the spear, he burns the shields with fire."Be still, and know that I am God; I will be exalted among the nations, I will be exalted in the earth." - NIV: Psalm 46:8-10

DEVELOPING STILLNESS IN POSTURE:

Novices in the art and practice of prayer struggle with a wandering mind as they try to stay focused on God. This difficulty creates restlessness in their bodies and they tend to fidget and move about. Sometimes they are so scattered they are not able to immerse themselves into prayer. Hence developing stillness in prayer is a priority, as it paves the way towards creating a listening heart. As previously mentioned, paying attention to a proper transition to prayer is an effective way of creating stillness. Another big help is to practice remaining motionless for the whole period of prayer. Initially, your threshold might not extend beyond a few minutes. With perseverance you will gradually be able to sit still for thirty minutes. Your body will become an integral part of your prayer and no longer a hindrance to your communion with God. You will pray with your whole being – heart and mind and spirit. Psalm 46 encourages us to heed the LORD's advice to develop stillness in prayer: "Be still, and know that I am God, exalted among the nations, exalted in the earth!"

PRAYING WITH YOUR HEART:

Scripture is replete with instances where the disciple is encouraged to relate to God with the heart which is the core of one's personality and being. In Psalm 51 the psalmist proclaims: "Restore to me the joy of your salvation and grant me a willing spirit, to sustain me…The sacrifices of God are a broken spirit; a broken and contrite heart, O God, you will not despise (NIV: Psalm 51: 12, 17)." In Luke 18, the tax collector "stood at a distance. He would not even look up to heaven, but beat his breast and said, 'God, have mercy on me, a sinner.' (NIV: Luke 18:13)'" Jesus pronounced judgment on him by saying that this man went home from the temple justified because he was humble of heart.

The saints offer the unanimous opinion that prayer is a matter of the heart as well. Our minds serve an important function in that they help to satisfy our curiosity about God and spiritual matters. But it is repentance or a life pointed in the direction of God that really matters as it leads to love and service of God. Repentance is a matter of the heart. The saints encourage us to use methods in prayer that quicken our hearts, or else no conversion will take place. The anonymous author of The Cloud of Unknowing states quite categorically that God can be reached only by love and not by intellectual knowledge. And in The Spiritual Exercises, St. Ignatius says, "It is not much knowledge that fills and satisfies the soul, but the intimate understanding and relish of the truth (Paragraph 2)." Prayer from the heart lets God's word seep into our beings the way a slow, steady drizzle sinks into the soil, to bring about the required change of heart. However, there are exceptions. Some people are very intellectually oriented. Their wills are moved to commitment and action through a thorough probe of the reasons as to why they should do something. They take the same approach to their discipleship. It is important to respect one's approach to God and trust one's insights into oneself.

INTEGRATING YOUR BODY INTO YOUR PRAYER:

As humans we are creatures who are determined by space and time. Our bodies express who we are in concrete and tangible ways. Our bodies tell us much about ourselves, and life in general. We can only come to God in and through our bodies. Many prayers have failed to germinate because the disciple sought to keep the body outside the realm of prayer. During prayer it is important that you listen carefully to what God might be saying to you through your body. It is equally important to see what your body is saying to God about you. Listen to both your feelings, moods, and bodily sensations and you will better understand the book of your life authored by the Holy Spirit.

PRAYING WITH YOUR BODY:

The wandering mind is an issue for many. They seek different ways of quieting the mind, to no avail. The wandering mind gets the better of them and creates fatigue and discouragement. A simple and effective way of dealing with distractions is to take an indirect approach. Let the body bring about a creative solution. During your periods of distraction in prayer, pay attention to the body by focusing on your breathing or bodily sensations, and remaining still during prayer. As a result of engaging the body actively in your prayer, you will begin to notice some changes taking place. Your mind is ceasing from its restlessness and is becoming more focused. You are now better able to return to God's presence and your heart is experiencing increased devotion.

CREATING A CONDUCIVE ENVIRONMENT FOR PRAYER:

As human beings we are greatly influenced by our environment. The sights and sounds around and within us influence our prayer positively or negatively. This is one important reason why our churches are built in such a way that they create the proper sacred space for us to encounter God. Similarly in her liturgy, the Church has always striven, in keeping with Biblical tradition, to provide the ideal environment so that God's life can be appropriately celebrated in the Eucharist. Through form and ritual the Church has given great importance to fostering a sacred environment. When worshippers are ignorant of the Sacred in our liturgical celebrations, their participation and benefit from the Eucharistic Celebration runs the risk of being minimal. It is very helpful, therefore, to get to Church several minutes before the commencement of Eucharist in order to transition properly into the Sacred Space within which the Eucharist is offered.

It makes sense to create a proper environment for prayer at home as well. Some like to pray in the same place where they have a candle burning before a crucifix or icon. Others like to pray in the dark, assuming that they have done their spiritual reading earlier in preparation for prayer. As creatures of habit, praying in the same place and possibly at the same time will foster an easier transition into communion with the Divine.

HELPFUL ATTITUDES FOR PRAYER:

- Make sure you learn to make your body an ally when you pray. By learning to keep motionless for longer periods, you will help your wandering mind stay more focused on God.
- Stillness in time of prayer is best engendered when there is stillness in your heart and mind during the day as you immerse yourself in the affairs of your life. Developing acts of constant gratitude and trust in God's love for you will create this stillness in your soul during the day.
- Scripture is replete with instances where the disciple is encouraged to relate to God with the heart which is the core of one personality and being. Psalm 51 proclaims: "Restore to me the joy of your salvation and grant me a willing spirit, to sustain me...The sacrifices

of God are a broken spirit; a broken and contrite heart, O God, you will not despise (NIV: Psalm 51: 12, 17)."
- Our minds serve an important function in that they help to satisfy our curiosity about God and spiritual matters. But it is repentance or a life pointed in the direction of God that really matters as it leads to love and service of God. Repentance is a matter of the heart.
- Prayer from the heart lets God's word seep into our beings the way a slow, steady drizzle sinks into the soil, to bring about the required change of heart.
- During prayer it is important that you listen carefully to what God might be saying to you through your body. It is equally important to see what your body is saying to God about you. Listen closely to both your feelings and bodily sensations and you will better understand the book of your life authored by the Holy Spirit.

III - PRAYING AS JESUS TAUGHT

SCRIPTURE:

"And when you pray, do not be like the hypocrites, for they love to pray standing in the synagogues and on the street corners to be seen by men. I tell you the truth, they have received their reward in full. But when you pray, go into your room, close the door and pray to your Father, who is unseen. Then your Father, who sees what is done in secret, will reward you. And when you pray, do not keep on babbling like pagans, for they think they will be heard because of their many words. Do not be like them, for your Father knows what you need before you ask him (NIV: Matthew 6: 5-8)."

DEFINING OUR PRAYER WITH GOD:

This passage from Matthew 6 gives us a keen insight into the nature of prayer. Prayer is relational, between God and the disciple, and is therefore a dialogue where the disciple is impacted by the Divine Presence. When prayer is one-dimensional, with the exclusive focus on self, then it runs the risk of contamination and mockery. So Jesus tells us not to behave like the hypocrites who love to stand and pray in synagogues or on street corners in order to be noticed. Prayer is really about God: engaging in adoration, worship, and praise of our God who is both our beneficent Creator and our crucified Savior. It can only be about us if our intentions for ourselves are in the service and for the Glory of God.

So Jesus asks us to pray in private and to become transparent before God, our Father. There is an interesting verse in Genesis: "The man and his wife were both naked, and they felt no shame (NIV: Genesis

2: 25)." Before the Fall Adam and Eve were naked and they knew no shame. Shame is an emotion that gives us a keen insight into the way we think and feel about our identity. Adam and Eve were naked before each other. There were no secrets, nor any reservations about who they were and how they felt about themselves and each other. And so they could appreciate and be totally comfortable with each other. The purpose of prayer is to become naked before God and feel no shame. God will make straight what is crooked, heal what is broken, and make us "participate in the divine nature (NIV: 2 Peter 1: 4)," when we open ourselves to the outstretched arms of the Crucified One and receive forgiveness and transformation in the acknowledgment of our sins and commitment to Jesus our Way, Truth, and Life. According to Jesus, it is our heart that matters in prayer, not our words or the sheer multiplication of them. But because we will use words in relating to God, they need to come from our hearts, honestly and humbly.

TEACH US HOW TO PRAY:

Let us continue listening to Jesus as he teaches us about prayer. Luke begins chapter 11 by telling us that Jesus was praying in a certain place. One of his disciples seemed quite intrigued by Jesus' behavior. Apparently his curiosity and hunger for prayer were aroused because he proceeded to ask Jesus to teach them to pray. In response Jesus taught them the familiar 'Lord's Prayer' that we have recited since we were little children.

It is interesting that through the Lord's Prayer Jesus chose to teach us the Prayer of Petition and Intercession. Many saints like Teresa of Avila have chosen to comment on the 'Our Father' and regard it as sublime prayer. Why then did Jesus teach us to use the Prayer of Petition? Is it really an inferior kind of prayer as some have purported it to be? Or is it a prayer that can lead the disciple into the depths of God's heart?

WHY THE PRAYER OF PETITION?:

In acknowledging ourselves as creatures, we declare that we have a Creator on whom we are totally dependent for everything. Our life and being comes from God. No matter how autonomous and independent we might become, it will always be an illusion to think that we can exist outside of God. The prayer of petition highlights the reality that God is the source of our being and we owe everything to our Creator and Savior. At the heart of every prayer, no matter what its form, lies the truth that we are creatures, always in need of God for all our needs, material and spiritual.

In adoration, praise, gratitude, and petition we recognize the same bottom line, our total dependence on God. We create a mockery of our true nature every time we move away from our dependence on God. No wonder, then, that Jesus offers us the 'Lord's Prayer' as a way of ensuring that we live our lives in the shadow of God's wings. As we comb through the Gospels and see Jesus in action, it becomes clear that he wanted us to have certain dispositions or attitudes when approaching God in prayer. They could be categorized as the attitudes of faith, forgiveness, perseverance, and abiding in God's will, all of which highlight the different dimensions of total dependence and obedience to God.

FAITH:

Jesus always evoked faith in the listener, either before or while he was working a miracle. Salvation was only possible if there were faith in the seeker. Jesus' miracles attested to the fact that humans were desperate without God's saving Presence and full of joy and salvation when they came to believe in God's Power and Mercy. In John 9, we have the story of the blind man whom Jesus chose to heal. In recovering his sight, the man became a witness of the saving power of Jesus in his life. Salvation and new life came to him when he bowed down and acknowledged Jesus as his Savior even though by then he had been cast out of the synagogue.

Mark has an interesting turn of phrase in 11:24: "Therefore I tell you, whatever you ask for in prayer, believe that you have received it, and it will be yours (NIV)." Faith is engendered in the heart of seekers when they know that God is indeed their only true Source and they have learnt to put their total trust in their God and Savior for all their needs, indeed for their very life. This is what it means to know God as Abba, Father.

FORGIVENESS:

In numerous places Jesus made it clear that the context for asking and receiving God's blessings and graces was conversion and discipleship. Immediately after giving us the 'Our Father' Jesus says, "For if you forgive men when they sin against you, your heavenly Father will also forgive you. But if you do not forgive men their sins, you Father will not forgive your sins. (NIV: Matthew 6: 14-15)." Simply put, salvation or becoming God-like is the reason for petitioning God. While forgiveness of others is Jesus´ explicit condition for the Prayer of Petition, it also implies forgiving ourselves. The inability or unwillingness to forgive ourselves makes it difficult to approach God for mercy and forgiveness.

PERSEVERANCE:

There are several examples where Jesus seemed disinclined to grant a petitioner's request. Upon their insistence he relented and granted them their heart's desire. The parable of the corrupt judge in Luke 18 captures this attitude as exemplified in the widow. As a widow she had no rights in society. She knew that the judge was corrupt. Yet she persisted and finally in exasperation the judge answered her plea. In Matthew 7, Jesus asks us to persist in our asking, seeking, and knocking until we receive what it is we are asking from God. Why then would Jesus make perseverance such a key attitude in our prayer? A simple answer is that we are devious and it takes much honesty to find out if we truly mean what we say in prayer. Perseverance in prayer tells us whether we sincerely and wholeheartedly desire God's saving grace and conversion. When we pray like the hypocrites who love to stand and pray in synagogues or on street corners in order to be seen by men, we fall by the wayside.

ABIDE IN JESUS AND PETITION:

Jesus makes us a wonderful promise in John 15: 7-8: "If you remain in me and my words remain in you, ask whatever you wish, and it will be given you. This is to my Father's glory, that you bear much fruit, showing yourselves to be my disciples (NIV)." When we abide in God and live by God's word, we are truly dependent on God and living according to our nature of being God's image and child. Jesus seems to say that disciples who abide in him and live according to his teaching have an irresistible power with God. The Holy Spirit tells them what to pray for and God listens to them. Indeed, saints can change the destiny of humans.

Finally, this passage from John's first letter can act as a resounding 'Amen' to our discussion: "This is the confidence we have in approaching God: that if we ask anything according to his will, he hears us. And if we know that he hears us – whatever we ask – we know that we have what we asked of him (NIV: 1 John 5:14-15)."

HELPFUL ATTITUDES FOR PRAYER:

- Prayer is relational, between God and the disciple, and is therefore a dialogue where the disciple is impacted by the Divine Presence.

When prayer is one-dimensional, with the exclusive focus on self, then it runs the risk of contamination and mockery.
- Prayer is really about God: engaging in adoration, worship, and praise of our God who is both our beneficent Creator and our crucified Savior. It can only be about us if our intentions and desires for ourselves are in the service and glory of God.
- The purpose of prayer is to become naked before God and feel no shame. God will make straight what is crooked, heal what is broken, and make us "participate in the divine nature (NIV: 2 Peter 1: 4)," when we open ourselves to the outstretched arms of the Crucified One and receive forgiveness and transformation in the acknowledgment of our sins and commitment to Jesus our Way, Truth, and Life.
- Try always to come into God's presence in the spirit of Psalm 139: God is passionate and immensely tender about your creation as God's image and likeness. You have been fearfully, wonderfully made.
- If your prayer is based on these four attitudes or conditions that Jesus requires of you, your prayer will bear fruit in your life and in the world.

PASSAGES ON THE PRAYER OF PETITION:

Exodus 32: 30-35: Moses makes atonement
1 Samuel 1: 9-23: Hannah's Prayer;
2 Samuel 7: 18-29: David's Prayer
Psalm 51: The Prayer of Repentance
Psalm 88: Lament and Prayer in Affliction
Psalm 139: The All-Knowing and Ever-Present God
Matthew 6:9-13: The Lord's Prayer
Mark 11: 20-25: The Power of Faith in Prayer
John 15: 1-8: The Vine and the Branches

IV - THE EXAMINATION OF CONSCIOUSNESS

THE GENERAL EXAMINATION:

I have chosen to call this section 'The Examination of Consciousness' rather than 'The Examination of Conscience.' Ordinarily when we do the examination of conscience, we are focusing on the sins we have committed as a way of preparing ourselves for the sacrament of reconciliation or to move toward repentance and ask God for forgiveness and mercy. The examination of consciousness includes the examination of conscience (steps 1,2,4 and 5) and goes beyond it to examine as well God's Presence in our lives, and graces we have received (Step 1 through 5).

The Examination of Consciousness has been a significant spiritual discipline and practice in Catholic Spirituality. St. Ignatius of Loyola chose to do it twice a day. Any disciple who is serious about their walk with Christ will have recourse to the examination, formally or informally. Here are some steps that St. Ignatius of Loyola offers for the daily examination of consciousness:

Step One: Bring yourself into God's presence through an act of faith. Taking a reverent stance can help smoothen your transition into God's presence.

Step Two: Ask the Holy Spirit to help and guide you in your prayer.

Step Three: Recall the blessings and graces you have received from God during this day. You can also recall the blessings and graces God has offered others through you. This step focuses on gratitude, on increasing your wonderment at God's constant providence and presence with you.

Step Four: Recall the instances during your day when you were absent from God. In other words, you are focusing on your sins, your missed opportunities, your resistance to doing God's will as manifested to you in the daily tasks and invitations.

Step Five: You make a sincere act of contrition and amendment and once again ask the Holy Spirit for guidance, strength, and wisdom as you go back to your everyday life.

THE PARTICULAR EXAMINATION:

The Particular Examination of Conscience was St. Ignatius of Loyola's idea. From his own experience of discipleship he came to the realization that he was led astray from God through the same particular weakness or sin which by habit or human condition had become deeply ingrained. It was important therefore to work assiduously at weakening and/or uprooting this vulnerability by replacing it with a virtuous habit or developing the habit of avoiding it immediately.

The Particular Examination is a way of telling God and yourself that you are serious about cooperating with God's plan of salvation and holiness for you (Read Ephesians 1:3-10). You do the Particular Examination along with the General Examination. In the Particular Examination you focus on one particular area of your life that needs attention. This area could be a chronic weakness or susceptibility, which you need to correct or else it keeps undermining your resolve. Or it could be a good habit that you need to develop as a way of deepening your walk with God. Examples: cutting down on the gossip you engage in; praying for those you resent every time thoughts of anger and hurt arise in you, etc. During steps three, four, and five, you do with the particular examination what you would ordinarily do with the general examination.

V - SPIRITUAL READING

Spiritual Reading

Spiritual Reading has always been regarded as a very important spiritual discipline in discipleship. In fact as one's discipleship deepens, the need for spiritual reading grows, sometimes even becoming an intense yearning. Since we are talking about our relationship with God, we need to know who God is as He has revealed himself to us as well as become familiar with the writings handed down to us by our Christian forebears who have shared their insights and experiences of discipleship from which we can benefit. Our saintly forebears, under the guidance of the Holy Spirit, have incarnated the spirit and life-style of Jesus and His message in their lives. Through them we get a deeper appreciation of how the gospels have been lived out in the nitty-gritty of everyday life.

In the early stages of this practice, the disciple will have a tendency to read and devour as much information as possible, partly from a deep craving for knowledge about God which yearning has been placed in our hearts by the Holy Spirit, and partly from the mistaken idea that knowing about God is the same thing as knowing God. In the worst case scenario you can have a seeker gathering erudite information and knowledge about God and His life as revealed to us in Jesus, and resisting the invitation to sit before God in loving and transparent communion. Hence it is important to note that spiritual reading is always at the service of our discipleship. If avid spiritual reading is not accompanied by daily prayer and communion with our Triune God, its noble purpose could well be defeated, promoting an inflated 'spiritual self' instead of surrender to God. Spiritual Reading has one purpose only which is to facilitate our coming into the presence of God where the Holy Spirit brings about the transformation and participation in God's life about which we have been reading. In the spiritual life it is a constant hazard to inflate the ego while supposedly pursuing the holy!

In the latter stages of the practice, the seeker will start moving into Lectio Divina, also called the Benedictine Method of Prayer. Spiritual Reading will no longer be done primarily to gain knowledge and information in the service of discipleship. Rather, spiritual reading will start becoming an expression and extension of prayer where at one and the same time, the seeker is both knowing about and knowing God. Spiritual Reading will become more of an exercise in pondering and savoring the Truth about whom one is reading. This will be especially true of our reading of Scripture. Like Mary, we will cherish in our hearts the Persons and Presence of the Trinity as revealed to us in Jesus. And very significantly, Spiritual Reading will become an experience of the Holy Spirit illuminating the text in ways that the human mind could never do. Verily, the seeker is now drinking from the source of divine life as he/she reads.

In our program, we are offering you an extended bibliography from which you can make a selection. You will find this bibliography at the end of the manual. More importantly, we suggest strongly that you steep yourself in **FOUR SOURCES** on a *daily basis*: the Bible, The Catechism of the Catholic Church, The Imitation of Christ, and your Manual.

The Bible:

The Bible is God's Living Word. The Triune God will be revealed to you when you read with faith and repentance. You can choose whichever option is convenient for you. My suggestion is that you read the New Testament first, from the Gospel of Matthew to the Book of Revelation. After that you can alternate between the Old and New Testaments, reading first one book from the Old Testament beginning with Genesis, and then one book from the New Testament beginning with Matthew.

It would help if you could discipline yourself to do about ten pages on a daily basis. Don't be discouraged if you do not understand much of what you read. It does help, however, to read up on the background information offered about every book in the Bible. Gradually the Holy Spirit will enhance your education and formation. But you need to be steadfast. The spiritual life is built on consistent practices which become life-giving once they are done habitually.

At the end of every session, in the Spiritual Reading section, you will be offered a suggestion as to which books of the Bible you can read as they relate to the theme of the sessions. This suggestion will be consonant with the recommendation made above.

The Catholic Catechism:

There are four sections to the Catechism:
1. The Profession of Faith: Pages 1 through 276: 276 in all.
2. The Celebration of the Christian Mystery: Pages 277 through 420: 143 in all.
3. Life in Christ: Pages 421 through 612: 191 in all.
4. Christian Prayer: Pages 613 through 688: 75 in all.

A helpful way of going through this very rich source of our Catholic Faith is to read five pages on a daily basis. Once again, much of the information might go over your head. As you get more familiar with the teachings and traditions of our Faith, you will find the Catechism to be an inestimable source of inspiration and strength for your discipleship.

At the end of every session, as with the section on the Bible, you will be offered a suggestion as to which sections of the Catechism you can read as they relate to the theme of the sessions. This suggestion will be consonant with the recommendation made above.

The Imitation of Christ:

The Imitation of Christ by Thomas a Kempis is a 15th century classic. After the Bible, this classic is the most widely read Christian book. There are four books and 114 chapters in all. During this formation program, each year you can savor this book three times over if you read *a single chapter each day*. This book has to be pondered slowly because the teaching about true discipleship is profound. It is more a book of formation rather than information.

The Manual:

The Manual will be a rich source of spiritual reading as well. You will want to read again the commentary on the themes of the sessions as well as the passages you prayed over on a daily basis. And there are Helps to Prayer, Methods of Prayer, Necessary Practices for Committed Discipleship that you will need to read over and over as there is a multi-splendored wisdom handed down to us through the ages and it takes time and patience to absorb this wisdom.

Finally, if you are to read the Bible, The Imitation of Christ, The Catechism, and the Manual on a daily basis, you will be doing roughly 25 pages, or about 30 minutes. You might not be able to give 30 minutes daily to spiritual reading. Start out with 15 minutes daily, and on the weekends try to make up the difference. Remember, in the spiritual life it serves you well to be the tortoise rather than the hare! Slow and steady wins the race!

VI - SUGGESTIONS FOR JOURNALING AND SPIRITUAL DIRECTION

Journaling

Every day you will be reflecting on your relationship with God as you experience it in your prayer, spiritual reading, and daily circumstances of life. As your most significant relationship, you will evaluate every aspect of your life from the perspective of this relationship with God. The Holy Spirit will enlighten your mind and strengthen your heart towards a deeper union with the Triune God.

Some saints, like Ignatius of Loyola and Teresa of Avila considered journaling or a written reflection upon their relationship with God to be a significant spiritual practice. Such a practice will help you prepare for the sacrament of reconciliation as well as for spiritual direction. During the program you will have opportunity for both. Here are some questions that you can reflect on in writing:

- What special consolation/insight/urging, did I receive in my daily prayer?
- Did I experience any desolation/resistance/anxiety, when praying on the Scripture passage or during my conversations with God?
- Is the Holy Spirit stirring my soul toward repentance/acts of service/invitation to renew my present calling/ to a new mission?

Spiritual Direction

Your answers will help you prepare for reconciliation and spiritual direction. Here are some other areas of your relationship with God that you can reflect on in preparation for reconciliation and spiritual direction:

- Did I spend time alone with God five days a week as asked for?
- What new learning have I received in the past weeks about the Trinity and myself?
- What have I learnt from the spiritual reading I have done in the past weeks?
- Is my life style becoming more Christ-centered? If so, in what way? And what have been some of my challenges?
- Am I becoming more focused on God and others than on myself?
- Is the practice of the Presence of God becoming more consistent and vibrant?
- Is Church as the Body of Christ beginning to make sense?
- Is God inviting me to renunciation of any kind, be it in the matter of food, money, material possessions, and relationships?

VII - THE PURGATIVE STAGE OF DISCIPLESHIP[1]

Saints like Ignatius of Loyola and Teresa of Avila have maintained that no meaningful relationship with God is possible *without a serious renunciation of sin*. It is a severe illusion to think that we can enter into union with God without repentance or a serious turning away from sin toward God. The Purgative stage of discipleship focuses on the necessary conditions required for discipleship or true surrender to Jesus Christ. It focuses on surrendering to the Holy Spirit to lay a sound foundation on which a solid relationship with the Trinity can be built, resulting in covenant living.

NO DELIBERATE SIN:

According to St. Teresa of Avila, serious discipleship can only really begin when a disciple has made an unequivocal rejection of deliberate sin. Teresa believed that the main reason for her mediocrity stretching over twenty years was the fact that *she paid very little attention to avoiding venial sin*. She attributed this negligence in part to liberal and permissive advice given to her by priests; "What was venial they said was no sin at all, and what was serious mortal sin they said was venial. This did me so much harm (*Her Life, chapter 5, no. 3*)." However, she took full responsibility for her dissipated life and at the age of 39 made the firm commitment to surrender herself completely to God. Another reason for our mediocrity is the fact that *we all look for advice that will let us follow our selfish desires.* We tend to seek selective counsel. Paul says it very well: "For the time will come when men will not put up with sound doctrine. Instead, to suit their own desires, they will gather around them a great number of teachers to say what their itching ears want to hear. They will turn their ears away from

---

[1] For a more detailed explanation of this stage of discipleship you would do well to read Ralph Martin's "The Fulfillment of all Desire." Much of this information is taken from his wonderful work.

the truth and turn aside to myths (NIV: 2 Timothy 4:3-4)." St. Teresa has a profound understanding of the gravity of sin. In her mind, *every deliberate sin is grave*: "It seems to me a sin is very deliberate when, for example, one says: "Lord, you see it, and I know you do not want it, and I understand this; but I want to follow my whim and appetite more than your will." It doesn't seem to me possible that something like this can be called little, however light the fault; but it's serious, very serious (*Way of Perfection, chapter 41, no. 3*)."

AVOIDING THE OCCASIONS OF SIN:

One occasion of sin is *our disordered relationships and attachments* which constantly place us in danger of sin. Not avoiding situations involving certain persons or places associated with sin will in turn weaken our resolve to avoid sin and is one of the main reasons why many don't make much progress in the spiritual life. Some people clearly have a harmful influence over us, yet we are reluctant to confront them about this unhealthy relationship. One reason is because we think it is easier to deal with the negative and sinful impact upon us rather than confront the situation and deal with 'all hell breaking loose.' And yet we know that the Holy Spirit is convicting us about this soul-disease and gently but persistently drawing us back to God. For some of us it is our addictive or harmful behaviors like drinking, pornography, gambling, and so on that delay and even prevent any meaningful covenant relationship with our Triune God. Those who have struggled with addictions know that no recovery and serious relationship with God is possible without giving up the addiction altogether. One cannot serve God and mammon at the same time.

Another common reason for failure in the spiritual life is *self-reliance.* It takes patience and humility to understand and accept graciously the reality that we cannot save ourselves. If we could, there would be no need for prayer or for God's help. To accept Jesus as Savior means that we learn to trust Him completely to bring about the transformation that the Holy Spirit will accomplish in us. For us to be like a weaned child in its mother's lap, we will need to learn to be honest about our sins, to acknowledge them without excuse, and to ask and receive God's forgiveness. Such a process of becoming like a child in order to enter the reign of God takes a long time and is an essential ingredient of the Purgative stage of discipleship. When we have not learnt true dependence on God, we find ourselves failing, getting frustrated and discouraged, and white-knuckling it rather than relying on the Lord.

Some saints are of the opinion that *it is important to strike while the iron is hot.* The Holy Spirit will offer us graces and insights and it is important that we act upon them promptly. St. Francis of Assisi prayed immediately wherever he was, even in the middle of a street, if he felt moved to pray. St. Francis de Sales describes a frequent, careful, and prompt response to the will of God and his inspirations as an important characteristic of the spiritual life. One reason for being lukewarm in the spiritual life is our hesitation to act upon the Holy Spirit's invitations to deeper intimacy and surrender. As the saying goes, 'Well begun is half done!'

VARIOUS TEMPTATIONS IN THE EARLY STAGES OF DISCIPLESHIP:

Strange as it may sound, being in a state of consolation could become a slippery slope in the spiritual life if we do not monitor carefully our thoughts and conclusions that accompany or follow from our consolations. One assumption that we could easily make is that God is now at the center of our lives because we are in consolation. Therefore we have our priorities straight. Many a spiritual life has gone awry because of misplaced priorities. Inadvertently at first, we begin to neglect what is our first priority and assume that doing things for God as we understand them is really the way to go. Almost always we are resistant to any advice that is given to us when it is contrary to our spiritual propensities! Generally, when our priorities are misplaced, we experience confusion, turmoil, and disunity. What began well begins to deteriorate, and ends up in disaster. So _it is important that we bloom where we are planted._ God's will is manifested in the daily nitty-gritty circumstances of our lives!

It takes a long time in the spiritual life _to accord God His absolute Sovereignty, to trust His loving Providence in our lives,_ and not give in to envy and anxiety over global events or in our lives. This is a conclusion that we cannot arrive at through the mind, because life is much too complex for our little minds to fathom, however intelligent we might be. It is an attitude that is gifted to us by the Holy Spirit and is given to the disciple who practices constant gratitude and childlike trust. As the Psalmist says, "Be still before the LORD and wait patiently for him; do not fret when men succeed in their ways, when they carry out their wicked schemes. Refrain from anger and turn from wrath; do not fret – it leads only to evil (NIV: Psalm 37:7-8).

Immature zeal could be an obstacle in the progress of a beginner-disciple. It is the characteristic of an inflated ego to mistakenly think we are transformed when the process has only just begun! One result is to think we are better than others, or that others are much worse than they really are, or that the world needs renewal and we are just the right person to do it. And there will always be like-minded flatterers around us to encourage us on this spiritual highway leading to futility and frustration. It is for this reason that frequent reception of the sacrament of reconciliation as well as being in spiritual direction is so helpful. A good spiritual mentor can help us live out our discipleship with integrity and humility.

DEALING WITH TEMPTATIONS:

The first purgation is from mortal sin, or sin that violates fundamentally our covenant-relationship with God. Some of us might not experience much difficulty in this regard. By God's grace and our cooperation we have lived within God's Embrace allowing the Holy Spirit to fashion us after the image and likeness of Jesus. And we have the first degree of humility which according to St. Ignatius of Loyola would be a commitment to God's will that is so strong that we would rather die than commit a mortal sin! The best way of avoiding serious sin is to live in such a way that we are constantly alert to avoid every deliberate sin, and be focused on doing much good. Being lax in the matter of venial sin is a recipe for making ourselves vulnerable to committing serious sin! *The second purgation deals with our affection for sin:* not only sin in general but particular sins and habits of sin that we have developed over a long period of time. Even after we have repented and pointed ourselves in God's direction, we still retain our affection for these habits which we keep alive in our memories and imagination through regret about all the sacrifices we have to make, through nostalgia about the good old times we had when drinking or gambling, etc. *The third purgation is purification from deliberate venial sin.* This stage of purification will not happen unless mortal sin is rejected and affection for sin is tackled assertively.

What then are some of the helps that our saints offer us in the matter of dealing with our temptations? Here are some suggestions that have come down to us from their accumulated spiritual wisdom:

- *Resist every temptation small and big*. If we don't resist the small temptations immediately, we will fall a prey to our serious temptations. As the wisdom passed on to us from Alcoholics Anonymous would suggest: you can't afford to entertain a temptation for more than five seconds, because by then you will be too vulnerable and will capitulate!

- Don't dialogue with the temptation but *perform some contrary act of virtue*, like praying your Jesus Prayer, engaging in gratitude, or doing some good deed immediately.
- *Bring the temptation out into the light,* especially if it is of an addictive nature. We are prone to commit our sins in secrecy. Talking about our temptations to a wise mentor is an excellent way of being accountable. Temptations only get stronger when they are allowed to grow in secrecy. Expose them and they lose their vigor!
- A daily practice of prayer, spiritual reading, and formation in spiritual practices is essential to tackling our affection for sin.

VIII - THE PRACTICE OF RENUNCIATION

Renunciation or the Practice of Penance/Fasting has always had an important place in the Spiritual Life. Renunciation has always been viewed as a necessary practice engaged in by committed disciples. The reason for giving the practice of renunciation a prominent place in the Spiritual Life is because of the reality of sin in our lives. Had there been no sin, there would be no need to practice renunciation or penance, as nothing would thwart us from seeking and finding God. As a result of sin, we experience a constant battle within us. On the one hand, God has placed an intense yearning in our hearts for union with Him and we are restless unless we find our rest in God. On the other hand, evil lurks within us and we have the shocking tendency of sabotaging this intense longing that God has placed in our hearts for intimacy and union with Him. As a result we are hell-bent on serving our own selfish interests and denying our dependence on the Source of our being!

In his teachings, Jesus is constantly urging us to stay on the straight and narrow road that leads to heaven and avoid the slippery slopes and detours that only bog us down in misery and turmoil: "Enter through the narrow gate. For wide is the gate and broad is the road that leads to destruction, and many enter through it. But small is the gate and narrow the road that leads to life, and only a few find it (NIV: Matthew 7:13-14)." The saints advocate renunciation and penance as an effective help to enter through the narrow gate and stay on the narrow road that leads to life. In summary, the fundamental meaning of Penance is detestation or hatred of sin as an offense against God and a firm purpose of amendment by living one's life in repentance. Penance is not just the detestation of sin, in general, nor of that which others commit, <u>but of one's own sin</u>. The motive of this detestation is that sin offends God: "Repent! Turn away from all your offenses; then sin will not be your downfall. Rid yourselves of all the offenses you have committed, and get a new heart and a new spirit (NIV: Ezekiel 18:30-31)."

ST. IGNATIUS OF LOYOLA ON PENANCE:

As a way of staying repentant so that we are pointed in God's direction in the decisions we make and the way we live, St. Ignatius of Loyola distinguishes Penance into Interior and Exterior. "*Interior penance* consists in sorrow for one's sins and a firm purpose not to commit them or any others (Spiritual Exercises, Paragraph 82)." *Exterior penance* is the fruit of the first kind and its purpose is to help the disciple maintain a healthy control over his/her evil impulses in thought, word, and deed. According to Ignatius the first kind of exterior penance concerns *eating*. Ignatius distinguishes between temperance and penance in the matter of food. When we do away with what is superfluous, we are practicing temperance. We do penance when we deny ourselves something of what is suitable for us. We all know those moments in our experience of eating when we are indulging ourselves and creating an imbalance in our bodies and a certain opaqueness of spirit. Foregoing that food item as a way of preserving and strengthening our one-pointed direction toward God is doing penance. Ignatius suggests that we make a habit of foregoing regularly, suitable and delectable food items. The more we do this, the better the penance, provided only we do no harm to ourselves and do not cause any serious illness.

The second kind of exterior penance concerns *sleep.* Here, too, doing away with the superfluous in what is pampering and soft is not penance. It is penance when in our manner of sleeping we take something away from what is suitable. Obviously, Ignatius is referring to creature comforts that we surround our beds with. His suggestion would sound strange to the modern ears. But you need to know what he says. According to him, the more we do in this line, the better it is, provided we do not cause any harm to ourselves, and do not bring on any notable illness. But we should not deny ourselves a suitable amount of sleep, except to come to a happy mean in case we had the habit of sleeping too much.

Ignatius offers various reasons for doing exterior penance. Two of them are worthy of note: "To overcome oneself, that is, to make our sensual nature obey reason, and to bring all of our lower faculties into greater subjection to the higher; and to obtain some grace or gift that one earnestly desires. Thus it may be that one wants a deep sorrow for sin, or tears, either of his sins or because of the pains and sufferings of Christ our Lord; or he may want the solution of some doubt that is in his mind (*Spiritual Exercises*, Paragraph 87)."

RENUNCIATION OF THOUGHTS:

St. Anthony of the Desert made the momentous decision of selling all his possessions and moving into the desert. However, in the desert he realized the vicissitudes of renouncing wealth, honor, status, relationships, and comfort. These desires were alive and thriving in his heart and they followed him into his solitude. Instead of experiencing and enjoying intimate union with the Divine, he was preoccupied with his previous life and its attractions. _He realized he had a second renunciation to undergo._ His thoughts mattered. They needed to be taken seriously and dealt with so that the spiritual life did not become a case of the tail wagging the dog. Or else St. Anthony would not be able to pray! This holy father of monasticism then learned to redirect his thoughts: either by placing a prayer alongside the thought, or filling his mind with inspired and traditional prayers.

In this first year we will concentrate on practicing the Particular Examination of Consciousness to control and dissipate thought-patterns that are laced with strong emotion and passion and tend to derail our relationship with God. We will practice praying for those who wish us harm/wrong, and replacing our fear and anxiety with joy and thanksgiving. We will practice living in the present moment and engaging ourselves wholeheartedly with the task at hand, because we can only experience God in the present moment.

PRACTICING RENUNCIATION THROUGH TITHING:

An effective way of practicing renunciation is to engage in the continual practice of tithing or sharing with others our time, talent and resources. At the heart of tithing is the realization that all of my life is a pure gift. All I have is the doing of my Creator and Lord. This realization creates a profound sense of gratitude which engenders a great desire and even obligation to share our talent and resources with others. A salutary way of offering God praise and adoration is to share with others who have been created in the divine image and likeness. They and we are indeed the delight of the Original who wants us to live in covenant with the Trinity as well as with one another.

BIBLIOGRAPHY

Prescribed Reading:
Manual
The Imitation of Christ
The Bible
The Catechism of the Catholic Church

Recommended Reading
The Way of Perfection by St. Theresa of Avila
Living in God's Embrace by Michael Fonseca
The Practice of the Presence of God by Brother Lawrence of the Resurrection
Opening to God, Guide to Prayer, by Thomas Green, S.J.
The School of Prayer or Beginning to Pray by Archbishop Bloom
The Way of a Pilgrim by Anonymous Author
Hinds' Feet on High Places by Hannah Hurnard
The Journey toward God by Benedict J. Groeschel, CFR with Kevin Perrotta
Listen to the Desert by Gregory Mayers
The Fulfillment of All Desire by Ralph Martin

VOCAL PRAYER

SCRIPTURE:

One day Jesus was praying in a certain place. When he finished, one of his disciples asked him, "Lord, teach us to pray, as John taught his disciples." He said to them, "When you pray, say: "Father, hallowed be your name, your kingdom come. Give us each day our daily bread. Forgive us our sins, for we also forgive everyone who sins against us. And lead us not into temptation." – NIV: Luke 11: 1-4

INTRODUCTION:

Most believers have taken their first steps in prayer at their mother's knees when they were taught some simple prayers. As children, we learnt these prayers by heart. By the time we reached the age of reason we had learnt a number of prayers by rote, including the Lord's Prayer, simple Acts of Faith, Hope, Love, Contrition, etc. Thus began our initiation into prayer in general and our introduction to Vocal Prayer.

PRAYING WITH THE WORDS OF OTHERS:

One form of vocal prayer is to take the words others have cobbled together and make them our own as we communicate with God. It is fairly easy to resonate with these composed prayers. In many instances holy women and men have put them together when they were experiencing significant communion or lack of it with the Lord. These prayers, therefore, have a ring of authenticity and authority about them. For many committed Christians, vocal prayer has been their staple communication with God. They derive comfort from walking in the footsteps of their holy forebears. It nourishes them as they resonate with these prayers and slowly but inexorably make these holy words their own. For many years, St. Teresa of Avila prayed out of a book because she was very distracted otherwise. Praying out of a book, or praying vocally, seemed to help her stay focused on God. The Psalms are probably the best example of praying with the words of others.

PRAYING WITH YOUR OWN WORDS:

When we have entered into a personal relationship with God, invariably we begin to feel the need to express our relationship with the Divine in our own words. While other people's prayers can sometimes better express our deepest sentiments, often it seems more appropriate and authentic to speak to God with our own words, sentiments, and images. Using our own words is especially appropriate when we are burdened and distraught, as well as when we are experiencing deep consolation. Hannah, Samuel's mother, is a good example of a person who prayed to God from the depths of her burdened heart. In response to Eli, Hannah answered, "Not so, my Lord. I am a woman who is deeply troubled. I have not been drinking wine or beer; I was pouring out my soul to the LORD. Do not take your servant for a wicked woman; I have been praying here out of my great anguish and grief (NIV: 1 Samuel 1: 15-16)."

As mentioned earlier, the Psalms are wonderful examples of prayers that were composed in various life-circumstances. They are powerful and riveting, sobering and ecstatic. They were prayers composed in the midst of danger and travail as well as in moments of intense joy and peace. There will be times when we ourselves will pray like the Psalmist. There will be other times when we will deem it best to use the Psalmist's words because ours are either inadequate or non-existent.

VOCAL PRAYER COMBINED WITH OTHER FORMS OF PRAYER:

There are several vocal prayers that have been handed down to us through centuries. These prayers have been hallowed by generations of faithful believers. They are a combination of vocal prayer with some other forms of prayer. Some such prayers are the Liturgy of the Hours, the Rosary, the Stations of the Cross, etc. The Rosary can be done as vocal prayer where the focus is on the meaning of the words. It can also be done as imaging prayer where the disciple enters into the heart of each mystery that is being contemplated while the prayers of the decade are being prayed aloud or with one's lips. The words act as a backdrop that helps with the contemplation of the mystery. Some like to go back and forth between paying attention to the words of the prayers and contemplating the mysteries. The same is true with The Stations of Cross. Regarding the Liturgy of the Hours when one prays the divine office by reading the Psalms and prayers with loving attention to the words and the Presence of God, vocal prayer truly becomes contemplative and restful.

THE HEART OF VOCAL PRAYER:

Prayer is the vehicle by which we express our relationship with God. It is the place where we speak to God, and as we mature in the relationship, God speaks to us and we learn to listen and recognize God's voice. The purpose of vocal prayer is the same as with any other form of prayer. It is to bring us into the presence of God where we move from communication to communion to union with the Divine. It is important, therefore, whether we are using the words of others or our own, that we pray these words from our hearts and claim them as our own. These words are expressing who we truly are or want to be before God. And as we seek to mean what we say, we pay loving attention to the Presence of God to whom we are offering our supplication.

HELPFUL ATTITUDES FOR PRAYER:

- Contrary to what some may think vocal prayer is an exalted form of prayer that has been used by holy women and men throughout the ages. It is very effective prayer that can and does lead one into the heart of God.
- When you pray vocally, either by using your own words or those of other believers, make sure you claim these words as your own and mean what they say.
- Remember that the Holy Spirit is praying in your spirit. At times you will sense that your prayer could not have come from you. Only the Holy Spirit could have prayed those words.
- Take a few minutes every now and then during the day to be present to God. Listen to your heart. If there are words given to you by the Holy Spirit, speak them to God. Or abide in loving silence, attentive to God's Presence.
- If you are losing your sense of joy, hope, and loving attitude, maybe you are not engaging enough in the prayer of gratitude and recollection of God's presence in your life.

BIBLICAL PASSAGES:

Matthew 6: 5-15: Prayer
Matthew 18: 19-20: The Power of United Prayer
Luke 11: 5-13: Two Parables on Prayer
Ephesians 3: 14-21: Prayer for the Readers
Ephesians 6: 18-20: Assiduous Prayer
Colossians 1: 9-14: Prayer for Continued Progress
Colossians 4: 2-6: Prayer and Apostolic Spirit
Revelation 4:1- 11: Vision of Heavenly Worship

THE METHOD OF MEDITATION

SCRIPTURE:

"Blessed is the man who does not walk in the counsel of the wicked or stand in the way of sinners or sit in the seat of mockers. But his delight is in the law of the LORD, and on his law he meditates day and night. He is like a tree planted by streams of water, which yields its fruit in season and whose leaf does not wither. Whatever he does prospers." – NIV: Psalm 1: 1-3.

A WORD OF CAUTION:

The method of prayer known as meditation has been in vogue since the Middle Ages. Saints Ignatius of Loyola and Teresa of Avila used the method themselves and taught it too. In his Spiritual Exercises, Ignatius offers extensive help as to how one goes about using the method of meditation in prayer. He uses this method almost exclusively in the First Week of the Spiritual Exercises.

Before we go into this method, it will help to remember that prayer is not about techniques or mechanics, so that if one took the right steps, the results would automatically follow. Such an approach would reduce prayer to a purely human activity where the results would depend on us. This attitude would take away the faith dimension in prayer which is supported by the foundational reality that Jesus is our Savior and any good in us is pure grace!

PRAYER IS A MATTER OF THE HEART:

Prayer must always be seen and practiced in the context of a personal relationship with God. In prayer we are on God's turf, and are there to listen and follow the divine bidding. So any method we use in prayer is a help towards deepening our relationship with God. It is at the service of the relationship. The same is true of meditation. It is interesting to note that in the second of his twenty annotations or footnotes at the beginning of the Spiritual Exercises, Ignatius says, "it is not much knowledge that satisfies the soul but the intimate understanding and relish of the truth." Keeping in mind then that prayer is a matter of the heart rather than an accumulation of knowledge about God through the mind, let us look at the method of meditation.

MEDITATION AS A METHOD OF PRAYER:

In the way Ignatius envisages the method of meditation, there are six steps: preparatory prayer, two preludes, three points, and a colloquy at the end.

- **The Preparatory prayer** is a significant first step. Ignatius assumes that we need to pay the utmost reverence and attention to God's Presence in prayer, especially when we address God directly. After all, we are in the Presence of our Creator, Savior, and Lord! The Preparatory Prayer acknowledges God as the Sovereign Ruler of our life. In his words, "I will beg God our Lord for grace that all my intentions, actions, and operations may be directed purely to the praise and service of His Divine Majesty (Spiritual Exercises, Paragraph 46)." Clearly prayer is serious business for Ignatius. The context of our relationship with God is set at the very beginning: we are there on God's terms and it is important immediately to declare our earnest commitment to the Lord.

The Two Preludes are preparatory steps as well.

1. **The First Prelude** is also known as the Composition of place. Ignatius was of the opinion that our whole being needed to be involved in our prayer. If utilized well, imagination can be an

effective help to our prayer. On the other hand, it can be a great source of distraction if it is not harnessed properly. In the first prelude Ignatius suggests that we create an image of the Scriptural scene or theme on which we will be praying. By situating our prayer within an image or context, our imagination becomes an active player in our prayer and our chances of being focused and attentive to the Lord increase. We can create whatever image we believe would help our prayer. In the first exercise of the Spiritual Exercises which is a meditation on sin, Ignatius suggests "to see in imagination my soul as a prisoner in this corruptible body, and to consider my whole composite being as an exile here on earth, cast out to live among brute beasts (Spiritual Exercises, Paragraph 47).

2. **"The Second Prelude** is the step we take and ask God for what we want and desire from our prayer. Ignatius assumes that we spent some time deciding what our subject for prayer would be, prior to beginning our prayer. So already at the start of our prayer we know what we desire from God. Some critics have accused Ignatius of voluntarism, implying that we are telling God what needs to be done. Nothing is farther from the truth. Ignatius believed strongly that Jesus had called him to serve at his side in establishing God's reign. On his part he saw the need of doing everything humanly possible to aid God. He never hesitated to ask God for what he believed he needed so that he could be the best possible instrument in God's hands. His only desire was to attain "the greater glory of God." It is this kind of thinking that is behind his second prelude.

3. **The Three Points** move us into our prayer session proper. Being a methodical person Ignatius divides up the subject matter into three points, as a way of breaking it down into manageable parts. We could do it in a way that suits us. In each point we ponder on God's truth as being presented *for us,* in the Scripture

passage. We spend time reflecting, comparing and contrasting, and deriving lessons for our own life. We would be seeking responses to questions such as: "Why is Jesus saying this? What is Jesus asking of me? What do I want and need to do for Jesus? This kind of reflection, if done purposefully and with care, will stir our heart deeply and we will be moved to offer Jesus a response. As mentioned earlier, Ignatius was adamant about tasting and relishing the truth in prayer. If one point suffices in this regard, there is no need to go through all three points.

4. **<u>The Colloquy</u>** is the time when we express directly to God in conversation the stirrings of our heart. In our sentiments the Holy Spirit is beckoning us toward repentance, commitment, and action. Through this step Ignatius wants to make sure that we spend time <u>*in face-to-face dialogue with God*</u>. As we become familiar with this method, we will speak directly to God as we reflect on Jesus. The ideal would be to reflect and converse simultaneously. However, if we haven't spent much time conversing directly with God, Ignatius suggests that at least we end our prayer with a colloquy.

<u>HELPFUL ATTITUDES FOR PRAYER:</u>

- It is not much knowledge that fills and satisfies the soul but the intimate understanding and relish.
- Imagination can be an effective help to our prayer if utilized well. On the other hand, it can be a great source of distraction if it is not harnessed properly.
- You pray with your whole being. God desires and deserves all of you when you come into the Presence. Hence it is important that you take time to dispose yourself for your daily encounter with God.
- Jesus has called you to serve at his side in establishing God's reign. Your discipleship requires that you will do everything humanly possible to aid God in this endeavor. Ignatius never hesitated to ask

God for what he believed he needed so that he could be the best possible instrument in God's hands. His only desire was to attain "the greater glory of God." It is this kind of thinking that is behind his second prelude. You can consider making it your own.

- Jesus made the decision to have you work by his side in establishing God's reign in our world. This is an awesome privilege, always to be taken seriously. Prayer, therefore, is serious and privileged business.

THE METHOD OF IGNATIAN CONTEMPLATION OR IMAGING

SCRIPTURE:

"Sovereign Lord, as you have promised, you now dismiss your servant in peace. For my eyes have seen your salvation, which you have prepared in the sight of all people, a light for revelation to the Gentiles, and for glory to your people Israel."
- NIV: Luke 2: 29-32

INTRODUCTION:

Saint Ignatius of Loyola popularized the method of prayer that uses imagination as a major vehicle. He makes extensive use of this method in the Spiritual Exercises. It is therefore called Ignatian Contemplation. In ordinary parlance it is generally known as the method of imaging. While Ignatius used the term 'contemplation', the method is a discursive form of prayer, meaning that the disciple engages in the use of words, images, symbols, gestures, feelings, and primarily imagination in his/her contact with God. It is not to be confused with contemplative prayer as understood by Saints John of the Cross and Teresa of Avila.

IMAGING AS A METHOD OF PRAYER:

Saint Ignatius begins using this method in the Second Week of the Spiritual Exercises. He asks you to use your imagination in creating the Scriptural scene on which you are praying. For instance if you were praying on the Nativity of Jesus, you would begin by seeing the persons in the mystery as though present before you, and "you would look upon them, contemplate them, and serve them in their needs with all possible homage and reverence" (Spiritual Exercises, Paragraph 114).

Next, you would consider, observe, and contemplate what the persons are saying, and then to reflect on yourself and draw some fruit from it. Lastly, you would see and consider what they are doing, for example, "making the journey and laboring that our Lord might be born in extreme poverty, and that after many labors, after hunger, thirst, heat, and cold, after insults and outrages, He might die on the cross, and all this for me" (Spiritual Exercises, Paragraph 116). Briefly, the method engages our imagination to better see God's mystery and to observe what is being said and done. This method highlights the fact that our sense faculties are an integral part of our beings and therefore have to be an integral part of our relationship with God and our prayer.

BENEFITS FROM USING THE METHOD:

The method works best for those who have arrived at internal solitude and quiet in their relationship with God. They are at home with themselves. Scripture is becoming God's living word, being spoken to them personally, and Jesus is establishing an intimate Presence in their lives. It does not take them long to enter God's Presence when they come to prayer because Jesus has become a very significant focus of their thoughts and desires during the day. Their visits with God seem to be a continuation of the prayerful relationship they have established during the day.

Ignatian contemplation is an affective method of prayer. It engages all the human faculties. What starts out as pure imagination as one tries to engage God's mystery, ends up in imaginative faith. Many who use this method will say quite categorically that they experienced God's Presence and Mystery and were awed and subdued by it. For those who enjoy using the imagination in prayer, this method can be restful and productive.

In the Spiritual Exercises, Saint Ignatius seems to presume that this method could lead to a greatly simplified form of discursive prayer or even contemplative prayer where God's Mystery is experienced in silence and awe. After he asks the retreatant to make several repetitions of say, the Nativity Scene, he invites him/her to do the Application of the Five senses. Using the same method he invites you to experience the mystery through hearing what "they are saying, or what they might say," through smelling "the infinite fragrance," and tasting "the infinite sweetness of the divinity." He asks you to apply the sense of touch as well, "by embracing and kissing the place where the persons stand or are seated, always taking care to draw fruit from this" (Spiritual Exercises, Paragraphs 123-125). The application of the five senses generally happens to the person who has learnt to ponder things in his/her heart the way Mary did, and is favored by the Holy Spirit to "sense" God's mystery.

DIFFICULTIES WITH THE METHOD:

This method does not seem to work too well for some. Saint Teresa of Avila did have difficulty using her imagination in presenting God's mystery to herself. Those with a logical and intellectual bent, or "left-brainers," might experience frustration with this way of praying. To each his/her own is the rule of thumb. If the method works for you, use it. If it doesn't, find one that does. It is important not to assume that something is wrong with you because you cannot use this method effectively.

I have made this observation in spiritual direction that some have difficulty imaging God's mystery because they are trying too hard. It is important not to force the method on God and yourself in prayer. Rather, it does you well to remember that the Holy Spirit is in charge. The right disposition would be to wait on the Holy Spirit to produce the images in you. You are like a canvas on which the Holy Spirit is painting God's Mystery for you to observe, participate in, and relish.

Lastly, some have found to their relief and delight that when they stopped trying to paint God's Mystery on the canvas of their hearts, paradoxically, the images started to appear and they could enter into God's Mystery through this method.

HELPFUL ATTITUDES FOR PRAYER:

- You can use this method whenever you wish. It seems to work well when the noise in your being has abated and your heart has become the Holy Spirit's temple. Practicing the Presence of God during the day enhances the chances of this method working well.
- Imagination can be an effective help to our prayer if utilized well. On the other hand, it can be a great source of distraction if it is not harnessed properly. This method is a good way of using imagination in the service of prayer.
- Imaging is a method that children and adolescents would take to rather easily. It could be used effectively for family prayer.
- Saint Anthony of Padua used this method very effectively and often it led him into the contemplative depths of God's Mystery. He would image himself at the manger where he would receive the Baby Jesus. He would cradle the infant in his arms and let his heart and being speak and be spoken to. This is the reason he is always portrayed as holding the Child Jesus in his arms.
- Advent, Christmas, and Lent are liturgical seasons that lend themselves very effectively to this method of prayer.

BIBLICAL PASSAGES FOR IMAGING PRAYER:

Luke 2: 1-40: The Birth of Jesus
Matthew 2: 1-23: The Astrologers and Flight into Egypt
Luke 10: 25-37: The Good Samaritan
Luke 18: 1-10: Zacchaeus the Tax Collector
John 9: 1-41: The Man born Blind

Luke 22: 39-53: The Agony in the Garden
Matthew 28: 1-15: The Women at the Tomb
Luke 24: 13-35: Emmaus

LECTIO DIVINA OR THE BENEDICTINE METHOD OF PRAYER

Lectio Divina, also known as The Benedictine Method of Prayer, is a very ancient method of prayer going back to the early Christian centuries. This ancient practice has been kept alive in the monastic traditions of the Church, especially by the Benedictines. Hence, the alternative name for this prayer expression is The Benedictine Method of Prayer. Given that this method originated in monasteries, it was very conducive to the monastic lifestyle which developed into a balanced and natural rhythm of life with the equally important strands of solitude, prayer, work, and rest.

While Lectio Divina could be classified as discursive prayer, meaning that it uses words, thoughts, images, and gestures, much like human communication, to relate to God, in many ways it could also be classified as contemplative prayer because it leads the disciple into God's Mystery. Lectio Divina becoming contemplative prayer would be especially true of a disciple who has been taught by the Holy Spirit to wait on God in quiet and loving expectation.

There are basically four steps to Lectio Divina:

1. **LECTIO OR READING:**

In his Prologue to the Rule, St. Benedict encourages us to hear "with the ear of our hearts" the Word of God as we read it. This is the first step in Lectio Divina or divine reading. For one to be able to listen with the ear of the heart, one must be finely attuned to the Holy Spirit. For that to happen, one has consciously eschewed all deliberate sin and has made an unequivocal commitment to keeping God at the center of their life. Such a person then is in harmony with God's Holy Spirit. This step of reading God's Word and listening at the same time to God's voice is then done in the spirit of the Prophet Elijah: "After the earthquake came a fire, but the LORD was not in the fire. And after the fire came a gentle whisper (NIV: 1 Kings 19:12)," which was the voice of God. It is the Holy Spirit who will teach us how to listen to the Scriptures while we read them. The ancient prophets exhorted the Israelites with the joy-filled command: "Hear, O Israel! The LORD is our God, the LORD is one (NIV: Deuteronomy 6:4)!" In Lectio Divina we are obeying this exhortation to listen to the Lord with our hearts. This first step is therefore done very slowly and reverently, listening in a spirit of silence and awe. In Lectio we read slowly, attentively, trustingly, gently listening for a word or phrase that is God's word for us this day. Our attitude must be one of peaceful anticipation and confident hope that we will be mentored by the Holy Spirit.

2. **MEDITATIO/REPETITIO OR MEDITATION/REPETITION**

In the course of our reading, once we have found a word or phrase that moves us or stirs our hearts, we move into the second step of Lectio Divina which is meditation or repetition. We ponder this morsel given to us by the Holy Spirit, chewing on it, tasting and relishing it as well as allowing it to interact with our thoughts, hopes, desires and memories, in short, with our lives. Our ancient Christian brethren took a cue from ruminant animals and saw this second step as the equivalent of "chewing the cud" that is God's revealed food to us. Mary, Mother of Jesus, in the way she "treasured up all these things and pondered them in her heart (NIV: Luke 2:19)" is our Scriptural role model when it comes to doing this second step of meditating on God's word. Through meditation we allow God's word to become His word for us. It is God's Living Word in the Person of Jesus Christ who touches us and transforms our lives. The term 'repetition' instead of 'meditation' emphasizes the fact that repeating God's word to us over and over is strikingly similar in action to chewing the cud.

3. ORATIO – PRAYER

The third step is Oratio/Prayer. The best way to describe this step is to say that the disciple now addresses God in and through the Scriptural word or phrase that he/she has received from reading/hearing God's word. Then pondering on it the way Mary pondered the events surrounding the birth of her Son, Jesus, the disciple makes an offering of self as it is shaped by the living word of God. In this prayer of consecration we allow our real selves to be touched and changed by the word of God.

4. CONTEMPLATIO – CONTEMPLATION

When Lectio Divina has been practiced for a long time, the disciple becomes quite familiar with this fourth step. In this step, we simply rest in the Presence of the One who has used His living word to invite us into His loving Embrace. This is a moment of intimacy and quiet rest. Words are unnecessary to express the deepest sentiments of our heart. On the contrary silence in the loving Presence of the Beloved seems to be the more appropriate way of communing with God. In our Christian tradition this wordless, quiet communing with God is called Contemplatio or contemplation. We practice loving silent attention to the loving Presence of God, simply enjoying the experience of basking in his Presence. The following quote from "Living in God's Embrace" by Michael Fonseca, page 156, sums up appropriately our discussion on Lectio Divina: "The Benedictine Method of Prayer has been used by countless holy men and women through the centuries. It has the uncanny knack of unlocking the precious treasures of God's heart and bringing us to the cusp of contemplation. It unlocks the treasures of our own hearts as well, bringing about a deeper integration between our hearts and minds."

PRAYING WITH THE PSALMS

SCRIPTURE:

"The Lord is my shepherd, I shall not be in want. He makes me lie down in green pastures, he leads me beside quiet waters, he restores my soul, he guides me in paths of righteousness for his name's sake. Even though I walk through the valley of the shadow of death, I will fear no evil, for you are with me; your rod and your staff, they comfort me."

– NIV Psalm 23: 1-4

INTRODUCTION:

The Book of Psalms is a significant part of the Wisdom Literature. The Jewish believer was very familiar with the Psalms, committing many of them to memory and using them frequently in prayer. They are an excellent way to connect our hearts to the heart of God. David is considered the author of most of the Psalms. He had a passion for intimacy with God and was characterized as "a man after God's own heart." Despite his major failings, he placed great priority on his relationship to God. He also had the heart of a shepherd and the creative gifts, both in terms of his poetic genius and musical ability, to achieve this masterpiece of expression.

The Book of Psalms is appropriate for all believers in every season of their spiritual life. Wherever you are in your spiritual journey, whatever emotions your heart may be encountering, whatever struggles you may be going through, you will find a place in the Psalms that resonates and draws you closer to the Lord. The Psalms are the language of the believer's heart. They were composed and prayed in time of mourning for sin, thirsting after God, rejoicing in Him, thanking God for

His mercies, or admiring the Divine Perfections. Every expression of prayer can be found in the Psalms. Their value is very great, and their use will enhance and deepen one's relationship with the Triune God. The Holy Spirit helps us to pray through the Psalms. In the language of this Divine book, through the Liturgy of the Hours, the prayers and praises of the Church have been offered up to the Throne of Grace from age to age.

BASIC OUTLINE:

The Psalms are divided into 5 books, each ending with a doxology:
1. Psalms 1 through 41;
2. Psalms 42 through 72;
3. Psalms 73 through 89;
4. Psalms 90 through 106;
5. Psalms 107 through 150.

TOPICAL GROUPINGS:

Analysis of the content of the Psalms is one way of classifying them, according to their themes or topics:

1. Prayers of the Individual: Psalms 3, 4, 5, 6, 7
2. Praise from the Individual for God's Saving Help: Psalms 30, 34
3. Prayers of the Community: Psalms 12, 44, 79
4. Praise from the Community for God's Saving Help: Psalms 66, 75
5. Confessions of Confidence in the Lord: Psalms 11, 16, 52
6. Hymns in Praise of God's Majesty and Virtues: Psalms 8, 19, 29, 65
7. Hymns celebrating God's Universal Reign: Psalms 47, 93-99
8. Songs of Zion, the City of God: Psalms 46, 48, 76, 84, 122, 126, 129, 137

9. Royal Psalms: Psalms 2, 18, 20, 45, 72, 89, 110
10. Pilgrimage Songs: Psalms 120-134
11. Liturgical Songs: Psalms 15, 24, 68
12. Instructional Psalms: Psalms 1, 34, 37, 73, 112, 119, 128, 133.

WHY STUDY THIS BOOK?

- The Psalms help us to enhance our Life of Prayer. They are an appropriate response to the disciples' pleas, "Lord, teach us how to pray."
- The Psalms enhance our Praise and Worship. They are used extensively in the Liturgy of the Eucharist and Liturgy of the Hours: "Lord, teach us to worship."
- The Psalms encourage us to be authentic and transparent before God and others.
- Through the Book of Psalms we learn more about the Character and Person of God: His Goodness, His Sovereignty, His Holiness, His Wrath, His Loving Kindness, His Mercy, His Power, His Majesty, His Transcendence balanced with His Immanence.
- Finally, through the Psalms we learn more about our Lord Jesus Christ as we see the Messiah in the Psalms.

NOTABLE QUOTES:

Spurgeon: "More and more is the conviction forced upon my heart that every man must traverse the territory of the Psalms himself if he would know what a goodly land they are. They flow with milk and honey, but not to strangers; they are only fertile to lovers of their hills and vales. None but the Holy Spirit can give a man the key to the Treasury of David; and even he gives it rather to experience than to study. Happy is he who for himself knows the secret of the Psalms."

Baxter: "This Book of Psalms is a limpid lake which reflects every mood of man's changeful sky. It is a river of consolation which, though swollen with many tears, never fails to gladden the fainting. It is a garden of flowers which never lose their fragrance, though some of the roses have sharp thorns. It is a stringed instrument which registers every note of praise and prayer, of triumph and trouble, of gladness and sadness, of hope and fear, and unites them all in the full multi-chord of human experience."

St. Ambrose of Milan: "Although all Scripture breathes the grace of God, yet sweet beyond all others is the Book of Psalms. History instructs, the Law teaches, Prophecy announces, rebukes, chastens, Morality persuades; but in the Book of Psalms we have the fruit of all these, and a kind of medicine for the salvation of men."

HELPFUL ATTITUDES FOR PRAYER:

- Wherever you are in your spiritual journey, whatever emotions your heart may be feeling, whatever struggles you may be going through, you will find a place in the Psalms that resonates and draws you closer to the Lord.
- No part of the Old Testament is more frequently quoted or referred to in the New than the Book of Psalms. Every Psalm either points directly to Christ or leads the believer's thoughts to Him.
- The Psalms are the language of the believer's heart, whether mourning for sin, thirsting after God, or rejoicing in Him. Whether admiring the Divine perfections, thanking God for His mercies, meditating on his truths, or delighting in His service, they form a divinely appointed standard of experience, by which we may judge ourselves.
- In the language of this Divine book, through the Liturgy of the Hours, the prayers and praises of the Church have been offered up to the Throne of Grace from age to age.

PRACTICING THE PRESENCE OF GOD

SCRIPTURE:

"And pray in the Spirit on all occasions with all kinds of prayers and requests. With this in mind, be alert and always keep on praying for all the saints. Pray also for me, that whenever I open my mouth, words may be given me so that I will fearlessly make known the mystery of the gospel, for which I am an ambassador in chains. Pray that I may declare it fearlessly, as I should."- NIV: Ephesians 6: 18-20

"I thank my God every time I remember you. In all my prayers for all of you, I always pray with joy because of your partnership in the gospel from the first day until now, being confident of this, that he who began a good work in you will carry it on to completion until the day of Christ Jesus. I give thanks to my God every time I think of you – which is constantly, in every prayer I utter – rejoicing, as I plead on your behalf, at the way you have all continually helped promote the gospel from the very first day." – NIV: Philippians 1: 3-5

PRACTICING THE PRESENCE OF GOD

When a believer becomes a committed follower of Jesus, prayer ceases to be an obligation. It now expresses the disciple's relationship with Jesus who is claimed as Savior and Lord. A personal relationship has developed between Lord and disciple, resulting in an ardent desire on the disciple's part to be in the Master's company continually. The desire to know Jesus and his ways grows incrementally, resulting in a firm commitment to walk in the Master's footsteps. At this stage prayer becomes the vehicle to express and experience intimacy and communion with the Lord.

Such intimacy can no longer be confined to some stipulated time on the daily schedule. It becomes a necessity to be with the Lord throughout the day. Jesus takes on the role of itinerant Teacher, Friend, and Beloved. The marketplace becomes holy because God resides there. It is now as holy a sanctuary as is Church, because in both places the Lord is present and wishes to commune with the disciple.

Practicing the Presence of God throughout the day is a tradition that dates back to the early Church. Paul was definitely a person who lived and breathed God. He and countless others have shaped their lives in God's presence and under God's directions. We will look at three different expressions of this practice of God's Presence.

THE JESUS PRAYER TRADITION:

If you wish to get a good understanding of the Jesus Prayer tradition, a wonderful source would be The Way of a Pilgrim, by an anonymous Russian author. It is the story of a pilgrim who experienced transformation and union with Jesus through the recitation of the Jesus Prayer. Briefly, the Jesus Prayer originated in the deserts of Egypt and the Middle East in the first centuries of Christianity. By the Sixth century this practice became a well-established tradition, and Saint John Climacus is commonly held as the founder and consolidator of this practice.

What is the Jesus Prayer? It is the constant recitation of the prayer formula, "Lord, Jesus Christ, have mercy on me, a sinner." The longer version is, "Lord Jesus Christ, Son of the Living God, have mercy on me, a sinner." Various individuals in the New Testament who needed healing uttered this prayer-exclamation, in one form or another. The most prominent of these individuals is the blind Bartimaeus in Mark 10: 47: "Jesus, Son of David, have mercy on me." In the parable of the

Pharisee and Publican in Luke 18, the publican utters a similar formula, "O God, be merciful to me, a sinner."

This prayer-exclamation is both simple and profound. These words capture the very heart of Christian discipleship, namely, that salvation comes from God and can never be something that we carve out on our own, or merit through our own efforts. Salvation can only be a gift, or Jesus can only be our Savior when we acknowledge the reality of sin in our thoughts, words, and actions. Whoever prays these words with simple faith, as did Bartimaeus, will experience salvation and God's life in Jesus.

There are three simple steps to follow: Locate Jesus' Presence in your heart; recite the prayer with loving attention to the words and the Presence of Jesus in your heart; and recite the prayer to the accompaniment of your breathing, praying the first half as you breathe in, and the second half as you breathe out. Try to make it a practice to say this prayer throughout the day.

You will grow in this practice in stages. In the beginning it will not be possible to do it throughout the day. A valuable tip is that whenever you remember to say it during the day, to recite it several times in a row. Using Rosary beads along with the recitation seems to help some people. If the recitation distracts you from the task at hand, do it during your countless moments of transition during the day, when you move from one task to another. Gradually you may be able to do it even while you are concentrating on your various duties. As for saying the prayer to the accompaniment of your breathing, it would do you well to use this step only when you are seated and at rest.

THE BENEFITS OF THE JESUS PRAYER:

The benefits of the Jesus Prayer are many and beyond measure. As disciples get into the practice of reciting this prayer continually throughout the day, they begin to have a strong sense of God's Presence within them. They recognize that they have become temples of the Trinity. There is a deep recognition of the Sacred within and outside of them. They belong to God and everything else is to be used for the greater praise and service of this indwelling God.

At first they are reciting the prayer with their lips. Gradually they recognize that they are praying it in their hearts. An abiding sense of God's Presence and the recitation of the prayer in their hearts emerge in their consciousness. They might recognize that even in their sleep this prayer is being prayed within them. They might have this sense upon awakening in the middle of the night. This practice creates the mind and heart of Jesus in the disciple. A slow and steady transformation is taking place. The disciple wants to follow in the Master's footsteps in every way. There is a strong commitment to choose God and avoid evil. There is as well a strong commitment to choose the better of two good options in decision-making. One's awareness moves drastically from focus on self to focus on God and serving others.

FINDING GOD IN ALL THINGS:

At the end of his month long Spiritual Exercises, Saint Ignatius of Loyola offered a special prayer exercise as a way of transitioning into the marketplace. He called it "Contemplation to Attain the Love of God." Ignatius was well aware that the daily circumstances after the retreat would change dramatically. They would be far from idyllic in terms of solitude and freedom from everyday pressures of life. At the same time he was confident that the retreatant could preserve and deepen the intimacy with God and familiarity with prayer developed during the retreat amidst the hustle and bustle of the marketplace. Ignatius was convinced that obligations and pressures of everyday life are not a distraction or hindrance to union with God. Rather they are stepping-stones to God as our duties and obligations are part of God's will for us. We would attain union with God if we did our everyday duties for God generously and solicitously. Keeping this conviction in mind he offered a great help to do God's will in our daily tasks and encumbrances. He offered the "Contemplation to Attain the Love of God" during the last days of the retreat and to continue practicing after the retreat.

What then is this way of praying? It is a very simple practice that has far reaching effects on the life of the disciple. Throughout the day you make it a practice to be gratefully aware of God's providence and largesse in every circumstance of your life. Consequently throughout the day you will experience first-hand how God is providing and taking care of your every need. Before long your consciousness is suffused with God's ardent love and compassion for you in Jesus Christ.

THE BENEFITS OF CONTINUAL THANKSGIVING:

The benefits of this way of praying are immense. Ignatius suggests the chief benefit in the title. He believes that anyone who focuses on God's continual providence to him/her, will invariably come to a deep experience of love – God's love for the disciple in the first place, leading to an ardent and serious commitment to loving God in deeds, or doing God's will in the nitty-gritty of life. A second and equally important benefit is that a person focusing on being loveable and loving is invariably joyful and hopeful. Such individuals know what Paul is talking about in the Scripture passage quoted above from Ephesians 6. They experience God's comforting presence even in affliction.

CONTINUAL CONVERSATION WITH GOD:

In "The Practice of the Presence of God," Brother Lawrence tells us that God gave him this method of being with God. He was told to converse with God during all of his waking hours. From after his year of novitiate till he was an old man, Brother Lawrence learned to be with God continually through an ongoing conversation. There would be times when he would speak his heart out to God. There would be other times when God would speak to him and he would receive answers to questions and dilemmas as well as deeper understanding of God's Mystery through special graces. He speaks of being overwhelmed with profuse tears for over thirty years, so that at times he would have to remove himself from human company. Clearly he lived with the Trinity, and the Holy Spirit was his Teacher and Mentor. And if anyone asked him for one piece of advice, he would recommend very strongly this simple and profound method of prayer.

HELPFUL ATTITUDES FOR PRAYER:

- *The Jesus Prayer:* Pay loving attention to the words as well as to the presence of God whom you place before you or in your heart.
- Pray this prayer with the simple faith of a child.
- You can use any prayer formula that suits you. Obviously the Jesus Prayer has stood the test of time, and it makes sense to give it a good try.
- Recite the prayer to the accompaniment of your breathing only when you are seated or lying down and at rest.
- If you are losing your sense of joy, hope, and loving attitude, maybe you are not engaging enough in the prayer of gratitude and recollection of God's presence in your life.

THE PRAYER OF REMEMBRANCE

SCRIPTURE:

"I always thank God for you because of his grace given you in Christ Jesus. For in him you have been enriched in every way – in all your speaking and in all your knowledge – because our testimony about Christ was confirmed in you. Therefore you do not lack any spiritual gift as you eagerly wait for our Lord Jesus Christ to be revealed. He will keep you strong to the end, so that you will be blameless on the day of our Lord Jesus Christ. God, who has called you into fellowship with his Son Jesus Christ our Lord, is faithful (NIV: 1 Corinthians 1: 4-9)."

GRATITUDE AS THE BASIS OF OUR PRAYER:

In almost every letter, Paul is giving thanks to God, sometimes ceaselessly, sometimes exuberantly. In this passage from his First Letter to the Corinthians, he is amazed and full of gratitude at the marvelous favor and gifting that God has bestowed on the Corinthians. His gratitude fortifies his trust that God will strengthen the Corinthians to the end so that they will be "blameless on the day of our Lord Jesus." And this trust is based on God's faithfulness to His people, rather than on the faithfulness of the Corinthians to God.

In his letter to the Philippians, for instance, Paul gives thanks to God _constantly_ at the way the Philippians have continually helped to promote the gospel from the very first day. "I thank my God every time I remember you. In all my prayers for all of you, I always pray with joy because of your partnership in the gospel from the first day until now, being confident of this, that he who began a good work in you will carry it on to completion until the day of Christ Jesus (NIV: Philippians 1: 3-

5)." In Paul, gratitude always seems to be the outflow of amazement and praise at God's marvelous favors and works among His people. As a result, his gratitude moves into earnest petition on behalf of the people he is ministering to, asking God to provide them with the grace to remain faithful and covenanted to Him.

What then is the basis of our prayer of remembrance or gratitude? As creatures we are beholden to God our Creator for the essence of our being. God upholds us in existence every waking and sleeping moment. In God we live and move and have our being, regardless of whether we choose to have a relationship or not. What is even more striking is that God has chosen to enter into a union of likeness with us. "For He (God) chose us in him (Jesus Christ) before the creation of the world to be holy and blameless in his sight. In love he predestined us to be adopted as his sons through Jesus Christ, in accordance with his pleasure and will – to the praise of his glorious grace, which he has freely given us in the One he loves (NIV: Ephesians 1:4-6)." Several imponderable truths strike us in this passage. They are truths we will never be able to comprehend adequately. However, they will always inspire and nourish us deeply as they reveal the deepest recesses of God's Love and Compassion for us. They are the following:

- God chose Jesus Christ to be our Savior by dying on the cross for the forgiveness of our sins. Jesus' death is the perfect sacrifice that has bought our forgiveness and salvation. We have now entered into a new and everlasting Covenant with our Triune God.

- God adopted us and made us sons and daughters of the living God and brothers and sisters of Jesus Christ. Knowing full well our sinful and flawed lineage, God did not balk at making us divine heirs, giving us all the rights and privileges that belong to the sons and daughters of God's family.

- Not only did God not hesitate to adopt us and change our blood lines in a manner of speaking, God then proceeded further to do the impossible by human standards, to make us holy, blameless, and full of love through Jesus Christ. Even though we have feet of clay, through God's power and passionate investment in us, we can and will be transformed if we follow in the footsteps of Jesus, obeying his commandments and heeding his teachings with all our hearts, minds, and souls. In surrender to the Holy Spirit, our generosity and steadfastness will be provided to us by our Advocate. Already in this life the Father of our Lord Jesus Christ "has blessed us in the heavenly realms with every spiritual blessing in Christ! (NIV: Ephesians 1: 3)"

THE PRAYER OF REMEMBRANCE:

Various traditions have developed around the central core of Christian discipleship, which is that our God is a gracious God, slow to anger and abounding in mercy. Our God is ever ready to forgive and bless. As a result, the disciple's basic attitude is gratitude, praise, and deep joy at experiencing such largesse at the hands of God. These traditions could be summed up in three categories:

- The first category would focus on being deeply grateful to God for all the gifts and blessings one has received and continues to receive on a daily basis from God. Such a practice leads to a grateful and trusting heart. Even in lean times, God continues to pour out the divine largesse upon us. *The ability to experience God's bountiful harvest in time of famine is a special grace that is given to the disciple who has staked his or her discipleship on trusting the Master completely.*

- The second category would emphasize all the gifts and blessings God has offered others through us. The emphasis would be on God choosing to use us as an instrument of salvation for others, and not on us being the author of our good works. This practice would gradually give us an understanding that our life is not our own. We belong to God and our life on earth is a mission and pilgrimage.

- *In essence we are part of the mystical Body of Christ and our function in life is to help establish the reign of God.*

- The third category would focus on thanking God for the trials, tribulations, and even failures we have experienced and committed in our life, as a way of understanding that God can and does bring good out of everything if only we trust God's forgiveness and guidance in our lives. For someone who has experienced extensive abuse this step will be a difficult one to take. It is important that such a person not do violence to self. When the time is right for this step to be taken, the Holy Spirit will initiate the practice. *Disciples who have engaged assiduously in thanking God for every single happening in their lives have come to a deep serenity and peace. They have also developed an abiding trust in God's protection and guidance.*

HELPFUL ATTITUDES FOR PRAYER:
- Try to follow Saint Paul's advice by thanking God continually for all that happens in your life. Try to be unwavering in your commitment to interpret life's circumstances from the point of view of faith which is to believe without seeing.
- When anxiety and fear, or any other desolation threatens your state of joy and trust, return to thanking God even though you might not *feel* gratitude.
- Pray for your enemies, do good to those who hate you, keep a non-violent and compassionate heart and mind.
- No matter what is happening in the disciple's life, all is well because God is at the helm.

- It does not matter how unreliable and corrupt our spiritual gene pool might be, God decided to adopt us regardless, believing that through Jesus Christ the Holy Spirit could and would accomplish the good work of making us sons and daughters of the Living God.
- It is more important in our relationship with God to focus on God's love for us rather than on our love for God. When our hearts and minds have been saturated with God's magnanimous love for us, our own love and commitment for God will blossom and become passionate.

PASSAGES FOR PRAYER:

Psalm 103: Praise of Divine Goodness
Psalm 136: Hymn of Thanksgiving for the Everlasting Kindness of the Lord
Psalm 138: Hymn of a Grateful Heart
Luke 1: 46-55: Mary's Canticle
Luke 1: 67-79: Zechariah's Canticle
Romans 8: 28- 39: God's Love for Humans
Ephesians 1: 3-23: The Father's Plan of Salvation
Colossians 1: 3-23: Thanksgiving and Prayer
Revelation 5: 1- 14: The Scroll and the Lamb

RECOGNIZING GOD'S VOICE AND PRESENCE – I

SCRIPTURE:

"We have not received the spirit of the world but the Spirit who is from God, that we may understand what God has freely given us. This is what we speak, not in words taught us by human wisdom but in words taught by the Spirit, expressing spiritual truths in spiritual words. The man without the Spirit does not accept the things that come from the Spirit of God, for they are foolishness to him, and he cannot understand them, because they are spiritually discerned – (NIV: 1 Corinthians 2: 12-14)."

PROMISE & CHARACTERISTICS OF THE HOLY SPIRIT:

The whole discussion on the discernment of spirits or recognizing God's voice and presence in our lives hinges on the gift of the Holy Spirit from the Father that Jesus offered us on the eve of his crucifixion and death. In John 14 and 16, Jesus describes the characteristics and function of the Holy Spirit in our lives. He begins by telling us that the Holy Spirit will be another Counselor who will be with us forever! (John 14:16). Like Jesus the Holy Spirit will be an advocate who will stand in our corner and go to bat for us. The Holy Spirit will be intimately committed and deeply concerned about our welfare as children of God. And this commitment will go on forever, always, with no let up! The Holy Spirit is the Spirit of Truth whom the world cannot accept or recognize (John 14:17), because the world's spirit and modus operandi is diametrically opposed to God's Spirit. As disciples of Jesus we will recognize Him because he lives with us and will be in us (John 14:17)! In a very real sense, then, the Holy Spirit will be Emmanuel, God-with-us. And the Holy Spirit will dwell within us, making us temples of the

Holy Spirit. In John 14: 23 Jesus says, "If anyone loves me, he will obey my teaching. My Father will love him, and we will come to him and make our home with him." In other words, we will truly be temples of the Trinity!

In John 16 Jesus tells us a lot more about the Holy Spirit. In 16: 7, Jesus tells us the sober truth that if He does not return to His Father the Holy Spirit will never come to us. After His Ascension, Jesus will bring glory to His Father in heaven, with the heavenly hosts joining Him in continual adoration, praise, and glorification of His Father. And on earth the Holy Spirit will fashion us into the Body of Christ through our participation in the Risen Jesus' Eucharistic Sacrifice, offering praise and adoration of His Father in heaven!!

The Holy Spirit's function will be to prove the world wrong about sin: the refusal to believe that Jesus is indeed the Savior of the world! (John 16:9); about justice: even though Jesus was found guilty and apparently died in disgrace, in reality justice has triumphed because Jesus rose from the dead and has returned to His Father! (John 16:10); about condemnation: Satan, prince of this world, has been condemned through the Risen Lord's triumph over death! (John 16:11).

Finally, in John 16: 13-15, Jesus tells us that the Holy Spirit will guide us to all truth. The Holy Spirit will not speak on His own behalf, but only what He receives from Jesus. And He will announce to us the things to come! Jesus and the Holy Spirit will always act as ONE! And just as Jesus sought constantly to bring glory to His Father by always doing His Father's will, in the same way the Holy Spirit will give glory to Jesus! In summary, then, the Holy Spirit will be our divine Mentor and Guide, forming and transforming us into Christ! Our lives are intimately and inextricably intertwined with the life of the Trinity in and through the Power of the Holy Spirit! The Holy Spirit is continually forming us into the Body of Christ or Church!

COMMITMENT TO GOD'S WAYS:

In light of the Holy Spirit's role and purpose in our lives, what then would be some of the underpinnings of prayer? The obvious disposition would be that the disciple seeks an intimate relationship with God. Intimacy cannot be had without honesty and transparency. In seeking intimacy with God the disciple makes a sincere commitment to live according to God's ways, under the guidance and direction of the Holy Spirit. A covenant relationship with God is the context. Prayer thus takes on a serious dimension because it petitions God for help to do right and avoid evil, and asks for repentance when one has sinned. In accepting Jesus as Savior and Lord, the disciple begins to grow in the ways of God. The Holy Spirit is not the world's spirit but God's Spirit as Paul tells us in the passage from 1 Corinthians.

Thus prayer has become a serious and elevating experience as it transforms life and conduct. The disciple, indeed, hears and recognizes God's voice and presence. Saint Teresa of Avila's opinion is that a serious relationship with God can only begin when the disciple has made a serious commitment to avoid all deliberate sin. Until then the relationship with God will be half-hearted and lukewarm. Without a sincere commitment to God, prayer will be superficial and tenuous, lacking real connection with God. A willingness to surrender totally to the hegemony of the Holy Spirit is the bedrock of serious prayer and discipleship!

EXPERIENCING CONSOLATION:

Saint Ignatius of Loyola observed carefully the different movements in his soul as he developed in his relationship with God. Before long, it became clear to him that God responded in a very personal way in our lives. The Holy Spirit was indeed our Counselor and Advocate who dwelt among us and within us. Ignatius discovered that when he was following God's ways in everyday life, the Holy Spirit made known the divine Presence through consolations.

Movements like peace, joy, trust, patience, and similar sentiments would be present in him moving him in God's direction, towards deeper commitment as a disciple. The Holy Spirit acted like a cheerleader making things easy and giving him strength and courage in difficult situations. In other words, the disciple was not alone in this journey into the heart of God. The Holy Spirit was an itinerant and constant mentor and guide.

MAKING DECISIONS IN CONSOLATION:

Ignatius realized as well that he did experience desolation or movements in his soul that took him away from God. Some of these desolations were caused in his soul in spite of his best intentions to live under the mantle of the Holy Spirit: "In the case of those who go on earnestly striving to cleanse their souls from sin and who seek to rise in the service of God our Lord to greater perfection...it is characteristic of the evil spirit to harass with anxiety, to afflict with sadness, to raise obstacles backed by fallacious reasoning that disturb the soul. It is characteristic of the good spirit, however, to give courage and strength, consolations, tears, inspirations, and peace. This he does by making all easy, by removing all obstacles so that the soul goes forward in doing good (*Spiritual Exercises,* Paragraph 315)."

He also realized that there were times when he did resist the promptings of the Holy Spirit and slip into desolation or movements in his soul that took him away from God. When he was under the influence of desolation, he was attracted toward tendencies that were evil that dissipated his commitment to God. Prayer was a chore and was resisted because he would have to confront himself before God. Slowly he understood that when he made decisions in a state of desolation, they never bore good fruit because they originated in confusion, reaction, and turmoil. On the other hand, when he made decisions in a state of consolation, they bore good fruit because he was influenced and strengthened by the Holy Spirit in his decision-making.

CONSOLATIONS COULD LEAD TO COMPLACENCY:

In a state of consolation it is easy to hear God's voice and feel God's Presence. Still there is the lurking presence of our deviousness even in this sacred space! Instead of treating our consolations as gifts, and offering thanksgiving and praise to our gracious God, we could quite easily succumb to the temptation of thinking that these consolations have come to us through our own merits and consequently we can produce them at will. Such a conclusion would put us in the unenviable position of judging others unfavorably and making us our own saviors! The Spirit of Truth will not tolerate such foolish complacency and conceit! When we indulge in conceit and arrogance we run the risk of slipping into desolation.

HELPFUL ATTITUDES FOR PRAYER:

- Like Jesus the Holy Spirit will be an Advocate who will stand in our corner and go to bat for us. The Holy Spirit will be intimately committed and deeply concerned about our welfare as children of God.

- This commitment will go on forever, always, with no let up!

- The Holy Spirit will be _Emmanuel_, God-with-us. And the Holy Spirit will dwell _within_ us, making us _temples_ of the Holy Spirit.

- Meanwhile, the Holy Spirit here on earth will continue to fashion us into the Body of Christ, through our participation in the Risen Jesus' Eucharistic Sacrifice and Prayer of praise and adoration of His Father taking place continually in heaven!!

- Our lives are inextricably intertwined with the life of the Trinity in and through the power of the Holy Spirit! The Holy Spirit is continually forming us into the Body of Christ, into Church!

- Decisions made in a state of consolation bear good fruit because they are influenced and strengthened by the Holy Spirit in the discernment process.

- Slowly he understood that when he made decisions in a state of desolation, they never bore good fruit because they originated in confusion, reaction, and turmoil.

- Instead of treating our consolations as gifts, and offering thanksgiving and praise to our gracious God, we could quite easily succumb to the temptation of thinking that these consolations have come to us through our own merits and consequently we can produce them at will.

PASSAGES FOR PRAYER:

John 14: 16- 17; 26: Promise of the Holy Spirit.
John 16: 7-15: The Holy Spirit's job description
Romans 8 1-13: The Flesh and the Spirit
1 Corinthians 2: 12-14: God's Spirit of Truth
Galatians 5: 16-26: Proper Use of Freedom

RECOGNIZING GOD'S VOICE AND PRESENCE - II

SCRIPTURE:

"The acts of the sinful nature are obvious: sexual immorality, impurity and debauchery; idolatry and witchcraft; hatred, discord, jealousy, fits of rage, selfish ambition, dissensions, factions and envy; drunkenness, orgies, and the like. ..But the fruit of the Spirit is love, joy, peace, patience, kindness, goodness, faithfulness, gentleness and self-control. Against such things there is no law – (NIV: Galatians 5: 19-23)."

HEEDING ONLY THE HOLY SPIRIT'S VOICE:

Saint Ignatius of Loyola observes that when the disciple is making progress and living in God's will, he or she is experiencing consolations or movements from the Holy Spirit that are encouraging and supportive. Peace, joy, patient endurance, generosity, transparency of spirit, etc, would be some such stirrings from the Holy Spirit. The Holy Spirit also acts as a supporter and friend, instilling confidence and courage in the disciple so that he or she is not daunted by difficult tasks. The Holy Spirit works things out in such a way that even in difficult situations the challenge becomes possible to accomplish.

However, there is another voice that is at work in the disciple's heart. This is a negative and destructive force, obviously not originating in God (*We alluded to this scenario in the previous section when we quoted from Paragraph 315 of the Spiritual Exercises*). This source is the evil spirit, either Satan and/or our own propensity toward evil and destruction. This voice seeks to diminish and ensnare us by suggesting thoughts and movements that disturb and cause anxiety, and in the process lead to discouragement and stagnation. So if we are making progress and overcoming a bad habit by stringing together several successful attempts at healthy behaviors, we might hear the following or such-like remarks within us: "Do you really believe you are capable of changing your behavior when you have had so many failures in the past? Don't you think your efforts will amount to very little?" Ignatius advises us to train ourselves to ignore the evil spirit's promptings in time of consolation when we are under the influence and guidance of the Holy Spirit. Oftentimes, after we have successfully resisted such negative suggestions we will see clearly that they were a web of deceit and delusion.

RECOGNIZING THE HOLY SPIRIT IN TIME OF DESOLATION:

St. Ignatius presumes that the disciple will struggle against temptation and succumb to it every now and then. Such capitulation will result in desolation or movements within the soul that would encourage us to move away from God. In other words, when we are in desolation through our own fault, our tendency will be to move away from God and towards the spirit of the world and the flesh. Quite simply, we are under the influence of evil and our thoughts and desires will be preoccupied and focused on what is not conducive for our spiritual well being.

Once again there are two forces at work. This time the evil spirit's presence seems to be more dominant and the disciple is encouraged to move away from God through specious arguments and excuses. Such arguments could be described in the following slogans: 'To err is human,' 'God understands,' 'How am I to learn compassion and understanding unless I experience my own sinfulness.' 'Why bother to be holy when church and so-called believers are so hypocritical and scandalous!' Meanwhile the Holy Spirit's Voice and Presence is disturbing. The disciple's conscience speaks up and convicts him or her with feelings of healthy guilt and shame. There is a strong appeal to reason as well. The disciple is left with disquiet and sadness until there is a move toward repentance and spiritual well being.

REASONS FOR DESOLATION:

We are easily prone to live in falsehood and denial rather than face the truth. We like to appear better than we are spiritually. Consequently, we might create a pseudo-consolation, which is not really a consolation because it is founded on a lie. Salvation can only come to us from an honest admission of our hypocrisy and sin, without which the Holy Spirit can't be recognized. We can never usurp God's sovereignty which is what sin tries to do.

Desolation can be the result of our own wrong-doing. In such an instance we will feel separated from God on the level of our feelings and sentiments, as well as on the level of our values and convictions. As mentioned above, the Holy Spirit's voice will be disturbing, calling us back to repentance and being right with God and ourselves.

Desolation can also be present as purification. The saints tell us that the Holy Spirit needs to subject us to purification as we will never be able to do an exhaustive clean-up job of our sinful attachments and disorders. In such a case one is not really in desolation. Sensible consolations or movements towards God on the level of feelings and sentiments will be absent, creating a sense of 'God's absence.' However, spiritual consolations, in the sense of a yearning for God and a deep commitment to Him in daily actions, will continue to be present and might even intensify.

HOW TO BEHAVE IN TIME OF DESOLATION:

Ignatius offers several suggestions about spiritual self-care in time of desolation. It is necessary to stick to one's resolutions that were made in time of consolation. The temptation will be to renege on them and adopt self-serving and destructive decisions in time of desolation. During desolation it is important to remind ourselves that God has not abandoned us and God's grace is still available to aid us in our struggle. Desolation is a time for extra prayer and taking stock. It is a time for suitable penance and self-discipline. Lastly, it is important to remember that consolation will return and the Holy Spirit will again be a lively and familiar presence.

BEING DECEIVED UNDER THE GUISE OF GOOD:

Even when our consolations are genuine because they come from God, we have the tendency to contaminate them by either distorting or embellishing them to serve our own pride and self-aggrandizement. If we deal with our consolations in the right way, they will produce lasting results in our lives. On the other hand, if the source of our consolations is anything other than God, there is a good likelihood that we will be led astray if we are not observant of the process as it unfolds in us.

Such consolations will be experienced as authentic, at least initially, and they will produce all the results of a true consolation, including peace, joy, fervor, enthusiasm to do God's will, and so on. However, such consolations are meant to lure and seduce with the purpose of throwing us into confusion and doubt. So the middle and end of the process will lead to a state of desolation, creating decisions that have our misguided selves as their center rather than God. *When a consolation is from God, the beginning, middle, and end of the process move us towards God and being committed to His holy will.* As you can see, there is a need to be constantly vigilant over the movements in our soul in order to make sure we are on the same page with the Holy Spirit.

CONCRETE SLIPPERY SLOPES IN DISCERNMENT:

Anxiety and Fear:

- _About tasks that have to be done:_ We will always have time and will be in consolation if we stay in the present moment and do our tasks as asked of us by God. Staying in the present moment is a necessary spiritual discipline that needs to be practiced rigorously because God can only be experienced in the present moment.

- When fear leads to the prospect of impending humiliation, negative outcome, or ongoing tension in a dysfunctional relationship or situation, _the only way to remain in consolation and under the influence of the Holy Spirit is by asking for peace and trust, thanking God for our critics and detractors, and letting go of any thoughts and emotions that keep us locked up in anxiety and its legion of negative emotions. Practicing loving acts is the antidote in time of anxiety and fear._

Criticism and Rejection:

- To stay in consolation, we must learn to act and respond rather than react and retaliate. For that to happen we would need to engage in thanksgiving for the detractor, and being grateful for the painful situation and the formation that it brings to us. It is the time to wait on the Holy Spirit to tell us what the best course of action is. Sometimes, after we have arrived at calmness, the storm seems like an illusion. Sometimes, an appropriate opening will be given to us by the Holy Spirit to bring about greater transparency with the person concerned, _after_ we have surrendered the desire to get even or explain ourselves.

- We also need to remind ourselves that to be in communion with others we don't need to be understood and accepted in every situation. *Often times if we can be at ease with ourselves, we can allow others to be different and even disagree with us.*

Disquiet and Doubt:

- There will be times of disquiet and doubt. *It is important to keep plugging away, doing what we have to do, and amidst groaning and sighs, asking God to give us strength to stay with Him and do His will.*
- When in doubt about God's existence, presence, and/or love, or all of the above, it is important to remind ourselves that Jesus is real. His death for us is beyond doubt. After how he has demonstrated His love for us, *we do not need* his assurances that we are loved by God, even though we might want them

Resentments and Unforgiveness:

- They are a plague and lead to desolation. They destroy us! *We need to understand very clearly that we will not have a meaningful relationship with God as long as we hold on to our resentments and are unwilling to forgive.*

- *As disciples of Jesus we cannot have enemies* even though others might choose to have us as theirs. And so Jesus gives us 490 times each day to get rid of our resentments and practice love and compassion!

Envy and Jealousy:

- *Envy and jealousy are a lack of gratitude for the abundance of God's love and blessings that we have all received.* They make us focus on someone else's abundance as if our own plate is empty! Thus they target an innocent person, be they God or a human being, as the scapegoat!

- Envy and jealousy are desolation. The longer you stay in them, the deeper the hole you dig for yourself. *Prayer is difficult and surrender is not possible without a spirit of gratitude!*

Bloom where you are planted:

- *It is an illusion and great distraction to think that we should be elsewhere and not where we have been planted!* We were born of specific parents, in a specific culture and environment, in a specific country. Learn to consider them as special gifts!

- It is an illusion to feel bad and self-disparaging because you seem to be in a better living condition. You will be in peace and joy if you try on a consistent basis to do what the Holy Spirit is prompting you to do in your everyday circumstances and life. Put out your own fires as best as you can, be of help to others as much as you are able, and trust the affairs of the world to God!

Sudden change in consolation or desolation:

- You can have consolation without a previous cause! Wait on God before you make any decisions based on the consolation. *Let the Holy Spirit clarify how you are to act upon your consolation so that you are not adding your own egotism to the decision.*

- You can also have desolation come upon you suddenly and furiously! These will be rather rare times. *In such cases it is important to have recourse to prayer immediately and remember that the Holy Spirit is greater than your travail.*

ABIDING IN THE HOLY SPIRIT:

Continual Gratitude:

- Hopefully the time will come when you will feel you are being inundated with blessings and brushes of divine tenderness either directly or through creatures. *More and more the Holy Spirit will be the Spirit oozing with love, compassion, and profound joy, expressing divine life in the Trinity.*

- In continual gratitude, you will discover the depths of God's life in the Trinity!

Towards Total Surrender or Indifference:

- The Holy Spirit will move you towards greater surrender and submission. You will practice surrender constantly.

- *In surrender you will experience at one and the same time both cross and resurrection*.

- You will develop a vague, and then again a not-so-vague, sense that indeed the Mystery of God's life is being infused into you. You are the grateful recipient, the action is the Holy Spirit's, and transformation is taking place!

Towards Continual Prayer:

- Your life will be more about God and less about you.
- *You will be focused on giving your best effort and being detached from the outcome.*

- You will sense within you a transparency and freedom, and as a result, God is easily reflected in your limpid waters!

- There is a profound peace in your heart and a profound love and concern for the universe and humanity!

- Contemplation leads to action and action leads to contemplation.

FOUR WEEKEND RETREATS

FIRST WEEKEND RETREAT

FRIDAY EVENING: 8:00-9:30

Introduction to the retreat:
- Be open: do not anticipate anything other than what God desires to give you/us. Be very much like a sponge ready to absorb whatever and whenever God wishes to grace you with and whenever.

- We are praying as members of the Body of Christ, as COMMUNIO. Hence we bring both the Triune God and one another into our prayer. All you need to do is have the intention. Whether you feel/experience it or not, the reality is that we are COMMUNIO in the Trinity.

Introduction to Liturgy of the Hours

Prayer Session: Practicing Stillness: Refer to Living in God's Embrace, Ch 1 Prayer

Session on Names of God

Compline

SATURDAY

MORNING PRAYER SESSION: 9:00-12:00
Liturgy of the Hours: Morning Prayer

Practicing Stillness: LIGE, Chapter 1

<u>*Who is God for me?*</u>
God & You naming each other

Group Spiritual Direction

Practicing Stillness: LIGE, Chapter 1

<u>*Who is God for me?*</u>
Naming your blessings

Liturgy of the Hours: Midday Prayer

AFTERNOON PRAYER SESSION: 1:00-3:00 & 3:00-6:00

Individual Spiritual Direction

<u>*Who is God as He says He is?*</u>
Lectio Divina on John 10: 1-18

Group Spiritual Direction

<u>*Who is God as He says He is?*</u>
Lectio Divina on John 15

Evening Prayer

EVENING PRAYER SESSION: 7:00-10:00
Adoration before the Blessed Sacrament

Sacrament of Reconciliation

Compline

Eucharist

<u>SUNDAY</u>
MORNING PRAYER SESSION: 9:00-12:00
Morning Prayer

<u>*God's Vision for us*</u>
Lectio Divina on God's Plan of Salvation: Eph 1:1-10

<u>*God's Vision for us*</u>
Lectio Divina on The World renewed: Isaiah 65: 17-25

Midday Prayer

AFTERNOON SESSION: 1:00-2:30

Lectio Divina on John 3: 16-18

Group Spiritual Direction

SECOND WEEKEND RETREAT

FRIDAY EVENING: 8:00-9:30

Introduction to the retreat: Same as in first weekend

Prayer Session: Practicing Stillness: Refer to Living in God's Embrace, Chapter 1

Session on Resting in God's Graciousness:
Image: You are all alone in a small and cozy chapel, in the dark of night, before the Monstrance, illuminated by a single flickering candle. You take your time getting used to your surroundings and the utter quiet around you. You are alone and face to face with Jesus.

Dialogue: Jesus thanks you profusely for coming to visit him and just desires to listen to you intently and thus to enter into every fiber of your being.

Very slowly and deliberately, with honesty and feeling you express your gratitude to him; you talk about your struggles and doubts; with hope and childlike trust you express your trust that He will bring you into deep union with Him.

Compline/Night Prayer

SATURDAY
MORNING PRAYER SESSION: 9:00-12:00

Liturgy of the Hours: Morning Prayer

Practicing Stillness

God's Vision for Us:
Image: The mystery, hidden from all ages, has now been revealed in Jesus. As you behold the tiny infant in his mother's arms, or in your arms, you are beholding the epiphany or manifestation of the Triune God in this little baby.

Dialogue: *Lectio Divina:* Emmanuel gazes into your eyes and speaks to your heart. You listen and ponder as He speaks to you:

- "This is my testimony: God has given you eternal life and this life is in me; anyone who has me has life, anyone who does not have me does not have life (1 John 5: 12)."
- "Yes, God loved the world so much that he gave his only Son, so that everyone who believes in me may not be lost but may have eternal life. For God sent me into the world, not to condemn the world, but so that through me the world might be saved. No one who believes in me will be condemned (John 3: 16-18)"
- "I am the gate. Anyone who enters through me will be safe; he will go freely in and out and be sure of finding pasture (John 10: 9)."

Practicing Stillness

God's Vision for Us:

Image: The Risen Lord: in Jesus the fullness of the ages has moved into the end times. You are in the upper room along with Mary and the disciples.

Dialogue: *Lectio Divina:*
- "'Peace be with you!' In a state of alarm and fright, they thought they were seeing a ghost. But he said, "Why are you so agitated, and why are these doubts rising in your hearts? Look at my hands and feet; yes, it is I indeed. Touch me and see for yourselves; a ghost has no flesh and bones as you can see I have. And as he said this he showed them his hands and feet. Their joy was so great that they still could not believe it, and they stood there dumbfounded (Luke 24: 37-42)."

Group Spiritual Direction

Liturgy of the Hours: Midday Prayer

AFTERNOON PRAYER SESSION: 1:00-3:00 & 3:00-6:00

Individual Spiritual Direction

Practicing Stillness

The Reality of Sin
Image: Jesus hanging on the Cross

Dialogue: *Lectio Divina:* Look at Jesus gazing into your eyes lovingly and humbly as he hangs and suffers on the Cross:
- 'Have you no fear of God at all?' he said. 'You got the same sentence as he did, but in our case we deserved it: we are paying for what we did. But this man has done nothing wrong. Jesus, he said, 'remember me when you come into your kingdom.' 'Indeed, I promise you,' he replied, 'today you will be with me in paradise (Luke 23: 40-43).'
- The Pharisee stood there and said this prayer to himself, "I thank you, God, that I am not grasping, unjust, adulterous like the rest of mankind, and particularly that I am not like this tax collector here. I fast twice a week; I pay tithes on all I get." The tax collector stood some distance away, not daring even to raise his eyes to heaven; but he beat his breast and said, "God, be merciful to me, a sinner." This man, I tell you, went home again at rights with God; the other did not (Luke 18: 11-14)."

Practicing Stillness

God's Compassion & Mercy:
Image: The Prodigal Son being embraced by his father

Dialogue: *Lectio Divina:* Jesus says to you:
- "Rejoice with me, I have found my sheep that was lost." In the same way, I tell you, there will be more rejoicing in heaven over one repentant sinner than over ninety-nine virtuous men who have no need of repentance (Luke 15: 6-7)."
- "Father, I have sinned against heaven and against you. I no longer deserve to be called your son." But the father said to his servants, "Quick! Bring out the best robe and put it on him; put a ring on his finger and sandals on his feet. Bring the calf we have been fattening, and kill it; we are going to have a feast, a

celebration, because this son of mine was dead and has come back to life; he was lost and is found." And they began to celebrate (Luke 15: 21-24)."

Group Spiritual Direction

Evening Prayer

EVENING PRAYER SESSION: 7:00-10:00
Adoration with Rosary & Night Prayer

Sacrament of Reconciliation

Eucharist

SUNDAY
MORNING PRAYER SESSION: 9:00-12:00
Liturgy of Hours: Morning Prayer

Practicing Stillness

Practicing the Presence of God

Practicing Stillness

Practicing the Presence of God

Liturgy of the Hours: Midday Prayer

Group Spiritual Direction

AFTERNOON PRAYER SESSION: 1:00-2:30
Lectio Divina on Colossians 1:15-23: Fullness and Reconciliation

Group Spiritual Direction

THIRD RETREAT WEEKEND

FRIDAY EVENING: 8:00-9:30
PRAYER SESSION

Introduction to the retreat: Same as in first weekend

Holy Hour to include Compline

SATURDAY
MORNING PRAYER SESSION: 9:00-12:00

Liturgy of the Hours: Morning Prayer

The Prayer of Remembrance:
Luke 1:46-55: Mary's Canticle;
Romans 8: 28-39: God's Love for Humans

God's Covenants with Us:
Isaiah 49: 17;
Jeremiah 31: 21-34;
Ezekiel 37: 1-14
Group Spiritual Direction
Midday Prayer

AFTERNOON PRAYER SESSION: 1:00-3:00 & 3:00-6:00

Individual Spiritual Direction

The Call of Abraham:
Genesis 15: 1-21: The Covenant with Abraham

The Call of Abraham:
Genesis 22: 1-19: The Testing of Abraham
Group Spiritual Direction
Evening Prayer

EVENING PRAYER SESSION: 7:00-10:00

Adoration with Rosary & Compline

Sacrament of Reconciliation

Eucharist

SUNDAY
MORNING PRAYER SESSION: 9:00-12:00
Morning Prayer

<u>The Call of Moses:</u>
The Burning Bush & Call of Moses: Ex 2: 23-3:1-22

<u>The Call of Moses:</u>
Exodus 12: 1-36: The Passover Meal
Group Spiritual Direction

Midday Prayer

AFTERNOON SESSION: 1:00-2:30
Final Sharing Session

FOURTH RETREAT WEEKEND

THEME: THEOSIS THROUGH THE CROSS
FRIDAY EVENING
PRAYER SESSION: 8:00-9:30

Introduction to the Retreat: Same as in First Weekend

Holy Hour: Jesus Prayer and Compline

SATURDAY
MORNING PRAYER SESSION: 9:00-12:00

Liturgy of the Hours: Morning Prayer

Matthew 11: 28-30: Jesus & Your Burdens:

Luke 18: 9-14: The Pharisee and Tax Collector

Group Spiritual Direction

Luke 9: 23-27: Conditions of Discipleship

Luke 9: 28-36: Jesus Transfigured

Midday Prayer

AFTERNOON PRAYER SESSION: 1:00-3:00 & 3:00-6:00

Individual Spiritual Direction

Matthew 5: 13-16: Discipleship

Matthew 5:43-48: Love of Enemies

Group Spiritual Direction

Luke 19: 1-10: Zacchaeus the Tax Collector

Luke 20: 45-21:4: The Widow's Mite

Evening Prayer

EVENING PRAYER SESSION: 7:00-10:00

Adoration with Rosary, Compline,

Sacrament of Reconciliation

Eucharist

SUNDAY
MORNING PRAYER SESSION: 9:00-12:00
Morning Prayer

John 1: 14-16: Prologue

Philippians 2: 6-11: Christ's Kenosis

Group Spiritual Direction

Acts: 7: 54-60: Stephen's Martyrdom

Acts 9: 1-9: Saul's Vocation

Midday Prayer

AFTERNOON SESSION: 1:00-2:30
Final Sharing Session

INDEX of Subjects

A

Abba, 30
Abraham, 1, 16, 22, 53, 61, 62, 63, 64, 65, 67, 68, 69, 70, 75, 83, 86, 90, 91, 154, 155, 262
Abram, 22, 59, 60, 61, 63, 65
Atonement, 116, 147, 149

B

Babylon, 12, 99, 106, 111, 113, 114, 121, 122, 123, 126

C

Cloud of Unknowing, 170
Compassion, 12, 25, 26, 43, 44, 46, 48, 52, 54, 55, 107, 115, 117, 118, 123, 146, 156, 157, 165, 231, 246, 250, 252
Composition of Place, 208
Consolation, 107, 116, 148, 189, 193, 204, 225, 243, 244, 246, 247, 248, 249, 251
Covenant, 5, 12, 45, 49, 51, 52, 53, 54, 55, 59, 60, 61, 62, 68, 75, 76, 78, 79, 83, 84, 85, 86, 87, 88, 89, 90, 91, 92, 95, 98, 115, 116, 118, 123, 140, 141, 146, 154, 155, 157, 191, 192, 195, 241

D

David, 42, 44, 45, 59, 85, 105, 180, 223, 225, 228
Desolation, 189, 236, 242, 243, 244, 246, 247, 248, 250, 251
Deuteronomic Reform, 112

E

Emmanuel, 2, 7, 14, 101, 139, 145, 147, 148, 149, 150, 239, 243, 258
Eucharist, 2, 7, 57, 78, 80, 81, 116, 147, 172, 225, 256, 261, 263, 265
Examination of Consciousness, 3, 5, 161, 181, 199

G

Goel, 105

H

Hagar, 61
Humility, 33, 88, 107, 108, 125, 192, 194, 195

I

Ignatius of Loyola, 4, 21, 38, 170, 181, 182, 189, 191, 195, 198, 199, 207, 208, 209, 210, 213, 215, 230, 231, 241, 242, 245, 246, 247
Immanence, 165
Isaac, 62, 63, 64, 65, 68, 69, 70, 75, 90
Isaiah, 2, 12, 21, 25, 26, 28, 34, 43, 45, 49, 50, 55, 56, 95, 96, 97, 98, 99, 101, 103, 104, 105, 106, 107, 108, 109, 110, 123, 124, 125, 126, 145, 146, 150, 155, 166, 256, 262
Israel, 12, 21, 22, 24, 43, 50, 51, 53, 54, 55, 59, 70, 71, 75, 76, 78, 79, 84, 85, 90, 91, 95, 96, 97, 98, 101, 103, 104, 105, 106, 107, 108, 109, 110, 112, 114, 115,

116, 117, 118, 119, 123, 124, 125, 146, 148, 154, 155, 156, 213, 220

Israelites, 22, 23, 24, 54, 68, 69, 70, 71, 75, 76, 77, 78, 79, 83, 84, 85, 87, 90, 91, 96, 97, 100, 106, 113, 116, 121, 123, 125, 146, 149, 220

J

Jacob, 21, 53, 55, 59, 67, 68, 69, 75, 83, 86, 91, 103, 107, 114, 146

Jeremiah, 2, 34, 50, 51, 54, 57, 107, 111, 112, 113, 114, 115, 116, 117, 118, 119, 120, 121, 122, 123, 125, 126, 155, 262

Jesus Prayer, 196, 228, 230, 232, 264

Judah, 51, 54, 59, 95, 96, 98, 99, 101, 103, 112, 113, 115, 118, 121, 122, 139, 142

L

Lectio Divina, 3, 6, 161, 186, 219, 220, 221, 256, 257, 258, 259, 260, 261

M

Magnanimity, 155, 164
Marriage, 13, 51, 75, 79
Meditation, 207, 208, 209, 220
Mercy, 1, 43, 48, 49, 50, 159, 177, 225, 260
Mosaic Law, 96
Moses, 1, 24, 27, 53, 67, 68, 69, 70, 71, 72, 75, 76, 77, 79, 83, 84, 85, 90, 91, 93, 97, 106, 107, 154, 155, 165, 180, 263

N

Noah, 44, 52, 83, 91, 154

P

Particular Examination, 182, 199
Passover, 1, 77, 78, 80, 81, 263
Penance, 197, 198
Persia, 106
Practicing the Presence of God, 3, 6, 161, 216, 228, 261
Prayer of Petition, 177
Prayer of Remembrance, 234
Preparatory Prayer, 208
Psalms, 3, 6, 44, 161, 204, 205, 223, 224, 225, 226

R

Red Sea, 23, 70, 81, 84, 93, 149
Redeemer, 40, 105, 107, 110, 123, 146, 148
Reverence, 15, 24, 38, 60, 89, 156, 164, 166, 168, 208, 213

S

Salvation, 4, 22, 34, 44, 46, 47, 48, 54, 55, 77, 78, 103, 104, 105, 106, 107, 108, 109, 139, 140, 143, 146, 148, 149, 154, 155, 156, 157, 164, 170, 172, 177, 178, 182, 213, 226, 229, 234, 235

Sarah, 22, 61, 62, 63, 64
Sarai, 22, 61
Sin, 15, 18, 31, 32, 33, 37, 38, 39, 40, 42, 43, 44, 46, 52, 54, 55, 79, 85, 90, 91, 95, 96, 100, 108, 115, 116, 117, 118, 140, 146, 147, 149, 157, 158, 178, 182, 191, 192, 195, 196, 197, 199, 209, 219, 223, 226, 229, 240, 241, 242, 247

Spiritual Exercises, 21, 38, 170, 198, 199, 207, 208, 209, 213, 214, 215, 230, 242, 245
St. Anthony of the Desert, 199

T

Teresa of Avila, 4, 176, 189, 191, 203, 207, 213, 215, 241
The Way of a Pilgrim, 201, 228

Theosis, 139, 142
Transcendence, 165

V

Vocal Prayer, 203, 205, 206

Y

Yom Kippur, 147, 149

CPSIA information can be obtained at www.ICGtesting.com
Printed in the USA
267588BV00003B/1-74/P